To Myanmar With Love

A Travel Guide for the Connoisseur

To Myanmar With Love
Edited & with contributions by Morgan Edwardson
Photography by Steve Goodman

To Asia With Love series created by Kim Fay
Cover and book design by Janet McKelpin/Dayspring Technologies, Inc.
Editing assistance provided by Robert Tompkins
Book production by Paul Tomanpos, Jr.
Special thanks to Ma Thanegi and Janet Brown

For information regarding permissions, write to:
ThingsAsian Press
3230 Scott Street
San Francisco, California 94123 USA
www.thingsasian.com
Printed in Singapore

ISBN-13: 978-1-934159-06-4
ISBN-10: 1-934159-06-9

Table of Contents

INTRODUCTION PAGE 4

1. MOVEABLE FEASTS PAGE 12
A tasting menu of exotic flavors

2. SEEING THE SIGHTS PAGE 44
Fresh perspectives on exploring must-see attractions

3. CULTURAL ENCOUNTERS PAGE 66
Taking part in the ethnic traditions of Myanmar

4. MAKING FRIENDS PAGE 86
Discovering the country through local hospitality

5. RETAIL THERAPY PAGE 108
An insiders' primer to boutiques and markets

6. SECRET GARDENS PAGE 128
Where to hide away from the touring masses

7. INTO THE WILD PAGE 150
Outdoor experiences for adventurous travelers

8. ON THE ROAD PAGE 172
Reflections on how the journey becomes the destination

9. WHEN IN ROME PAGE 200
Lessons on living local and making yourself at home

10. PAYING IT FORWARD PAGE 220
Suggestions for giving back while you're on the road

11. RESOURCES FOR THE ROAD PAGE 248
Practical advice to help you prepare for your travels

12. EPILOGUE PAGE 270
One writer discovers family among friends throughout Myanmar

CONTRIBUTOR BIOGRAPHIES,
CREDITS, AND INDEX PAGE 278

INTRODUCTION

Imagine that on the eve of your upcoming trip to Myanmar, you are invited to a party. At this party are dozens of guests, all of whom live in or have traveled extensively through the country. Among this eclectic and well-versed group of connoisseurs are authors of acclaimed guidebooks, popular newspaper columnists, veteran gourmets, and pioneering adventurers. As the evening passes, they tell you tales from their lives in these exotic places. They whisper the names of their favorite shops and restaurants; they divulge the secret hideaways where they sneak off to for an afternoon or a weekend to unwind. Some make you laugh out loud, and others seduce you with their poetry. Some are intent on educating, while others just want to entertain. Their recommendations are as unique as their personalities, but they are united in one thing ... their love of Myanmar. If you can envision being welcomed at such a party, then you can envision the experience that *To Myanmar With Love* aspires to give you.

Kim Fay
Series Editor, To Asia With Love

Girl wearing leaf patterned thanaka paste

For many years while living in neighboring Thailand, I pondered whether or not I should visit Myanmar, also known as Burma, a country crippled by controversy and ruled by one of the most vilified governments on the planet. During my decade of indecision I talked to dozens of travelers who had been there, and every single one had nothing but praise for the experience. "You have to go," one person told me. "It's such an amazing place, and the people are so sweet."

After much consideration, I finally took the plunge and spent two weeks touring the country. I knew right away I was in a special place. *Longyi*-wearing locals, many with *thanaka* paste dabbed creatively on their cheeks, greeted me wherever I roamed. They invited me into their simple homes, offering snacks and tea and good conversation. Some insisted on giving me gifts even when I had nothing to offer in return except my sincere thanks.

I was so eager to experience more of the country that I returned three more times during the following year. Each visit was unforgettable. As I write about in this book, one morning I met sweet, elderly Sheila in a Shan Market and spent a morning touring the town with her, while another morning I had breakfast with twenty-seven hundred monks in Mandalay. I enjoyed a chilly but spiritually rewarding evening at Golden Rock, cooled off with the locals at a water park in Yangon, and discovered the pleasures of simply wandering the streets of every city, town, and village I visited.

Critics who support a tourism boycott of Myanmar are fond of slapping labels such as "selfish" and "misguided" on travelers who wish to visit the country. The condemnation only intensified after the suppression of monk-led street protests in Yangon in September 2007. Then Cyclone Nargis hit in May 2008. With the country's delta region reeling from the massive destruction and fatalities caused by the storm, the government came under fire for its delayed response and resistance to international relief efforts. Sadly, these incidents focused the world's attention—and wrath— on Myanmar once again, reinforcing the negative impressions that the average Westerner already had of the country.

Myanmar is an incredibly complex nation—culturally, historically, and politically—with an ethnically diverse population of more than fifty-two million people. They, and not the government, are the focus of this book. Instead of divisive politics, we want to shine a light on the remarkable people, culture, and sights, and the fact that Myanmar continues to be a safe and inviting destination for travelers. From the hill towns of the north to the beaches of the south, there are delightful places to explore, and even more importantly, delightful people eager to welcome you.

Whenever I talk to the people of Myanmar, I am moved by the enormous pride they have for their homeland. But they express sadness and bewilderment that Myanmar is subjected to economic sanctions and travel boycotts by the international community. They absolutely want more tourists. In fact, it's not uncommon for total strangers to stop me on the street and thank me for coming. Many of us who have experienced the wonders of Myanmar make return trips because we know how much our visits mean to the people, not only by putting money in their pockets (oops, *longyi* don't have pockets, do they?), but for moral support too.

Due to the controversy, I wasn't sure what sort of reaction I would receive when I started soliciting writers for this project. As expected, there were some who condemned the whole idea. But the vast majority of replies were overwhelmingly supportive. These people—some of whom have lived and worked in Myanmar—were eager to share their passion and enthusiasm for a country that they felt "deserves more positive exposure." One writer called his experience in Myanmar "profound," while another hailed the country as "one of the most unique travel destinations still available to experience." One comment in particular echoed what we are trying to do with this book: "So far not one of the guidebooks I have seen has touched the soul of Myanmar."

Response from locals I contacted was just as supportive: "Delighted to read the title *To Myanmar With Love* and love

your intention of writing this book to show the positive and good things ... That is an important thing for our country. We have been overly influenced by international media, all from a negative perspective." Another voiced hope that the book would "show people that my country is not some sort of hell."

By all means, we think more people *should* visit Myanmar and see things for themselves, although we don't want them to wander in blindly. Read about the history, customs, and Buddhist etiquette of the nation before you visit. Be aware of the political situation, and enter responsibly. Take advantage of the many independent travel agencies and guides that can show you how to discover the country's endless charms. Make the most of your trip by getting off the beaten path and breaking away from the tour bus contingent.

Hit the streets and get totally lost. Walk, cycle, hire a trishaw, or take a ride in a horse cart. Follow in the footsteps of the writers of this book and play guitar for the locals, sneak into the forgotten corners of a colonial hotel, mingle with pottery makers in a small village, get a massage at a blind school, and so much more. You are also encouraged to give back to this country that gives so much to those who visit. And of course, return those smiles and greetings of *"Mingalaba!"* with a big smile and greeting of your own.

Whenever I think about Myanmar and how important it is to build bridges between cultures, I am reminded of a 1970's song by the Staple Singers. In the chorus, Mavis Staples sings: "Reach out, touch a hand. Make a friend if you can."

I can think of no better place to do this than in Myanmar, where those hands are outstretched and eagerly waiting to greet you.

Morgan Edwardson
Editor, *To Myanmar With Love*

How This Book Works

A good traveler has no fixed plans, and is not intent on arriving.
~Lao Tzu

To Myanmar With Love is a unique guidebook with chapters organized by theme as opposed to destination. This is because it focuses foremost on the sharing of personal experiences, allowing each place to serve as the colorful canvas on which our writers overlay vivid, individual impressions. Within each themed chapter you will find the recommendations grouped by regions and then cities. Geographically, the essays move from south to north, beginning in the country's largest city and main point of entry, Yangon. "Yangon and Southern Myanmar" encompasses the area surrounding Yangon and down to the Myeik Archipelago at the southern tip of the country. "Mandalay and Central Myanmar" is comprised of the area encircling Mandalay, including the western part of Shan State. The remainder of Shan State and destinations in Kachin State are found in "Eastern and Northeastern Myanmar."

Each recommendation consists of two parts: a personal essay and a fact file. Together, they are intended simultaneously to inspire and inform. The essay tells a story while the fact file gives addresses, phone numbers, and other serviceable information. Because each contribution can stand alone, the book does not need to be read in order. As with an old-fashioned miscellany, you may open to any page and start reading. Thus every encounter with the book is turned into its own distinctive armchair journey.

To facilitate locating the recommendations in the essays, the index is organized by place. As well, additional information and updates can be found online at WWW.TOASIAWITHLOVE.COM/MYANMAR. Keep in mind that *To Myanmar With Love* is selective and does not include the practical information you need for daily travel. Instead, reading it is like having a conversation with a friend who

just returned from a trip. You should supplement that friend's stories with a comprehensive guidebook, such as Lonely Planet.

Confucius said, "A journey of a thousand miles begins with a single step." We hope that this guide helps you put your best foot forward.

Key Terms and Important Information

Addresses: Address listings may look confusing at first, but they are actually quite logical. For example, after a street address you will often see a pair of numbers or words, such as (25/26) or (40/Bo Aung Kyaw). This means that the address is between 25th and 26th Streets or 40th and Bo Aung Kyaw Streets.

Burmese: Myanmar is also known as Burma, and while the word Burmese is sometimes used to describe all the people in the country, in this book, for the most part, Burmese refers to the Bamar, the country's majority ethnic group.

Cyclone Nargis: Most of the destinations recommended in this book were not significantly affected by the cyclone. If a place was affected, it is noted at the end of the essay.

Longyi: This sarong-like item of clothing is the unofficial national attire of Myanmar. Both men and women have been wearing versions of it for centuries.

Metric system: Although we are an American publisher, we have used the metric system for all measurements. For easy conversion, go to: WWW.METRIC-CONVERSIONS.ORG

Names: You will often see *U* or *Daw* in front of a person's name. *U* means Mr. and *Daw* means Mrs. or Ms. As an alternate to those common forms of address, *Ko* is sometimes used for middle-aged men, and *Maung* for younger men. *Ma* is the preference for younger women.

Place names: There is much controversy about place names in Myanmar. Some people argue for the old colonial names (i.e. Burma rather than Myanmar), and others prefer newer government-changed names. While you will commonly find both used in news articles, websites, etc., we have chosen to use the current official place names.

Prices: Prices are based on costs at the time of writing. When including prices, we have used a rate of 1,200 kyat to the US dollar. This is an average, since prices and exchange rates fluctuate regularly. Though food and lodging can be a real bargain, other prices, such as transportation, guide fees, and permits, can be high compared to other Asian countries. If you have any questions about this before you go, check with a reliable travel agent (see page 267).

Spellings: The languages of Myanmar are based on characters rather than a Roman/Latin alphabet. Because of this, many words have never been Westernized. As you research your trip, you might find five different spellings for a single phrase or place. We have done our best to pinpoint common usage and offer consistent spellings.

Thanaka: Mainly women and children, but also some men, use this paste made from the bark, roots, and wood of local trees for sunscreen and to condition their skin. Because it is often applied in patterns, it also serves a decorative purpose.

Moveable Feasts

A tasting menu of exotic flavors

One of the great joys of travel is not just discovering new places, but new tastes. Forget the sightseeing tour, lead me to the kitchen. I want to sample as many of the local delicacies as time, and my stomach, will allow.

For discovering interesting cuisine, Myanmar is no different than any other Asian country: new flavors abound. Many travelers, however, are hesitant to sample the food after hearing reports that it's too oily. I too approached the food with trepidation the first time I arrived. But I was delighted to find that there were several intriguing dishes to choose from. Anyone care for fermented tea leaf salad, or the noodle dish known as "burn throat burn tongue"?

Almost all hotels and guesthouses in Myanmar offer their guests a free breakfast, usually an uninspiring plate of eggs and toast, and—if you're lucky—some fresh fruit. The best thing you can do is politely decline and head to a teashop for your morning repast instead. Teashops, as Win Thuya describes in this chapter, are the best places to sample the country's delicious noodle specialties, and also where you can rub shoulders with the locals.

Make no mistake about it: Myanmar is a noodle-crazy nation. In her essay on the country's "noodle wars," Ma Thanegi takes us inside the frontlines, where *monhinga*, *ohn no kauk swe*, and *mondhi* battle it out for supremacy. In another illuminating essay, she breaks down the many varieties of noodles in the outlying ethnic regions of Myanmar. Once you've read this, your appetite for regional cuisine will surely be piqued. Follow Janice Nieder to Kyaing Tong, the picturesque Shan State town that she dubs "the culinary mecca of Myanmar." There she falls in love with an addictive, if somewhat pungent, condiment called *ngapi*. If you buy any to take home, be careful how you pack it; this paste is not something you want smelling up your luggage!

Fisherman cooking in his home near Inle Lake

While most people don't associate Myanmar with wine, the country now boasts well-regarded vineyards. Not only does Manjit Kaur take you to a winery near Taunggyi in Shan State, she marvels at how the availability of vintages from other countries has improved dramatically in recent years, especially in the restaurants of Yangon. Coffee is something else not usually associated with Myanmar, but Viola Woodward found several wonderful cafés that helped to soothe her caffeine cravings. The cakes and pastries that she sampled were pretty darn tasty too.

Despite the abundance of local dishes, visitors will sometimes want to indulge in the comforts of Western food. Yangon is the country's biggest city, and it's not surprising that it boasts the widest range of culinary choices. It's also why most of the essays in this chapter are about eateries in Yangon. In addition to tons of Chinese and Indian restaurants, there are places specializing in French, Italian, Thai, Japanese, Korean, and other global cuisines. Find out which ones are the favorites of our writers in the roundtable discussion of Yangon restaurants, then head out and discover a few favorites of your own.

YANGON DIVISION

Ma Thanegi
hungers for ethnic noodles
around Yangon

When I am too lazy to cook, I stroll out to the shops in my neighborhood, where I can get oodles of noodles from dawn until midnight. This is one advantage of living in Yangon, the country's largest city: the availability of a large variety of noodles, some of which were previously found only in remote parts of the country. To a dedicated foodie like me, the diversity of the 135 ethnic groups of Myanmar is reflected in their food, and the noodle dishes in particular.

The majority ethnic group in Myanmar, the Bamar (Burmese), live in the central part of the country, and their two most common noodles dishes, *monhinga* and *mondhi*, battle it out for the honor of favorite. But the rest of the country's population, especially those ethnic groups living near the borders, ignore this rivalry and enjoy their own variety of noodles.

The Dawei people of the far southern coastal region prefer a noodle dish they call *kut kyee kite*, or "cut with scissors." As the name implies, flat rice noodles are cut, stir-fried with vegetables such as bean sprouts and steamed peas, along with shrimp, chicken, and squid, and then served with a sour spicy sauce. In this part of the country it's common to see customers bring their own veggies and other ingredients to local noodle shops and hand them over for the cook to fry along with their noodles. The last time I was in the region, I saw two male customers stroll up to one street-side noodle shop with little bags of shrimp, squid, and greens, and then take over the cooking process themselves. I asked them why they couldn't simply buy the stuff at the market, take it home, and cook it all there. It's just not the same, they told me.

There is another wonderful south coast Mon dish called *kaw yay kauk swe,* or "gooey noodles." Egg noodles are mixed with a rich chicken stock that is thickened with a little corn starch, making a soup as smooth as liquid silk. Bits of chicken and simmered strands of beaten egg float at the top. You eat it with a special sauce, a mixture of shrimp paste, lime juice, and some pounded green chilies. My cousin loves this dish and often makes it at home. I'm always standing in her kitchen, asking, "Can we eat now? Can we eat now?"

The Rakhaing race living on the western coastline call their noodle dish *ar pu shar pu,* meaning "burn throat burn tongue," and also known as *Rakhaing mondhi.* This is a recipe of thin rice noodles with fish flakes, served dry or in a soup of fish stock strongly laced with pepper and galangal. To make sure the dish lives up to its name, two types of chilies are added: fried, pounded red chilies and lightly cooked, pounded green chilies. I was once visiting the old Rakhaing city of Mrauk U with a friend from Australia, and before I could warn her, she took a hearty bite of *ar pu shar pu* and nearly set her mouth on fire.

The Kachin and Shan races, living, respectively, in the north and northeast, have some of the tastiest noodles in the country. The rice noodles of the Kachin sometimes have slivers of pickled bamboo shoots in them; the shoots can also be served separately as a relish. These noodle dishes tend to be spicier and sharper in taste than Shan noodles. The meats are usually chopped chicken or pork, whole chicken legs or wings, or pork ribs, all cooked until very tender.

Shan noodles have a milder taste, but their spicy herbs make up for it. Shan rice noodles are usually accompanied by crushed peanuts, a dash of salty pickled soybeans, and something similar to Hoisin sauce. They also have a ladleful of chopped chicken or pork cooked in watery gravy and flavored with a powdered mixture of herbs. The noodles are served with a relish of pickled mustard greens, much like Korean *kimchi,* but milder.

Around 1990, after peace accords were signed with various rebel groups, people from remote regions around Myanmar finally enjoyed the freedom to travel. This brought many of them to Yangon. So it was only somewhat recently that the city's residents first discovered these varied ethnic cuisines. Now, along with more well-known favorites like *monhinga* and *mondhi,* we have the benefit of the country's culinary diversity without having to leave the city.

Noodles around Yangon

Ah pu shar pu

"Burn throat burn tongue" noodles are usually served at roadside stalls. They are not found in restaurants serving Burmese (Bamar) and Chinese food.

Happy Café & Noodles

This café serves authentic Kachin noodles. The owner grew up in Kachin State.

62 Inya Rd.
Bahan Township
Yangon
(+95-1) 705-620

Kaw yay kauk swe

Gooey noodles are typically served in Chinese noodle shops. In the Chinatown district you will find numerous venues, including roadside stalls.

Kut kyee kite

For Dawei noodles, look for the stalls inside the compound of the Home Economics Technical School on the corner of Dhammazedi Road and Thanlwin Road, which runs beside the Savoy Hotel.

Giles Orr fortifies himself for Yangon's Shwedagon Pagoda

On my first full day in Yangon, I decided to visit Shwedagon Pagoda, Myanmar's most sacred landmark and the country's most popular tourist attraction. I was staying out in the suburbs with my cousin, who had already left for work that day, and had no idea what my transportation options were. After looking at a map, I discovered that the pagoda was about six kilometers away, and I decided to walk.

It was a clear sunny day with scorching temperatures, and I quickly began to sweat. In Yangon, unlike in Bangkok, there aren't any air-conditioned shopping malls lining the streets where you can slip in and cool down from the heat. After walking for a couple of very hot kilometers, I badly needed some water. I found a small shophouse that sold groceries. The woman running the place spoke no English, so I had my first experience in Myanmar with pointing-and-waving shopping

It was past noon and I was getting closer to Shwedagon, but I realized that I needed to sit down and eat and drink more water before I started my big pagoda tour. I stopped at Aung Thuka, a restaurant located about three blocks from Shwedagon. My first view of the place was not entirely reassuring. The building looked a little shabby, it was open on all sides (no air-con here!), and the ceiling was very low. But it was full of local customers, an encouraging sign that the food would be good.

After being seated, I was taken under the wing of a young waitress who spoke a little English, or at least more than the rest of the staff. Instead of giving me a menu to order from, she led me to a row of pots that were arranged on a long counter at the back, and did her best to explain what was in each one. Most of the choices were meat-based stews in various shades of brown. The stews of Myanmar are often called "curry" because they use similar ingredients, but those worried about spice will be relieved to know that curries in Myanmar are substantially milder than Indian and Thai varieties, while still being quite flavorful.

In addition to these stews, there was a wide variety of vegetables. I chose a crushed corn mix that was drier and less sweet than the North American creamed corn I'm used to eating; still, it was very good. The venison stew was likewise tasty, but the highlight was a dish I was least able to identify. The waitress told me it was "fish balls" in tomato sauce, but the look, texture, and taste all suggested tofu to me. With just a bit of spice, the flavors came together beautifully.

Along with my main meal, I was served traditional side dishes: large leaves to fold my stews in, generous servings of rice, and the famous fermented tea leaf salad *(laphet thoke)*

YANGON & SOUTHERN MYANMAR

to finish. The salad is very much an acquired taste. It has a strong, distinctive flavor, like wet, sour leaves. But don't let my dislike for it put you off. Sample it at least once when you are in Myanmar.

Except for the tea leaf salad, I loved all the dishes I tried. In fact, Aung Thuka offered the best local food of any place I visited during my month of travels around Myanmar. A filling meal cost less than $2, and the location couldn't be better, just a few blocks from Shwedagon Pagoda.

Aung Thuka

The restaurant is quite well known. It is located north of Shwedagon Pagoda, just across from the front entrance of the Savoy Hotel on a small side street between Dhammazedi Road and Shwe Gone Daing Road.

17A 1st St.
Bahan Township
Yangon
(+95-1) 525-194

Robert Carmack craves lobster thermidor at The Strand in Yangon

When I travel to a foreign land, I strive to eat only local foods, and particularly a country's specialties. It's a badge of pride. So while in Singapore, for example, I regularly have coconut-laden *laksa lemak*, and

in Hanoi I order *pho* noodle soup, specifying boiled or raw beef strips for added authenticity.

I don't travel to Bangkok for Indian dishes, nor do I patronize Asia's growing elite of French and Italian skyscraper restaurants. In Chicago I order simple sirloin and baked potato, not *stek frites*. But I must admit, I invariably break my rule when I visit Yangon. Here, I especially crave lobster thermidor—but not from just any place. I have to have it at The Strand, where the recipe's Belle Époque origins are matched with the colonial grandeur of this majestic hotel.

At The Strand Grill the recipe is transformed into a truly delicious dish, updated since Escoffier's time and tasting only subliminally of the heavy white sauce of olden days. Barely a soupçon of English mustard and Parmesan masks the lobster's sweet flesh, and I wouldn't have it any other way. The taste is sublime, tender and succulent, with no cloying quality. By comparison, it leaves the over-priced Phuket lobster dead in its tracks.

A century ago, The Strand was renowned for its lobster thermidor, and today the hotel is one of the few places in the city where you can order the crustacean still live and kicking. I've found scarce small "tails" in local eateries. Even in Yangon fish markets, you aren't likely to find lobster. If you do, it won't be the gargantuan size so prized by aficionados. As well, the cost is out of bounds to all but the most affluent resident of Myanmar. So lobster is relegated to the city's few top hotels, and even then it's rare. Seems most of the country's shellfish is labeled "product of Thailand" to avoid the West's boycott and shipped across the world, leaving very little for in-country consumption.

If you're lucky enough to befriend The Strand's dynamic young chef, Sandro Zimmerman, ask to visit his kitchen to view the critters in their tank. They vary in color from emerald to jade to jasper-tinged black. Locals pay a premium for orange hues, but query the chef and he'll confide there's scant difference in taste. They're all superb.

The Strand

Start saving your pennies, as lobster thermidor at The Strand will set you back about $40.

92 Strand Rd.
Dagon Township
Yangon
(+95-1) 243-377
www.ghmhotels.com

Viola Woodward catches a caffeine buzz in Yangon

"I'm running short on my Starbucks coffee," I overheard a new teacher at my school say one morning.

He's got to be kidding, I thought. Who needs Starbucks in Yangon? While the city is best known for its abundance of teashops, there are now numerous coffee shops, and the selection of domestically grown coffee has also improved greatly in recent years. Coffee is grown in the central region and northern mountains of Myanmar, and one of my favorite brands, Golden Triangle, is sold at City Mart, a chain of Yangon grocery stores. You can also buy fresh beans from Let Ywe Sin Tea and Store, a terrific little shop that's owned by the uncle of one of my students.

Right next door to Let Ywe Sin is Parisian Bakery and Café, which has a luscious assortment of cakes, all baked by a Korean chef. I discovered it the first week after it opened for business. A crew of eight waiters greeted me at the door, quickly seated me, and politely hovered as I perused each pastry on the menu. Along with a piece of ornately decorated chocolate layer cake, with chocolate swirls and shavings perched precariously on top, I ordered an iced cappuccino. Seizing a teaching moment, I mentioned to the waiters that iced cappuccino should be served with ice.

Continuing along Sule Pagoda Road, you will find Café Aroma, one of the more popular branches of a local chain. It serves Lavazza brand coffee at affordable prices, along with tasty desserts. The service at this outlet is always pleasant and attentive. And it's just around the corner from the Thiripyitsaya Sky Lounge, at the top floor of the Sakura Tower, which is home to many international airline offices. Here you can enjoy panoramic views, including Shwedagon Pagoda, from the twentieth floor while you savor every sip of your iced cappuccino or refreshing coffee float.

Another one of my favorite local chains is Moon Bakery. There is a big, popular branch on Mahabandoola Road, but I frequent a smaller one at the Orange Supermarket on Waizayandar Road, where the waiters know me well. As I step inside, usually dripping with sweat from my bike ride, I hear them murmuring, "Iced cappuccino. Iced cappuccino." Sometimes a waiter, seeing me in my hot and exhausted state, will come over and fan me. How embarrassing! Actually, I secretly love that kind of service. Every once in a while, just to see them laugh, I throw them off by ordering a strawberry juice. If I wait more than a week to stop by, they'll ask me where I've been. And they never blink an eye when I order a piece of my favorite Korean mocha cake for breakfast.

If you are a coffee lover and find yourself in Yangon, never fear. There are plenty of good coffeehouses to choose from, and chances are, you'll never give Starbucks another thought.

On a budget

Coffee and pastries are among the best deals for Western fare in Yangon. Depending on the establishment and the elaborateness of your drink, coffee prices range from about 800 to 3,000 kyat. Pastries are generally in that same range.

Sipping and snacking in Yangon

Café Aroma

246-248 Sule Pagoda Rd.
Kyauktada Township
Yangon
(+95-1) 241-943

City Mart

This supermarket chain has many locations around the city. Golden Triangle Coffee costs about $2 for a 280-gram bag (ground or beans).

www.city.com.mm

Moon Bakery

At the time of publication, Orange Supermarket is under repairs due to Cyclone Nargis. In the meantime, you can visit the Moon Bakery branch on the ground floor of Olympic Tower on Mahabandoola Road.

Orange Supermarket
Waizayandar Shopping Centre
Waizayandar Road
Thingankyun Township
Yangon

Parisian Bakery and Café

132 Sule Pagoda Rd.
Kyauktada Township
Yangon
(+95-1) 387-298

Thiripyitsaya Sky Lounge

Sakura Tower, 20th Floor
339 Bogyoke Aung San Rd.

Kyauktada Township
Yangon
(+95-1) 255-277

Let Ywe Sin Tea and Store

The beans here are kept in barrels that will be sealed for you in plastic bags for about $4 a kilo. They can also be ground, and you can sip a cup of coffee in the back with the locals while you wait.

128 Sule Pagoda Rd.
Kyauktada Township
Yangon
(+95-1) 246-313

Our writers share their favorite restaurants around Yangon

When it comes to dining in Yangon, our contributors have more favorite restaurants than we had room for in this chapter. Along with their essays, we are thrilled to include this round table discussion of their additional recommendations. Bon appetit!

Guillaume Rebiere

Feel 3 serves traditional Burmese (Bamar) food. You can choose from a wide variety of dishes in a clean and welcoming environment. I think it's really the best place to have Burmese food in Yangon. It appears the locals agree with me; it's always packed.

Another restaurant I like is Shwe Mi, a Burmese restaurant located near the Savoy Hotel. There is nothing special about the ambience, but the pork curry with mango pickles is the finest in the city.

Don Gilliland

I like Feel 3 too. Ma Thanegi was the first person to introduce me to it. There are dozens of dishes to choose from, all displayed behind a counter. You don't need a menu; just point to what you want. When I visited, it was one of those situations where my eyes were bigger than my stomach, and I couldn't finish everything I ordered. Still, I found room for dessert. I forget what it was called, but it was delicious. Maybe Ma Thanegi can remember the name of it.

Ma Thanegi

It was sago pearls in jaggery syrup, Don, with shavings of fresh coconut. We call this dessert *thargu* in Burmese—it's known as sago elsewhere. Jaggery (palm sugar) comes in dark or light versions (lumps or pellets, respectively). The darker lumps are simply lovely. They have a deep, rich, slightly bitter taste and are used to make syrup for dessert. The light-colored ones can be mixed with plum paste or coconut shreds. Yum! And let me explain about the restaurant's name, because some people get confused. Feel refers to feelings, not groping. People in Myanmar went crazy over that song "Feelings" back in the 1970s—"nothing more than *feelings!*"—and have not yet recovered.

Myriam Grest

When I need to chill out, I drive to the Marina Residence on Kaba Aye Pagoda Road and visit my friend Lisa, the owner of L'Opera restaurant. She is a real Italian, with her big gestures, smiles, and laugh. She is always bringing diners together. One table with a couple chairs can often end up with a dozen or more after a few hours. The Italian food here is excellent, and the service attentive. Whenever I have to cater for incentive groups or guests in my garden, I ask the head chef, Maurizio, to create a menu for me. I believe 100 percent that this is the best fine dining in Myanmar.

Roger Lee Huang

After eating a steak in a creamy white sauce at Onyx, a European-style café hidden down a potholed dirt lane, I became an instant fan of the restaurant's unorthodox semi-fusion cooking. The hearty feta cheese salad, certainly a rare treat in Myanmar, is a healthy alternative. Ask Martin, the owner, about his *kimchi* beef, a dish that has proven to be a great hit with the regulars. The sizzling hot Korean-style beef is piled on top of rice and comes on a sizzling hot plate. Besides the reasonably priced and delicious food, I enjoy the soothing jazz and most of all the friendly and relaxing company of Martin and his staff.

Don Gilliland

One of my very favorite restaurants in Yangon is Monsoon. The first time I went there was with Ma Thanegi ... of course. She knows how to pick the best places. Along with the expected bounty of well-prepared Burmese dishes, Monsoon also serves Thai, Vietnamese, Laotian, and Indonesian cuisine, and the blended fruit smoothies go well with anything you order. Monsoon is tastefully decorated with lovely artwork and photographs on the walls. Up on the third floor, you'll find a variety of local handicrafts and cool things to buy, such as glassware from the Na Gar Glass Factory and umbrellas from Pathein.

Kyaw Zay Latt

Sandy's Myanmar Cuisine is my favorite restaurant in Yangon. Not only does it have delicious food, but it's also a pleasant place to relax and enjoy the city's natural beauty, as you look out on Royal Kandawgyi Lake and the Karaweik Barge. The meals are a little pricey compared to other restaurants that serve local cuisine— an appetizer, main dish, soup, salad, and beer will cost me from $8 to $10—but the quality is always high. My favorite dinner begins with a starter of duck eggs filled with minced prawns, followed by boiled snakehead fish wrapped in moringa leaves, bean soup, and a vegetable salad. For dessert my choice is *shwegyi*, a cake of baked cream of wheat, rice flour, coconut cream, and palm sugar. The waiters at Sandy's are friendly and a good source for the best daily specials. Cooking demonstrations can be arranged by request. I always recommend this unpretentious restaurant to tourists and friends.

Sandra Gerrits

I always enjoy eating Indian food at Golden City Chetty. I walk in, order whatever I want, and minutes later—or, in the case of rice, just seconds—the food is on my table: *chapatti*, *puri*, or one of the excellent *thosa* choices. Fast food in the best sense of the word. And with dishes around 1,000 kyat, I can eat as much of it as I like. Brilliant. The combination of quality, price, cleanliness, and serving size (big!) is what draws me back every time. During lunchtime around noon, the place is a complete frenzy, packed with customers. It is not uncommon to be seated at a table with other people due to lack of space, but most speak a little English, so it can make for nice conversation during your meal.

Wyn Tin Tut

I adore Le Planteur, where great French cuisine (as well as French dishes incorporating local ingredients) is prepared by Boris Granges, the Swiss chef-owner, and his team of local sous chefs. The beautiful two-story mansion has a spectacular garden, where a craggy old cashew tree reigns. I go for either the lobster with delicate melt-in-the-mouth lotus stems, the leg of piglet with honey, or the pan-fried goose liver. The items

on the dessert trolley are sublime, especially the chocolate cake. As for when I want good Burmese food, plus a quiet place to talk with friends, I like Padonmar. The river prawn curry is rich and creamy, and the prawns are huge, like lobsters. Another one of my favorite dishes here is the pork cooked in bean paste, a Bagan specialty called *pone yay gyi*. All my expatriate friends who try it at my urging, after eyeing the dark brown gravy with suspicion, fall for it. The gourd fritters, served as appetizers, are crisp on the outside and so sweet and juicy inside.

Robert Carmack
and Morrison Polkinghorne

We are also impressed with Boris Granges' cooking at Le Planteur. We were there for his New Year's Eve menu of Swiss-French delights, including foie gras, gravlax, lobster, and beef filet. We adore his wine list, certainly the best in the country, and better than most we've seen in Bangkok. As well, a tour group that we were leading inaugurated Boris's new eatery in Nyaungshwe, near Inle Lake. View Point Restaurant serves Shan nouvelle cuisine. Very smart and delicious.

Sudah Yehuda Kovesh Shaheb

One of my favorite restaurants is Green Elephant. It's popular with tourists and expatriate residents. The enterprising owner is from Sittwe in Rakhaing State and is a shining example of a woman from this country succeed-

YANGON & SOUTHERN MYANMAR

ing in the business world. The service at the restaurant is courteous and pleasant. The food is purely Burmese in character and, in my opinion, appropriate to the romantic and relaxing atmosphere of this place. There is a variety of vegetable curries (okra, aubergine, watercress), soups, and salads. One can eat very well for about $10 per person. The elegance is in contrast to another restaurant that I like, the simple Thite Di Shin. Almost all the diners here are locals, gathered in small or large groups. The quality of food is very good, but the price is less than half of what you would pay at Green Elephant.

Ma Thanegi

Fook Mun Lau Seafood is another place I enjoy. Tucked away behind a huge cinema, the ambience is pure Old World Chinese. This is the type of restaurant you see in kung fu movies, where you expect Zhang Ziyi to come flying down from the upper gallery. The food is excellent, especially the Peking duck. Rare delicacies on the menu, such as bamboo clams and mantis prawns, are also excellent but can be expensive.

Feel Myanmar (Feel 3)

This popular branch is on the same road as the French and Indonesian embassies. Be careful not to go to one of the Feel "Burger & Snack" branches by mistake.

124 Pyidaungsu Yeiktha St.
Dagon Township
Yangon
(+95-1) 725-736

Fook Mun Lau Seafood

Kaba Aye Pagoda Rd.
Nawaday Cinema Garden Compound
Mayangone Township
Yangon
(+95-1) 663-743, 661-397, 247-389

Golden City Chetty Restaurant

170 Sule Pagoda Rd. (near Anawrahta Road)
Kyauktada Township
Yangon
(+95-1) 371-839

Green Elephant Restaurant

519A Pyay Rd. at Attiyar St. (Thirimingalar St.)
Kamayut Township
Yangon
(+95-1) 535-231, 720-375
www.greenelephant-restaurants.com

L'Opera Restaurant

Along with this original venue, L'Opera also has a newer branch at Inya Lake.

Marina Residence
8 Kaba Aye Pagoda Rd.
Mayangone Township
Yangon
(+95-1) 650-651
www.marinaresidenceyangon.com
www.myanmars.net/lopera/

Le Planteur

22 Kaba Aye Pagoda Rd.
Bahan Township
Yangon

(+95-1) 541-997
www.leplanteur.com

Monsoon

85-87 Thein Byu Rd.
Botataung Township
Yangon
(+95-1) 295-224, 705-063
monsoon-ygn@myanmar.com.mm

Onyx

Onyx is not directly on the main road, but tucked away on a small lane behind the Samurai Japanese restaurant, near the corner of Thanlwin Road and Dhammazedi Road. If you get lost, just ask one of the kids selling flowers at the intersection.

135 Dhammazedi Rd.
Bahan Township
Yangon
(+95-1) 524-271
casa92@hanmail.net

Padonmar

78C Inya Rd.
Kamayut Township
Yangon
(+95-1) 536-485

Sandy's Myanmar Cuisine

The Kandawgyi Palace Hotel
Kan Yeik Tha Road
Dagon Township
Yangon
(+95-1) 249-255
www.kandawgyipalace.com

Shwe Mi

This restaurant is located on a small side street between Dhammazedi Road and Shwe Gone Daing Road, just across from the front entrance of the Savoy Hotel in Bahan Township, Yangon.

Thite Di Shin (Theikdi Shin)

331/333 Anawrahta Rd.
(corner of 1st Street)
Lanmadaw Township
Yangon

Dining beyond Yangon

View Point Restaurant & Bar

Near Talk Nan Bridge and Canal
Nyaungshwe
(+95-81) 29062
(+95-1) 541-997 (Yangon office)
www.viewpoint.leplanteur.com

MANDALAY DIVISION

Don Gilliland discovers a jumping joint in Mandalay

The first time I visited Mandalay, I made plans one evening to attend the much acclaimed Moustache Brothers variety show. Not wanting my stomach to add any unwanted percussion to the performance, I decided it would be wise to grab a bite to eat beforehand. I consulted my dog-eared guidebook, hoping to find a good restaurant in the vicinity. Located only two blocks from the venue where the Moustache Brothers perform each night, Aye Myit Tar looked promising.

My trishaw driver dropped me off, and I was immediately greeted by a pair of smiling young waiters, ushered to a vacant table, and presented with an English-language menu. After a bit of ordering indecision, I settled on the beef curry and a bottle of Myanmar Beer. As I waited for my food to arrive, ceiling fans whirred overhead, and the room buzzed with the drone of diners chatting and enjoying their meals.

The waiters, mostly teenage boys wearing light blue T-shirts and *longyi*, glided around the room taking orders, serving food, cleaning tables, and occasionally singing along to songs playing on the sound system. Most of the tables were full, occupied by local diners. I sat right in the center of the room, the sole foreign patron, sticking out like a smear of *thanaka* paste on sun-baked skin.

Talk about fast food. My order appeared from the kitchen in less than two minutes. In addition to the curry I asked for, the meal came with a slew of free side dishes such as tomato salad, creamed corn, butter beans, roselle soup, and some mysterious dark green vegetable. A feast, indeed. I enjoyed everything I sampled—well, except a gooey, fishy-tasting dish—

but what impressed me the most was the extraordinary service.

The waiters attentively refilled my glasses of beer and water, and constantly offered extra servings of rice and the various side dishes, smiling the whole time. It was amusing the way these kids waited on me. I felt as if I were in the middle of some hidden camera comedy skit: the waiters whirling, pivoting, running around, and grinning as they battled it out for the prestigious opportunity to be the first one to plop more rice onto my already overflowing plate.

Second helpings? I must have received three or four extra portions of some of those side dishes. Between that and all the beer I guzzled, I felt close to bursting. Eventually, I decided to decline any additional portions. I had visions of the famous "wafer-thin mint" incident from *Monty Python's The Meaning of Life*, and I feared that if I ate just one more bite, my stomach might dislodge its contents in a grotesque shower of half-digested bits.

The quality of food and service at Aye Myit Tar was so outstanding that I took a fellow traveler there for a meal the next night. Once again, everything was fabulous and the joint was jumping. This time there were three tables of foreign customers, no doubt on their way to see that evening's Moustache Brothers' show. At one point, as the sea of attentive waiters temporarily parted, I exchanged bemused expressions with a Western woman at the next table, as if to say, "Can you believe how crazy and wonderful this place is?"

On successive trips to Mandalay, I've enjoyed both lunch and dinner feasts at Aye Myit Tar, proving that those initial, euphoric meals were no fluke. The restaurant continues to satisfy me with its meals—and entertain me with its memorable service.

Aye Myit Tar

Most dishes are around 2,000 kyat. One warning: curry selections can be on the oily side. Every trishaw driver and tour guide in town knows how to get to this restaurant. I tried to cycle there once by myself and promptly got lost, but a helpful trishaw driver—who appeared to be napping by the side of the road—gave me excellent directions.

530 81st St. (36/37)
Mandalay
www.aye-myit-tar.com
(+95-2) 31627

The Moustache Brothers

The Moustache Brothers are a traditional Burmese *Anyeint* troupe. A must-see if you are in Mandalay, their shows are this country's equivalent of a cabaret: a bit of song and dance, lots of comedy, a dazzling display of costumes, and even some bongo playing. They are held at the troupe's home every evening starting at 8:30 p.m. A donation of 8,000 kyat is requested. Shows are performed only when there are a minimum of four people in the audience.

39th Street (80/81)
Mandalay

Jeff Gracia goes bananas over dining in Bagan

With a total of sixteen customers, the Silver House Restaurant was unusually busy for a September evening. Never mind the fact that the customer count comprised only one party—me and my friends.

Seated at one very long table, we were all enjoying a supremely good meal and each other's company. Well, almost everyone was. One kid in the bunch couldn't stay in his seat and was darting around, sticking a camera in front of everyone's face and continuously snapping photos like a hyperactive paparazzo.

During our brief stay in New Bagan, my traveling partner and I had met a lot of very nice people: souvenir sellers, horse cart drivers, and village kids and their parents. It hadn't been hard to attract the attention of all these fine folks, as it was September, the tail end of the rainy season, and we were the only guests staying at our hotel. In fact, judging from the absence of other tourists on the street, we seemed to be the only ones staying in the town.

We were bound for Mandalay the following day and wanted to treat our new friends to a farewell dinner of sorts before we left. We could think of no better place to hold it than at the always splendid Silver House. We'd eaten nearly all of our meals there during the previous four days and had yet to be disappointed.

The first night we dined there, I ordered a tomato salad appetizer, the serving so large it could have sufficed as a full meal. The plate overflowed with juicy slices of red tomato (some places use green tomatoes in their salads), garnished with onions and crushed peanuts, and lightly covered with a flavorful dressing. In addition to that, I chose the beef curry. Served over rice, it was quite tender and tasty, not nearly as oily as some Burmese curries I'd sampled. A platter of fresh fruit (papaya, oranges, and banana) made for a nice, light dessert.

Silver House occupies a large building in the middle of New Bagan. The restaurant is not air-conditioned, but fans keep the air circulating during those frequently steamy times of the year. The owners, U Aung Koont and his wife, are personable hosts and made extra efforts to ensure that we were satisfied with our meals.

For example, for breakfast one morning I ordered the banana pancakes, but when the dish emerged from the kitchen, it looked as if the pancakes had been run over by a horse cart. Despite their misshapen appearance, they were hot and yummy, filled with chunks of bananas, and I devoured them in a few short minutes. No sooner had I done that, when U Aung Koont marched out of the kitchen with another plate of pancakes, apologizing for the lumpiness of the first batch. I said that wasn't necessary, assuring him that the first plate had tasted just fine, but he insisted on giving me this new batch for free, anyway.

Nice touches like that kept us coming back, and ultimately hosting our farewell dinner there. Near the end of that meal, as I sipped the last of my beer and the young photographer snapped away, I surveyed the table and noticed that every single plate was empty. Not a scrap of chicken or puddle of curry to be found. Was the food that good or were our guests that hungry? Probably a bit of both!

Silver House Restaurant

The restaurant is located on the Main Road of New Bagan, directly across the street from Ruby Guesthouse, and one block west of the Eight Faces Pagoda roundabout. Along with serving food, it also offers a variety of bicycles for rent. The cost is 2,500 kyat (about $2) for a full day.

(+95-2) 67036

Misan Restaurant

Another very good New Bagan restaurant is Misan. Unfortunately, its location on the dirt road that leads to the Thazin Garden Hotel makes it difficult to spot if you are venturing down the town's Main Road.

Laurie Weed confirms the hype in Nyaung U

Rarely does a tourist restaurant live up to its own hype, but Aroma 2 in Nyaung

U isn't bluffing. It really does have some of the best Indian food in Myanmar. Along with making this extravagant claim, the restaurant features a large sign out front that brags of a guidebook endorsement and includes the challenge: "Food No Good, You No Pay."

Set in a garden draped in fairy lights along the town's "Restaurant Row," Aroma 2 may look like every other café around it, but the exceptional food and attentive service make it worth seeking out. Dressed in a crisp summer suit and Panama hat, the ebullient owner, born in Myanmar to Indian immigrants, creates a lively, convivial atmosphere as he dashes around the tables every night, chatting with customers and micromanaging the staff. His compelling personality aside, family recipes are the secret to the restaurant's success, the sauces so perfectly balanced that I immediately pictured an ancient Indian granny presiding over the kitchen, grinding up herbs and spices with a mortar and pestle.

What to order? Any set meal including the popular *tandoori* chicken, fish, or one of three different vegetarian *thalis* is spectacular. The meals are served on large banana leaves and accented with five kinds of fresh chutney (tomato, ginger, mango pickle, tamarind, and mint), as well as *dhal*, rice, and all the piping hot *chapattis* you can consume. If you somehow manage not to stuff yourself, you can finish up with the complimentary fresh fruit that appears on your table for dessert.

As for the "No Good, No Pay" offer, when I asked the restaurant's owner about his customers' response, he told me no one ever takes him up on it.

Aroma 2

This Indian restaurant is located near the center of Nyaung U's "Restaurant Row," also known as Yar Kin Thar Hotel Road, which runs between Bagan-Nyaung U Road and Anawrahta Road. Look for the big yellow sign in front of a leafy garden.

SHAN STATE

Jeff Gracia is serenaded in a Nyaungshwe café

I had just taken a spoonful of pumpkin soup, a steaming bowl of savory goodness, when I heard the singing. The voices were like an aural kite, darting and soaring on currents of air, melodious notes climbing higher and higher. A few seconds later I saw the source of these sounds: three young men on bicycles, lazily pedaling down the road and singing joyfully. I put down my spoon and relished the moment.

At the time of this musical interlude, I was dining at Unique Superb Food House. As far as I'm concerned it is the best place to eat in Nyaung-shwe, the gateway to Inle Lake. The name might strike you as brash or boastful, especially when you see the place. You won't find air-conditioned dining rooms or plush verandas. Unique Superb Food House looks more like an ordinary patio, just half a dozen tables arranged under an aging wooden awning. But during my multiple visits, the restaurant certainly lived up to its moniker. Every single dish I had was indeed "superb." We're talking mouth-watering, finger-licking (I hope nobody saw me do this!) goodness.

The first time I came here, I was stumped for something to order, so I asked the waitress for a recommendation. She didn't hesitate to suggest what she claimed was the specialty of the house: the filet mignon. At a restaurant that serves mainly Shan food, I thought it an unlikely entrée to specialize in, but a juicy filet sounded good and so I took her advice. It wasn't quite like the filet mignon I get in US restaurants (it wasn't wrapped in bacon, for one thing), but that piece of meat was tender, succulent, and outrageously inexpensive. A filet of heaven for only 3,500 kyat (about $3)!

During the subsequent pumpkin soup visit, I was diving into a tomato salad when I heard a second pack of cyclists coming up the road, harmonizing even louder than the first bunch. Soup and salad finished, I was about to cut into another eagerly anticipated filet mignon when the electricity suddenly went out. Traveling around Myanmar, you come

to expect these occasional power cuts, so I wasn't annoyed. The locals are always prepared, and as if on cue, my waiter scurried over and set flame to a candle that was already on the table.

After I finished my meal I sat there and nursed a bottle of beer, absorbing the tranquility of this charming little town by candlelight. Before I left the restaurant, yet another singer passed by. To me, such exhibitions of outdoor crooning perfectly reflected the cheerful spirit and vitality of the people of Myanmar.

I encountered musical spontaneity in other cities I visited: street corner serenading in Yangon, guitar virtuosity in Mandalay, and chorusing children in Bagan. But the memory of those singing Shan State cyclists, from the patio of Unique Superb Food House, remains the most vivid in my mind.

Unique Superb Food House

Going north on Myawady Road, the restaurant is on the left-hand side, about two blocks past the Yone Gyi Road intersection. (The Golden Kite, a very good restaurant that specializes in pasta and pizza, is on that corner.) On the right-hand side, just before Unique, you will see a sign reading, "Win Nyunt traditional Burmese massage" (recommended). Dishes range from 1,000 to 3,500 kyat. The spicy braised chicken with mint is excellent.

3 Myawady Rd.
Nyaungshwe

Janice Nieder makes a culinary pilgrimage to Kyaing Tong

Even if you have the most sophisticated food palate, I bet you can easily count on one hand, if at all, the times you've said, "Gee, who feels like chowing down on some good Burmese food tonight?"

Naturally, as a food consultant, I was excited to be invited to visit Myanmar to write about the traditional cuisine. I felt a little like Columbus, sent to explore previously uncharted territories. After spending a few days in Yangon, though, I didn't feel as if I was close to unlocking any culinary secrets. I had eaten some tasty Chinese food, dined on fancy French food, and even stumbled across a Mexican wine bar, but where was the good local food? One reason this quest was so difficult was because most local restaurants use copious amounts of oil in cooking their dishes.

I found a few places that catered more to a traveler's palate by decreasing the amount of oil to just a small slick. However, they also assumed (big mistake in my opinion) that tourists would like a milder, less spicy—and not as authentic—version of local dishes. After querying everyone I met, the general consensus was that Shan State had the best traditional food in the country.

A few days later I excitedly boarded the plane for Kyaing Tong, in eastern Shan State. Although the flight took only about two hours, upon arrival I felt as if I had gone back one hundred years in time. In a valley around Naung Tung Lake, Kyaing Tong is surrounded by picturesque green mountains. Numerous Buddhist pagodas and monasteries add to the quiet beauty and serenity, most welcome after the hustle of Yangon.

On the first night, I ate at the Golden Banyan, where I prearranged to have a Shan dinner prepared. Although the atmosphere of this open-air restaurant may have left something to be desired, the food certainly did not. I began with a pot of vegetable soup, made up of fresh market vegetables and seasoned with a unique blend of herbs and spices. One of my favorite dishes was *ne sa*, a mound of minced pork that was sautéed with shallots and chilies, surrounded by a bed of crunchy cabbage, scallions, chive roots, and herbs, and accented with crispy fried onions and dried shrimp.

I was impressed with the beautifully presented *lakai en rok care*, an elegant local flower stuffed with delicately spiced minced meat and then deep fried. This colorful vegetable stir fry was lightly kissed with a touch of garlic and chilies. I ladled it over piles of fragrant sticky rice. This was also where I first encountered the ubiquitous *ngapi*. Shan people can't make it through a meal without abundant spoonfuls of this hot seasoning paste, made with fermented fish or shrimp. After my first taste, I was immediately hooked. I even began carrying small containers of my favorite *ngapi* with me in case the food I was served needed a fix.

With all this eating, some sort of exercise was mandatory. Taking day treks to visit the local hill tribes was an excellent way to burn off some extra calories. Since there were no restaurants in the area where I trekked, a picnic lunch was always in order. Starting off each morning with a trip to the Kyaing Tong market, I felt just like the locals, as I cheerfully elbowed my way through the crowds, visiting various vendors, and squeezing and sniffing the fruit to make sure it was at peak ripeness.

Every day I'd try a different sausage or jerky to go with my sticky rice selection, and a salad, perhaps made from freshly chopped sweet tomatoes, onions, and chili sauce, all packed in pristine little plastic take-away bags. Instead of my usual ketchup and mustard, here my favorite condiments were a salty piquant sauce made from pickled mustard greens, an intense smoky aubergine spread, or sour slivers of fermented bamboo shoots—definitely an acquired taste.

Kyaing Tong is a lovely destination with numerous hill tribe villages located nearby. And for those in search of undiscovered cuisines, it's a dream come true. After eating beautifully prepared meals, home cooked and at restaurants, and sampling from the endless selection of exotic foods at the market, I concluded that Kyaing Tong is indeed the culinary mecca of Myanmar. It's a pilgrimage that all foodies should make at least once in their lives.

Getting to Kyaing Tong

Yangon Airways and Air Bagan fly from Yangon to Kyaing Tong, the biggest city in eastern Shan State, but the flight is not direct. Normally, the plane will stop in Heho or Mandalay first. You can also reach Kyaing Tong by car from the border town of Tachileik. The border crossing between Thailand and Myanmar, as well as the road between Kyaing Tong and Tachileik, is sometimes closed. Therefore, if you plan on using this as an entry or exit point for the country, be sure to check on its status before you go. It's important to note that if you have entered Myanmar at the Tachileik border crossing, you must also exit the country from this same point. For those making such a land crossing you are allowed only fourteen days in the country. A normal twenty-eight-day visa must be obtained ahead of time before you fly to Yangon and continue your domestic travels from that point.

Golden Banyan Restaurant

Zay Tan Gyi Street (near Wat Chiang Jan and Pa Dung city gate) Kyaing Tong
(+95-84) 21421

Culinary caveats

An excessive amount of oil is used when cooking local dishes. Along with protecting food from bacteria, it is considered insulting to a guest to do otherwise, since it is considered a "luxury" to be able to use a lot of oil. After requesting that my food be made with only a little oil—and finding out that "a little" meant something quite different to the cook—I asked for "no oil" and was extremely satisfied with the results. The other warning is to be sure and ask for food to be prepared "without Ajinomoto." A brand name, Ajinomoto has become a generic term for MSG in Myanmar.

Wyn Tin Tut goes for all you can eat in Shan State

I was on the road in the north of Myanmar with two college pals, trying to recapture the freedom and fun we had enjoyed eons ago before the chaos of marriage, kids, divorce, careers, and grandkids. Along with wanting to reclaim a part of our youth, our aim was to go shopping at a border town in China.

We flew to Lashio in northern Shan State, and from there booked a car for the six-hour drive to Muse, a small town on the Myanmar-China border. As we crossed over the Lwai San Sit mountain range, its jagged tips rose to the skies like uneven teeth, making a strangely beautiful sight. On the seemingly inaccessible hilltops we saw a couple of pagodas. One had a group of glittering, gilded spires, and the other a mammoth standing Buddha image, starkly alone in its surrounding of thick woods.

After arriving in Muse, dumping our baggage at the hotel, and having a quick lunch, we went out to see some shops. Our program for the next four days was simple: breakfasting at noodle shops in the morning bazaar, changing our kyat into Chinese yuan, and shopping in Ruili, the Chinese town across the border, where you will find Chinese-made clothes, shoes, and bags, and carved figures from local jade. To explain how much we shopped, we arrived in Muse with a total of three bags and left with nine.

On our drive back to Lashio, we took the advice of a friend from Yangon who said we *must* try the buffet at a restaurant in Kut Khaing. He had raved about Aung Chan Thar, claiming that he has never eaten so well, for so little, anywhere. When we arrived, we found Aung Chan Thar to be an unassuming place: basically a large hall with a few tables.

But on the left side of the room were long tables with huge enameled basins, all brimming with food. We were each given a plate with a scoop of rice and encouraged to eat as much as we wanted. The owner, a Shan woman in her forties, walked around the restaurant and called out orders to her staff in a gentle but firm voice. "See to Table Nineteen, they need more green tea." "Clear the plates from Table Seven, and give more soup to Table Twelve."

We enjoyed tender pork stews, chicken cooked with herbs (sweet, sour, or spicy), several types of fish, and seven choices of salads. There were also vegetarian dishes of luscious greens, peas, corn, and mounds of succulent wild mushrooms. Altogether the restaurant offered thirty-four dishes, not including two varieties of steaming hot soup. Urged on by the owner to "please take a lot, eat a lot," we ate our fill. I even got a take-out box, as I simply could not leave without more of the fabulous stir-fried mushrooms.

After checking into our hotel in Lashio, my two friends went out for shopping and dinner at the night market, which was conveniently at the end of our street. I stayed behind in our suite, eating dinner alone: the takeaway I had bought at Aung Chan Thar. Even when stone cold, the slippery sweetness of the mushrooms was to be relished. Many months afterwards, I am still able to recall the taste, and I long for more.

Aung Chan Thar

This buffet restaurant is located on the main street in Kut Khaing, a town on the route from Lashio to Muse (about a four-hour drive from Lashio, and definitely worth the trip, in and of itself!). All the taxi drivers know where it is. You can book a taxi through your hotel. Meals are 1,500 to 2,000 kyat.

Dining in Muse

Tohu nwe, or warm tofu paste poured over rice noodles and garnished with pounded peanuts, fried garlic, and a sweet soy sauce, is served at the open-air food center at the morning and evening bazaar. Just pick a stall; they're all delicious. A great choice for vegetarians.

GENERAL MYANMAR

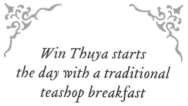

Win Thuya starts the day with a traditional teashop breakfast

Most people in Myanmar get up early, eat early, and go to bed early. This is especially true for anyone living in the countryside, where the day starts at four in the morning when monks at monasteries wake everyone in the area by beating on wooden bars. Unlike in the past, these villagers don't usually have breakfast at home, but instead go to a teashop for their first meal of the day.

I frequently travel around Myanmar, and when I do I'm always looking for good breakfast places. Following local tradition, I seek out teashops. Besides being reliable places to eat, they are where I can meet people and learn more about the area.

Depending upon the city or region, the types of teashop breakfasts are quite different. In Yangon and the lower parts of Myanmar, *monhinga*, a noodle soup with fish, is the most common morning meal. In downtown Yangon, Lucky Seven is a good place to try this dish. I was born in Bagan, and the Yar Kyaw Teashop in New Bagan remains one of my favorites. In the mornings it serves tasty vegetable *samosas* and steaming bowls of *monhinga*.

Also in the area, near the town of Nyaung U in Wetkyi Inn Village, the Myo Myo Teashop is a nice breakfast spot. I usually order the rice salad (*htamin thoke*) with beans and tomatoes. Or try the fried beef with chili if you're looking for a spicy choice. Myo Myo has a good selection of breakfast food, such as rice with grilled dried fish or boiled peas. The latter is a favorite meal for people living in northern Myanmar.

The teashops in Mandalay usually have a greater variety of dishes on their menus than those in other parts of the country. The Minthiha Teashop is my choice here. Not only does it have delicious noodle dishes such as *monhinga* and *ohn no kauk swe*, but also *mondhi,* the popular Mandalay style noodle dish. Other breakfast options include sticky rice with sesame or peanut powder, and an Indian-style *paratha* with beans.

The people in Shan State prefer to eat their beloved Shan noodles for breakfast, but many also like vegetarian dishes such as *tohu nwe* (warm tofu paste with noodles) You can find good noodle stalls at the markets in Shan State tourist towns such Kalaw and Nyaungshwe. But my favorite Shan breakfast food is not a noodle dish; rather, it's *htamin byar,* which is like a rice donut and can be found at Shan noodle shops.

In Rakhaing State, previously known as Arakan, there is a special soup dish for breakfast called *Rakhaing mondhi*. It is similar to regular *mondhi*, but this local version is much spicier. Rakhaing State is also the only place I know in Myanmar where the locals drink tea with salt. It sounds strange, but people here claim that it is good for your health.

In the ancient capital of Mrauk U, my chosen venue is not a restaurant but a small hut with one long table. It's located not far from the old royal palace site on the way to the Vesali Resort. The hut has tasty Arakan food such as gourd fruit and chicken, and a variety of fresh vegetables. The family that runs it does not speak English, so you might need help from a guide if you want to order some of the Arakan specialties.

In Myanmar we have a saying: "You shouldn't forget your friends when you find good food." If you visit a teashop, try to take at least one friend with you, or make a new one when you are there.

Yangon teashops

Lucky Seven

164 West Shwe Gone Daing Rd.
(near Shwedagon Pagoda)
Bahan Township
Yangon

Shwe Kayar Gyi Teashop

There are many branches of this teashop chain in Yangon. I prefer the one located on Gyo Phyu Street, on the east side of Aung San Stadium, near Upper Pansodan Road. Look for a sign in English that says, "Golden Big Kettle Tea & Snacks."

GENERAL MYANMAR

Dagon Township
Yangon
(+95) 379 572

Mandalay teashop

Minthiha Teashop

Corner of 28th Street and 72nd
Street
Mandalay
(+95-2) 33960, 64623

Bagan area teashops

Myo Myo Teashop

This teashop is located north of
Old Bagan near Nyaung U.

Main Road
Wetkyi Inn Village

Yar Kyaw Teashop

Main Road
New Bagan

Ma Thanegi referees Myanmar's battle of the noodles

I can never get enough of the three noodle dishes that compete for supremacy in the unofficial battle for the national noodle of Myanmar. This friendly rivalry between the country's upper and lower regions has been going on for ages, but which dish should take the honors? Is it *monhinga*, the aromatic fish-based broth with rice noodles? Is it *ohn no kauk swe*, a creamy coconut and chicken soup with egg noodles? Or is it *mondhi*, which is drier and more savory, with thick rice noodles in a gravy of roasted bean powder and onion oil?

Monhinga is the most popular dish in the lower Ayeyarwady Delta, where fish is abundant. To understand how complex the noodle battles are, you need only look at this particular dish, for when it comes to *monhinga*, even families are split in their preference. Some members like the soup to be thick, and others go for a clear, more peppery version.

In my opinion, the best *monhinga* should have lots of pepper and lemongrass in a good fish broth, thick with fish flakes and sliced hard boiled eggs, and with circles of banana stem giving it a necessary crunchy texture. If I am in the mood for an even crispier version, I can add gourd fritters, deep-fried in a thick coating of batter and cut into bits. And for a more luxurious taste, I use slices of fish cake and fish roe. A sprinkling of chopped coriander leaves adds an earthy fragrance. While these noodles are common for breakfast, they are also eaten for lunch, afternoon tea, dinner, and as a midnight snack. Anytime is fine!

In the upper part of the country around Mandalay, people insist on *mondhi* as their noodle of choice. To make it, thick rice noodles are mixed with roasted bean powder. When combined with onion oil, they form a delicious gravy, over which is poured a ladleful of chicken that has been cooked with garlic, onion, and a bit of ginger. A thin soup with boiled fish balls clears the palate. Lime wedges and roasted dry chili powder can be added to change the flavor to suit one's individual taste.

Those seeking the middle ground should dine on *ohn no kauk swe*, egg noodles in a creamy soup of good chicken stock and thickened with roasted bean powder, coconut cream, and chunks of chicken. For a piquant taste, add slices of raw onion and lime juice, and for texture, crisp deep-fried curls of flat noodles.

In the upcountry city of Mandalay there is only one shop that I know of selling proper delta-style *monhinga*, and to the south in Yangon, just one place selling true Mandalay-style *mondhi*. But in each respective city, the home grown dishes are common. Happily, *ohn no kauk swe* is easily available throughout the country, north or south.

My ancestors came from Mandalay, but I was raised in the south, so I am exempt from accusations of treachery from either side of the noodle wars— as are visitors to the country. Feel free to enjoy these dishes without getting caught in the crossfire, wherever you are in Myanmar.

Mondhi in the main cities

Sein Pan Pyar

For the best *mondhi* in Yangon, plus many other Mandalay noodles or breakfast dishes and good tea, I would recommend this eatery near the Myoma High School. It also sells other foods throughout the day.

Myo Ma Kyaung Street (at Sagawa Street)
Dagon Township
Yangon

Soe Soe Mondhi Shop

In the courtyard behind Malun Rice Donation Association.

31st Street (84/85)
Mandalay

Monhinga in Yangon

Feel Myanmar

This popular restaurant set in a wooden bungalow serves two types of *monhinga*, from the towns of Laputta and Pyapon in the delta. Laputta-style *monhinga* uses more chili. *Monhinga* is offered only in the morning.

124 Pyidaungsu Yeik Thar St.
Dagon Township

Food canteens at Bogyoke Aung San Market

A few of the shops in this market sell good *monhinga*. When you arrive, ask around.

Bogyoke Aung San Road
Pabedan Township

Tin Tin Aye Monhinga

Behind the Padonmar Theatre, this is the original branch of the Tin Tin Aye chain, which has restaurants all over Yangon. The *monhinga* is so popular here that people arrive in droves around 5 a.m., an hour before the shop opens, ready to wolf down double helpings (about 20 cents a serving). By nine thirty, it's sold out. The shop is dark and noisy, and the air is thick with the smell of lemongrass that wafts out to the street, drawing in yet more customers.

Sanchaung Street (off Pyay Road)
Sanchaung Township

Sagar Gyi Monhinga

This is a small café with stools spilling onto the pavement. It is popular with shoppers at nearby Hledan Market. It is located on the left side of the market; ask anyone in the area for directions. Servings here are also around 20 cents.

80 Hledan Street
Kamayut Township

Robert Carmack feasts on traditional Burmese curry

There are several sorts of eateries in Myanmar, from hawker stalls and teashops to small cafés and up-market restaurants. But my favorite remains the *htamin hsain*, the humble rice and curry shop. These restaurants typically offer a cafeteria-style range, with numerous dishes cooked and set behind a glass partition; in the hygienic West, we would call it a "sneeze guard." There is no need to consult a menu here. Just pick and point, and the establishment will round out the offerings, ensuring that you get "a balanced meal," as my mother was wont to say.

Myanma asar asa is a general term for most Burmese (Bamar) food, and at every *htamin hsain* I have visited, it's a veritable feast. Rice is always king, but the dozen or so side dishes crown its glory. A standard spread includes pulses such as butter beans or soybeans cooked with turmeric, or a lentil *dhal*; a clear-broth gourd soup or sour tamarind soup; and a light and mildly spicy salad of raw fruits or vegetables—locals like it "*chin-chin, ngan-ngan, sut-sut*," an expression they use meaning "sour, salty, and hot."

Mildly tart salads from pennywort to citron to crisp-fried chicken skin are all typically bound with chickpea flour. There will also be some curries, variously of fish, chicken, prawns, or "mutton," which is actually goat. Concurrently a relish is eaten with raw vegetables. Cooks prepare these sumptuous spreads in the early morning, and serve them throughout the day. But late morning and the noon hour are when I head to the roadside eateries, for local food at its freshest.

Unlike Indian and Thai food, the curries of Myanmar are mild and simply cooked without too many spices. I suspect it is a badge of honor amongst native Bamar to differentiate their food from their Bengali neighbors. As a matter of course, the cook fries onion and garlic as a base, which is then reserved and re-added shortly before serving. One cook explained to me that this procedure keeps the oil flavorsome, but prevents the dish from becoming overwhelmed by the pungency of onion and garlic kept in too long.

Other ingredients include ginger, turmeric, and chili powder, along with *ngapi*, which cooks commonly add in copious quantities. This came as no surprise to me. Whenever I wander through a local market, I spy humungous mounds of shrimp paste, double the size I've found at markets in any other Southeast Asian country.

Only occasionally do the people of Myanmar use an Indian-style curry powder, *masala hmont*, typically consisting of cinnamon (or its close relative cassia), cloves, cardamom, and black pepper. Even then, it is only frugally sprinkled atop a finished dish. In regards to chili, locals cook with two versions, but both are more akin to mild paprika than fiery cayenne. A slightly salty, bright red powder that primarily colors, *a yaung tin hmont* infuses dishes with a subtly complex flavor. The other is a richer, dark red pepper, slightly similar to paprika, and can be used by the heaping teaspoonful before the barest glimmer of sweat hits the brow. Deeply hued Alleppey turmeric finishes the spice trifecta. I always purchase bags of these spices before leaving the country, as it's fresher than anything found in the West, and is a fraction of the cost.

At Mar Lar Thein Gi in New Bagan, one of my favorite eateries in the country, I asked proprietor Ma Yin Teh to show me how to cook a Burmese-style curry. After adding meat and vegetables, plus a generous slop of oil,

she boiled down the stew. This simple gravy is the base for many dishes, which probably explains why tourists find Burmese cooking "too much of the same." Likewise, my Western friends complain that it is too oily. In fact, the oil is a protective coating against air-borne spoilage in a country without reliable refrigeration. Peanut oil is the most popular, but sesame and soy oils are also used to flavor. Unfortunately, cheap (and indigestible) palm oil from Malaysia is now entering the market.

Throughout the meal, a weak, Chinese-style green tea is offered for free, and afterward, hard lumps of jaggery (palm sugar) are taken. Otherwise, sweets are typically served at a teahouse. Surprisingly, one of my favorite Burmese dishes, fermented tea leaf salad (*laphet thoke*), is often eaten in place of dessert. Green tea leaves are steamed and buried to ferment for six months, then washed and pounded with garlic, and tossed variously with sesame seeds, nuts, fried beans or peas, dried fish, fried garlic, and ginger. Though unusual, it's a delicious finish to a rice and curry meal.

Curry buffets around Myanmar

Mar Lar Thein Gi

This restaurant is located just across the street from the market on the town's main road.

New Bagan
(+95-61) 60397

GENERAL MYANMAR

Pakokku Daw Lay May
73rd Street (29/30)
Mandalay
(+95-2) 35170

Sayarma Gyi
I consider this the best restaurant in the country!

46 21st St.
Panhlaing Quarter
Bago
(+95-52) 22508

Thite Di Shin (Theikdi Shin)
331-333 Anawrahta Rd. (corner of 1st Street)
Lanmadaw Township
Yangon
(+95-1) 223-503

Manjit Kaur pairs fine wines with local cuisine

When I first moved to Yangon in 1993, I couldn't help but notice all the red stains on the sidewalks and streets. As a first-time visitor, I thought I might have wandered into prime wine country—albeit it one where people spill a lot. Unfortunately, as I soon discovered, those weren't splashes of Merlot, but the expectorations of enthusiastic betel nut chewers.

I'm a wine lover, and back in those days finding a good bottle of wine in Yangon was difficult. If I was lucky enough, I might track down a bottle of red, white, or even something sparkling, but there was no guarantee that it would be any good. After all, how long had it been stored and where did it come from?

That was then and this is now. Thankfully, shopping for imported food, liquor, and wine in Myanmar has become much easier. The variety gets better every year, and you can now find wine at stores and supermarkets all around Yangon. The selection is especially good at a local chain, City Mart, which carries French, Italian, Australian, Chilean, Spanish, South African, and even local wines. The employees are familiar with the products and can provide appropriate suggestions. Another local food and wine distributor, Quarto Products, caters to both wholesale and retail markets, offering a wide selection of quality wines from a variety of countries at reasonable prices.

But what about the relationship between wine and the food of Myanmar? After all, what can you pair with a bottle of Rothschild? Yangon's Green Elephant Restaurant offers bell-ringing local cuisine that wakes up your taste buds. The sour roselle leaf soup in fish stock makes a wonderful starter when served with a chilled Chardonnay. The famous fermented tea leaf salad *(laphet thoke)* with ginger is offered as an interesting appetizer and excellently paired with a chilled Italian Soave. You might also try the pork curry with monkey nuts, a dish offering a betel-nut-like aroma and flavor that goes well with a light Pinot Noir.

Yangon's best French restaurant, Le Planteur, also offers fantastic cuisine and fine wines, served by a well-trained staff. It maintains a cellar with more than twenty thousand bottles. Owner and chef, Boris Granges, is passionate about vintages and will be able to advise you on what to order to complement his gourmet heaven of a menu: layered goose liver foie gras with banana flower and palm wine aspic; warm Japanese scallop salad with lentils; rack of lamb with tea leaf salad; black truffle ravioli with Pecorino cheese sauce; char-grilled potatoes au gratin; and many other memorable entrées, appetizers, soups, salads, cheeses, and desserts.

Eventually, my search for fine wine in Myanmar took me to Taunggyi, an old hill station in Shan State, where there is a vineyard near the village of Aythaya. This vineyard, Myanmar's first, was established in 2000 on ten hectares of land, at thirteen hundred meters above sea level. A pair of German wine experts and Myanmar enthusiasts, Wolfgang Schaefer and Peter Hoehnen, have proven that top-quality vines can be grown here by launching two brands: Aythaya and Kambosa. The winery's managing director, Bert Morsbach, told me that the selected grape varieties are from cuttings and grafted rootstalk of reds such as Cabernet Sauvignon, Shiraz, Tempranillo, Egiodola, Barbera, Moscato, and Dornfelder. The white wines are made from Sauvignon Blanc, Semillon, and Chenin Blanc, whereas the rosé is a cuvée from a special Italian Muscat and Shiraz.

After visiting the winery, I had the opportunity to sample some of their wonderful wines on the beautiful terrace of the Winegarden Restaurant, overlooking the vines. At first glance, this *terroir* reminded me of the vineyards in Burgundy, France. As I sipped my glass of wine and admired the view, the floral scents of grapevines and the smell of musty earth filled the air. I took a deep breath, closed my eyes, and listened to the sound of pruning shears clicking away in the distance.

In between sipping and admiring the view, I ordered lunch. My over-indulgence in good food and wine was followed by a stroll around the vineyards. Amongst the grapevines, female workers assisted with the irrigation. Dressed in traditional *longyi* and with *thanaka* paste smeared on their faces, they waved as I walked by. "*Mingalaba*," I called to them, and they replied with giggles and wide grins.

That evening I had dinner with friends at the Golden Kite Restaurant in nearby Nyaungshwe. We decided to open a lightly chilled bottle of Aythaya Sauvignon Blanc to accompany our Hawaiian pizza, which was absolutely delicious. Looking around the restaurant, I saw a familiar face: Boris from Le Planteur. He told me that he and his wife had just launched the View Point, a new restaurant in Nyaungshwe featuring Shan Nouvelle Cuisine. "Make sure you drop by sometime," he told me. Shan cuisine with French wine? Most definitely!

GENERAL MYANMAR

Wining and dining around Myanmar

City Mart

City Mart has numerous branches around Yangon. For addresses, check out the company's website.

www.city.com.mm

Golden Kite Restaurant

Yone Gyi Road
Nyaungshwe
(+95-081) 29327

Green Elephant Restaurant

519A Pyay Rd. at Attiyar Street
(Thirimingalar Street)
Kamayut Township
Yangon
(+95-1) 535-231, 720-375
www.greenelephant-restaurants.com

Le Planteur

22 Kaba Aye Pagoda Rd.
Bahan Township
Yangon
(+95-1) 541-997
www.leplanteur.com

Myanmar Vineyard

Along with offering tours and wine tasting, the vineyard is home to Winegarden Restaurant.

38G Myitzu St., Parami Avenue
(head office)
Mayangone Township
Yangon
(+95-1) 664 386
www.myanmar-vineyard.com
info@myanmar-vineyard.com.mm

View Point Restaurant & Bar

Near Talk Nan Bridge and Canal
Nyaungshwe
(+95-81) 29062
(+95-1) 541-997 (Yangon office)
www.viewpoint.leplanteur.com

Bowlful of bean sprouts

SEEING THE SIGHTS

Fresh perspectives on exploring must-see attractions

Myanmar has no shortage of captivating attractions. The glittering gold majesty of Yangon's Shwedagon Pagoda, the "far as the eye can see" splendor of Bagan's ancient pagodas, and the jaw-dropping beauty of the mountain-fringed Inle Lake area are obvious highlights. As any visitor will testify, impressive sights and scenery can be found no matter which part of the country you explore.

My favorite sort of "touring" consists of nothing more than walking or cycling around a town, absorbing my surroundings, and trading smiles and greetings with the locals. Who needs an itinerary? I'd rather wander and get lost. I think I've seen more interesting sights that way than on any guided tour I've ever taken.

Of course, this doesn't mean that you should discount the benefits of using a good guide or travel agency, a selection of which are recommended on page 267. There are many personable and knowledgeable guides who can enhance your experience. Whether it's a freelancer you meet on the streets or someone you hire for a specific excursion, a guide can be an invaluable addition to your trip.

Accepting an offer from a freelance guide, somewhat reluctantly at first, Leif Pettersen explores Yangon's famous Shwedagon Pagoda. This impromptu tour leads to not only an insider's view of the country's incredible "Buddhist theme park," but also a nap with locals in one of the resting areas. Being open to new experiences adds to Steve Goodman's experience, as well. In a quest to find snake blood vendors at a Yangon market, he strays up to the top floor, where he discovers a fish sausage factory and winds up sipping herbal whiskey with the personable factory owner. Mick Shippen also experiences the benefits of just meandering with no specific destination in mind, as he mingles with the pottery makers of Kyauk Myaung.

Stupas in Indein village near Inle Lake

From Yangon's historic Strand Hotel, where Robert Carmack sneaks behind the upscale façade for a glimpse of the old un-renovated section; to Kyaiktiyo's Golden Rock, where I climb to the top to find the incredible monument aglow in the halo of a nearly full moon; to colonial Mawlamyine, where Graydon Hazenberg follows in Kipling's footsteps, Myanmar offers diversity. One of its most photographed places is the longest teakwood bridge in the world, and the location of Serena Bowles' encounters with giggling monks, weathered fishermen, grumpy ducks, and oh what an incredible sunset! And just eighty kilometers from Yangon, Bago makes a perfect day trip, as Peter J. Walter learns when his attempt to catch a train leads to an unforgettable car trip with a few locals instead.

It's unlikely that you will encounter hordes of tourists during your travels around Myanmar, even at the more popular destinations. But once the masses find out how spectacular Myanmar is, that situation will soon change. Along with each of the intriguing recommendations in this chapter, this is yet another reason that you should make plans to visit soon.

YANGON DIVISION

*Morgan Edwardson
wanders the streets
of Yangon*

The insistent ring of my alarm clock jars me awake. It's four in the morning. I rub my eyes and groan. I don't especially want to get out of bed at such a wretched hour, but my flight from Bangkok to Yangon has an early departure, so I don't have much choice in the matter.

The flight is uneventful. Before I've read the first hundred pages in my Ian Rankin paperback, the plane has landed, and I've quickly passed through immigration and customs. I remember the funky time change—Myanmar is thirty minutes behind Thailand—and reset my watch. I hail a taxi outside the terminal. No working AC, as usual, but I roll down the window and let a soothing breeze wash over me.

Five traffic lights and thirty minutes later, I'm at my hotel. At check-in, the receptionist announces that the power is out. Unfortunately, this is a common occurrence in Myanmar. The electricity should be working later in the morning, she predicts. Up in my room I unpack my bags, brush my teeth, change shirts, and then rush down the stairs and out into the streets of Yangon again.

I love this city. No matter how many times I return, I never get bored of roaming, gazing at the dazzling kaleidoscope of faces, and absorbing the intoxicating stew of sights, sounds, and smells. Yangon's populace encompasses a staggering range of ethnic groups, and there is additional diversity amongst that lot: businessmen in dark suits, monks in red robes, students in green *longyi* uniforms, street vendors and office workers in their own *longyi* patterns, and the occasional tourist shuffling along in ripped jeans or baggy shorts, nose buried in a guidebook.

I hear a lot of people dismiss Yangon as a one-hit wonder. Go and see Shwedagon, they advise, and then get out of the city and explore the rest of Myanmar. That's nonsense. I'm not saying the rest of the country isn't spectacular—it certainly is—but there's much more to Yangon than one big pagoda. Take walking around, for example. It's never a lonely experience. I don't have to wander far before some friendly local strolls up alongside of me and strikes up a conversation.

"Hello, sir. How are you today? Would you like to change some money?"

I smile, say no thanks to the fellow with the red teeth, and keep walking.

Yangon is not a quiet city. Street vendors loudly proclaim the prices of their wares as pedestrians steadily stream past. Buses rumble down the streets, stopping to dislodge passengers, as conductors yell out destinations for the benefit of the next wave of commuters, who are all attempting to squeeze into the already packed vehicle.

I observe men drinking tea at makeshift sidewalk cafés, women shopping at no-frills street markets, and children flying kites or playing games such as marbles and badminton. Outdoor fun. What a concept! Besides the pastiche of people, the architecture of Yangon also offers striking visual contrasts: colonial-era courthouses and hotels, crumbling Chinese shophouses, golden pagodas, majestic mosques, stately old churches, and a sole serene synagogue.

"Hello, sir. Where do you come from? Would you like to buy some postcards?"

I smile, say no thanks to the small boy wearing a "World's Greatest Mom" T-shirt and keep walking.

Later in the morning, I stop at Yatha Teashop for some nourishment. After a couple cups of sweet hot tea, some good, greasy potato *samosas*, and an interesting conversation with a Yangon architect, I feel rejuvenated. Yatha is always busy and boisterous. Waiters shout orders to the kitchen, whip out rags to wipe tables, and refill thermoses of Chinese tea. The customers, a mostly male bunch, catch up on the latest news, rumors, and soccer scores, while enjoying the tea and grub. Where, I wonder, do the neighborhood women go for their tea and gossip?

"Hello. How are you? Where are you going? Do you need a taxi?"

I smile, say no thanks to yet another polite guy chewing betel nut, and keep walking.

For some strange, wonderful reason, used books are easy to find in Yangon, sold both at shops and sidewalk stands, especially on Pansodan Street. However, I see few that were printed in the past thirty years. Most of the tattered titles are Burmese-language tomes, but some dealers also offer English-language paperbacks. At one shop I find titles by Agatha Christie, Somerset Maugham, Nelson Algren, Dale Carnegie, Joseph Conrad, and Dostoevsky. Another stall has a Che Guevara biography with an introduction by none other than Fidel Castro.

"Hello, sir. Where are you from? Do you need a guide today? I can show you many interesting places."

I smile, say no thanks to the well-dressed fellow with surprisingly white teeth, and keep walking.

Okay, you get the point. There are lots of people in Yangon trying to offer their services as guide, driver, or money changer. My tendency as a solo traveler is to quickly dismiss these characters, avoid eye contact, and walk away. I'm the sort who prefers to aimlessly walk the streets without being bothered. I don't want a ride or a guide, nor do I want to buy any souvenirs. But I've come to the realization that in Yangon not all of the people saying hello are trying to take my money. Most of them are just curious, friendly folks who only want to chat with a foreigner. Sometimes I have to remind myself to take the time and do just that.

By one o'clock I'm hungry again. Where to eat lunch today? Nilar Biryani or the Golden City Chetty Restaurant? Both are in the Sule Pagoda vicinity, both are inexpensive, and both serve good Indian food. I settle on Golden City Chetty, mainly because it's on the same block as my hotel.

Speaking of which, I wonder if the electricity will be working when I return to my room. No matter. It only adds yet another unpredictable dimension to the Yangon adventure. As far as I'm concerned, keep the surprises coming.

Golden City Chetty Restaurant

170 Sule Pagoda Rd. (near Anawrahta Road)
Kyauktada Township
Yangon
(+95-1) 371-839

Nilar Biryani

216 Anawrahta Rd. (31/32)
Pazundaung Township
Yangon
(+95-1) 253-131
http://myanmarnilar.com/

Yatha Teashop

353 Mahabandoola Rd. (39/Seik-kanthar)
Botataung Township
Yangon
(+95-1) 349-341

Money honey

You can't walk for more than fifteen meters around the Sule Pagoda area, or nearby Mahabandoola Park, before being approached by some guy (and it's always men) asking if you want to change money. Around Bogyoke Market the money changers are also thick. By exchanging money on the street, you will get a substantially better rate than the "official" rate quoted at the airport. If you are uncomfortable with changing money on the streets, hotels are a good place to do this and offer exchange rates that are only slightly less than street rates—and you won't run the risk of getting short-changed. It is very important to bring clean, crisp US bank notes, since notes with marks or rips of any kind will not be accepted. Also, make sure to bring what you need with you. ATM machines are nonexistent, and few hotels, restaurants, and shops accept credit cards.

Leif Pettersen dozes off at Yangon's Shwedagon Pagoda

During my first afternoon in Yangon, as I made my random rounds through the city center, a local man sidled up to me, speaking excellent

English. He kept me company for several minutes before informing me that he was a tour guide. I really hate being approached by independent guides, but U Hla Toe was so nice, and provided the best conversation I'd had all day, that I didn't tell him to get bent.

In the end, I'm very glad I didn't. Toe turned out to be a great guy and quite knowledgeable. After he tagged along for my walk down the river, giving me his spiel and casually inserting some interesting nuggets about life in his country, I realized that I needed him. I had only one full day in Yangon and a lot of ground to cover. I could have stuck to my Independent Traveler guns and muscled through unassisted, but that would have opened me up to the usual energy-draining, foreigner-in-an-unfamiliar-city aggravation and delays. Not the best way to launch ten days of high-speed touring in a comfort-starved destination. We arranged to meet early the next morning at my guesthouse.

We kicked off the day at a bustling outdoor market, well off the beaten tourist track, where in essence I became the main attraction for shoppers rather than the other way around. Next we visited Chaukhtat-gyi Paya, home to Yangon's giant Reclining Buddha, followed by a lengthy five-course lunch at a local restaurant. Then, after a short walk, we arrived at the day's main objective: Shwedagon Pagoda. While in Myanmar I would eventually see more *payas* than most people see in

two lifetimes, but none could hold a candle to Shwedagon.

Shwedagon is immense, like a Buddhist theme park. Aside from the towering main *stupa*, there are more than eighty other buildings in the complex, some being simple *zayats* (small rest houses) holding a single modest Buddha figure, and others exceptional *pathos* (temples). The central *stupa* and several of the surrounding statues and religious artifacts date back more than one thousand years. Various members of local royalty and Myanmar's rich and famous have donated their weight in gold leaf to wallpaper the *stupa* over the centuries, and I was told it's estimated that there are fifty-three metric *tons* of gold covering the thing today. The only security? Monks. Very telling of the Buddhist mindset, eh? A similarly unprotected treasure, plopped down in central Los Angeles, would be plundered down to the foundations in a minute.

Despite my best efforts, I hadn't gotten enough sleep the night before, and our lunch feast dropped me into a lethargic food hangover. Toe suggested we join the dozens of locals napping in the *zayats*. Initially, I wasn't enthusiastic about this idea. I'm regrettably picky about my sleeping arrangements, and a filthy hardwood floor in a public place in mid-afternoon heat that was capable of liquefying hair provided far from my ideal napping conditions. Nevertheless, I was dead on my feet and willing to try anything for some relief. I fell asleep almost instantly.

Thirty minutes later, refreshed from my nap, I set out to take in the wonders of Shwedagon. We walked around the complex for several hours, during which time I rarely put down my camera. Every structure, every Buddha, every angle was stunning—and each time I focused, it was going to be the greatest picture ever. We ducked into a past-and-present photo display of the pagoda that included close-ups of the staggering amount of gold, silver, jade, and jewels hanging off the top of the main *stupa*: allegedly more than five thousand diamonds and two thousand rubies and emeralds.

While we were wandering through the compound, we came upon a ceremony for boys being initiated as novice monks. This was a big deal, and Toe was thrilled that I was going to see it. This rite, known as *Shin Pyu*, kicked off with a procession led by a woman throwing out candy to children. Next came the novitiates, boys who looked no older than ten, all being carried by a parent. Families can offer their children to the monasteries at a young age—some appeared to be only four or five—to begin their Buddhist training. Bringing up the rear of the procession were young female escorts.

The kids were dressed in ceremonial robes, orange for the boys and peach for the girls, and all wore odd little decorative hats. Everyone was arranged in front of the main *stupa*, and the kids took some sort of vow, while a team of photographers documented everything—including me at one point, standing to the side also taking photos.

Afterwards, Toe and I settled down at a good vantage point and waited for the sun to set. Huge spotlights are trained on the main *stupa* after dark, making this the best time to catch a good glimpse of the jewels twinkling high above. Then we left Shwedagon, taxied back to my guesthouse, and ate dinner at a nearby restaurant.

Though I asked him repeatedly, Toe would never volunteer his exact fee. He said he normally asked people to give him what they felt was appropriate. It was my first full day in Myanmar, and I had no idea how much that should be. Apparently, the amount I gave him was generous, because when I met him during my swing back through Yangon a week later, he was ecstatic to see me and treated me like an old friend.

Touring Shwedagon Pagoda

Yangon's Shwedagon Pagoda can be reached by climbing one of four covered stairways. The most popular entrance is on the south side, just off U Htaung Bo Road. The southern and northern entrances have the option of steps or an elevator, while the western entrance has an escalator instead of stairs. Entrance fee is $5. There is also a 500 kyat camera fee. Shwedagon is open daily, 5 a.m. till 10 p.m.

YANGON & SOUTHERN MYANMAR

Personal service

If you're heading to Yangon and would like to contact U Hla Toe for guide services, you can reach him by email. Sending and receiving emails in Myanmar is very expensive for locals, so be sure to include all information, including dates, times, and tour requests in your initial message.

batin@mptmail.net.mm

Suggestions for tipping

Many freelance guides will give an "up to you" response when you ask what you should pay them. Generally, a freelance guide is paid anywhere from $10 to $30 for a daylong tour of Yangon, depending on his experience and language skills. Freelance guides for Shwedagon Pagoda typically receive around $5 to $10 for a tour of a few hours. To find an official tour guide, you can start with the companies listed on page 267.

Robert Carmack explores Yangon's legendary Strand hotel

"Ooh la la, c'est magnifique," purred the French tourist as she strolled through the lobby of The Strand. Her almost inaudible reflection was said to herself, but as an involuntary eavesdropper, I suddenly felt a little proud that I was not a mere sightseer, but rather a guest at the hotel.

The woman was with a small group treating the property as part of a tourist circuit of "Colonial Rangoon." Some such seekers come for a very British afternoon tea, while most of the others sneak in on the subterfuge of surveying the hotel's gift shop. So how does a mere hotel warrant as a must-see stop, especially when, like The Strand, it is not ostentatious and its furnishings less than grand? The answer is history. This stately colonial remnant is one of those experiences unique to the annals of heritage travel. Moreover, there is nothing else like it in the entire country.

The Strand was opened in 1901 by the Sarkies Brothers, the same family that opened Singapore's famous Raffles Hotel. After witnessing an eclectic century of colonialism, war, independence, and economic isolation, this famous landmark closed in 1990 for a $15 million facelift, reopening three years later as the country's showcase hotel. Alas, I personally never knew the old Strand Hotel, neither the noble Edwardian establishment that hosted grandees such as Somerset Maugham, nor the later post-war structure of shabby dilapidation. I did, though, know where to find glimpses of both.

Only the original, front three-story building underwent renovation. I didn't realize this until one day when I meandered behind the lobby, between the business office and the River Gallery, and found a tower with an old birdcage elevator, complete with a sign warning against more than five passengers at a time. I couldn't resist the temptation, and took the stairs up to the old, un-renovated section, a rabbit warren of crumbling rooms and decades of dust. This vacant, ignored area gives an idea of how low the hotel sank before new management took over. You also get an appreciation for how well the renovations succeeded.

Stepping through the front doors today is a bit like entering a time warp, reinterpreted for modern sensibilities. I revel in it. The Georgian-style portico colonnade covers arriving guests from the elements, just as in yesteryear. Potted palm fronds look straight out of an Edwardian parlor, complemented by creamy cool tiles and slightly austere wicker and teak furniture. It's much more style than actual affluence, though. Looking at historic photos, I get the feeling that old hotels such as this were not as deluxe as Hollywood portrays. Here you could get a clean bed and private room, sometimes with en suite toilet, and—luck be willing—a gin and tonic with ice. Like a private club, such colonial hotels were little oases of European "civilization" in an alien environment.

Staying at The Strand today distinctly lightens my pocketbook, but it is still much less expensive than similar hotels in other countries. And not staying at The Strand while in Yangon would be like visiting Hanoi without sleeping at the Metropole; seeing Singapore and not drinking a Sling at the Raffles; or touring Bangkok without eating at the Oriental. The Strand is a true *grande dame*, but unlike its restored contemporaries welcoming busloads of affluent tourists, it uniquely continues an aura of quiet gentility.

Perhaps that's to do with the feeling that you are alone in this vast hotel. At full house, there are rarely more than sixty guests. The lobby is calm, with just a few people quietly mingling. No Louis Vuitton or Shanghai Tang outlets here. Tucked behind the signature Grill restaurant are just a couple of small shops and a contemporary art gallery. Surprisingly, there's not even a bakery to tempt the moneyed populace with the hotel's prestige tastes.

One block from the riverfront, The Strand's location is dead smack in the colonial heart of Yangon, but the river's current commercial shipping takes place far from surveying eyes, which is a pity, as the hotel's water view was once its best feature. Today, an ugly fence and scraggy plantings mask the fluvial setting. There's also a hawker market across the street along the riverfront, but restricted to locals, with "no foreigner" warnings posted. Still, The Strand capitalizes on its location by providing a charming pen-drawn walking map, printed on brown recycled paper, listing neighboring architectural treasures with a short history on each.

The Strand boasts much more than pedigree and location, though. Amongst the dilapidation of decaying Yangon, it is an oasis. Upon arrival at the airport, for example, I was personally escorted through customs and immigration by a member of the staff. Butlers surreptitiously attended my room while I had breakfast, and again while I was out on a short stroll. Then there were the smart-looking doormen in their sandals, checked *longyi*, dark jackets, and collarless white shirts. I adored the huge bathrooms, sky-high ceilings, and ceiling fans, as well as The Grill, The Café, and The Bar, all of which made me feel like a colonial traveler of yesteryear.

Strand Hotel

92 Strand Rd.
Dagon Township
Yangon
(+95-1) 243-377
www.ghmhotels.com

Steve Goodman encounters fishy business in Yangon

Theingyi Zei is one of Yangon's liveliest markets, located about a block from the more famous Bogyoke Market. While staying in the city, I stopped by one day with my travel buddy from San Francisco. We were looking for snake blood vendors or dealers that sold herbal medicines.

We weren't interested in buying anything, but simply curious about the exotic ingredients used to make such concoctions.

After finding only the usual assortment of clothing and dry goods for sale, we were about to leave when we decided out of curiosity to climb the stairs to the seemingly empty upper floors. On the top two floors of the enormous five-story building, we made an unexpected find: a fish sausage factory.

The owner, U Tin, seemed surprised to see a couple of foreigners, but was most welcoming as he enthusiastically showed us around his facility, one that not only makes fish sausage, but also—lucky for us—manufactures wine, vinegar, and brandy. The factory used to be a seafood restaurant, but over the years U Tin grew less interested in being a restaurateur and more interested in being an entrepreneur.

University educated as a chemist, he began with wine and then branched out. With mad scientist fascination, he experimented with snake-based remedies, vinegar, wine, brandy, frozen fish sausage, and fish cakes. One of his special mixtures stops women from excessive bleeding after childbirth.

As we explored, I noticed large glass cisterns containing snakes, turtles, lizards, scorpions, and other strange specimens marinating in a strong herbal whiskey. Accepting U Tin's offer to sample the brews, I drank some shots. Other than losing the feeling in my legs for awhile, I felt fine.

Inside the factory about a dozen young women with *thanaka* paste on their faces sat around a big stainless steel table cleaning fish in preparation for making the sausages. The freshly caught fish were beheaded and then washed before being gutted and cleaned again. Ingredients were portioned out and mixed into the final pungent slurry before the sausage was pressed into tubular skin forms. Finally, it was packaged and frozen for shipment to grocery stores throughout Myanmar.

As for the remains, nothing was left to waste. The fish heads were sold up the street in Chinatown and used to make the traditional Chinese delicacy of fish-head soup. The guts were sold back to fishermen and used as chum. But that wasn't all. Even the fish skins were carefully hung on long lines of thin rope strung across the roof, where they dried in the sun before being packed for sale as fish-skin chips.

Though the factory isn't known as an official tourist site, U Tin welcomes all visitors. Before I left he offered me another shot of one of his herbal brews. After I placed the empty glass on the table, he smiled and proclaimed, "When we drink a few brandies, life becomes oh so very beautiful!"

U Tin's fish sausage factory

The factory occupies space on the fourth floor, at the north side of the Theingyi Zei Market. Don't mistake the market for Theingyi Zei Plaza, located across the street, which features more modern—and more expensive—shops.

Shwedagon Pagoda Road
(Anawrahta/Mahabandoola)
Pabedan Township
Yangon

BAGO DIVISION

Peter J. Walter gets derailed on his way to Bago

During my first trip to Myanmar, I had a mere four days to spend, all of it in Yangon. After a few days of exploring the city and soaking up the usual sights, I was inspired to head for the central train station to see if it was possible to take a day trip somewhere.

I entered the station with no particular destination in mind, but after looking around I wondered whether I would be going anywhere at all. People lay about lethargically on benches and chairs, looking as if they'd been waiting a very long time. The silent tracks and lifeless ticket windows hinted at the possibility of even longer delays.

I walked up to the only attended window I could find and inquired about the next train. The response suggested that either there were no trains leaving that day, or that I, as a foreigner, wasn't supposed to be traveling by train to any place the trains were going. Even if I did find an outbound train, I questioned the possibility of a timely return, in order to make my flight back to Thailand the following day.

Fortunately, the ticket clerk gave me another option to consider, offering to arrange a taxi to take me to Bago, a city about eighty kilometers northeast of Yangon. Wanting to take advantage of any opportunity to see a new place, I agreed to the plan. The clerk led me outside to where his friend, the taxi driver, was parked. I thanked the clerk for his help and started to say goodbye, but he grinned and opened the front car door, announcing that he would be coming along. The train delays, apparently a frequent occurrence, meant that he could slip away.

We pulled out of the station and headed through town, bouncing along bumpy roads in the creaking old taxi. As the urban streets gave way to rural byways, I rolled down the windows and breathed in the pungent smells of roadside market stalls and cooking fires. We passed spots along the road where farmers had put down plastic sheeting, on top of which they spread rice to dry in the sun. In the distance, a range of low, gray mountains loomed, separated from the road by broad swaths of rice fields.

Our first stop in Bago was the local market. I hoped to pick up a few *longyi*, the sarong-like garment that many men in Myanmar wear. The indoor market was teeming with people, and it seemed twice as hot as it was outdoors. I quickly found several shops selling *longyi* and bargained for those that I liked. The next few destinations entailed a series of pagodas whose names I can't recall, but which were enjoyable and are certain to be included in any day tour of Bago.

Once I'd had a good look around at our final stop, the large reclining Shwethalyaung Buddha, I mentioned to the train clerk that I was thirsty. His face brightened, as if he thought I'd never ask. He motioned for me to follow him, away from the Buddha and through a path into the fields surrounding the adjacent monastery.

After our short walk, we arrived at a simple bamboo canopy under several shady trees. The clerk kicked off his shoes and sat down on the raised platform, signaling for me to follow suit. He yelled something, and suddenly a man emerged from a nearby hut. After a brief exchange, the man walked away, and the clerk proudly announced that he had ordered us some refreshments: a jug of toddy palm wine and some dried fish. My stomach quivered for a moment, but when the spread arrived, I tucked in.

Toddy palm wine is made from the juicy sap of the tree that bears its name. Farm hands collect the sap from taps inserted into the tree, and after fermenting overnight, the brew takes on a distinctly sour and fizzy character. The first sip caught my palate off guard, but each successive swig left me feeling a little more refreshed and revived. The small dried fish were forgettable, but crunching these salty snacks in between gulps of wine, I was reminded of just how important the rivers and fish are to the diet of the people in Myanmar.

We sipped and nibbled for at least an hour, lounging on the floor of the bamboo shelter. As we talked, I was told that toddy palm wine should not be consumed with pork, the unfortunate outcome being temporary intestinal distress. Thankful for my newly acquired knowledge, I made a mental note to avoid pork for the rest of the day, and took another deep swig. Later, as the car raced back to Yangon, I reflected on the ground we had covered, and marveled at my luck in stumbling upon the perfect one-day getaway, even if it didn't involve any trains.

Day tripping to Bago

Bago makes a perfect day trip from Yangon. It has several interesting pagodas, a vibrant market, and hidden treasures like toddy palm huts. Most street taxis in Yangon are happy to take travelers there. You will need to agree upon a rate before departure. Don't expect your vehicle to have working air conditioning!

MON STATE

Morgan Edwardson finds warmth on a chilly night at Golden Rock

I was waiting for the light to change before crossing a busy Yangon street when a monk walked up and introduced himself. There was nothing especially odd about that. Friendly fellows in robes are a common sight around the city, and many approach tourists for a chat. But this particular monk was persuasive, and after our introductory conversation, he convinced me to scrap my planned break at a nearby teashop and accompany him to his English class.

The monk's school was located on a side street just off Mahabandoola Road. I followed him up a flight of stairs to the second-floor classroom where about thirty students, half of them also monks, sat behind desks. The exuberant, long-haired teacher encouraged his class to bombard me with questions, and for the next hour that's just what they did. Aside from common ones, such as "What's your name?" "Where do you come from?" and "Are you married?" the question asked most often was "Have you been to Golden Rock?"

Not only had I never been, I'd never heard of the place. The students were more than happy to tell me all about it. Golden Rock, or Kyaiktiyo as it's officially called, is a sacred mountaintop boulder in eastern Myanmar. Thoroughly covered in gold leaf, it rests precariously at the edge of a cliff, looking as if it might tumble over the side of the mountain if given a good push. According to legend, a hair of the Buddha was placed in the small *stupa* that rests on top of the boulder, thus assuring its stability. For Buddhists, going to Golden Rock is the Myanmar equivalent of a Muslim making a trip to Mecca. Pilgrims from all over the country flock to the site to pray and make offerings.

The following year, after several aborted attempts, I finally visited Golden Rock. Getting to Kyaiktiyo was no easy task. From Yangon I took an old non-air-conditioned bus to Kinpun, a town located at the base of the mountain, and then boarded a large flatbed truck, packed with dozens of other passengers, for a back-wrenching roller-coaster-like ride up the mountain. Even after that tortuous ordeal was over, we still had not reached the summit. The final ascent required an exhausting walk up a steep trail, a workout that took me the better part of an hour.

Rather than stay at more affordable digs in Kinpun, I splurged for a room at one of the mountaintop hotels. Doing this enabled me to view both sunset and sunrise at Golden Rock, opportunities that wouldn't have been possible if I had to return before dark on the truck from hell.

After a late afternoon arrival, I checked into my hotel and was back outside ten minutes later, ready for what I thought would be a quick hike to the rock. I'm in very good physical shape for a middle-aged bookworm, but that "quick hike" more than humbled me. Even though it was a relatively cool December afternoon, I was sweating profusely after the first five minutes, and had to stop several times to catch my breath during the continuing ascent.

With each step that I took, I began to appreciate the importance of the pilgrimage to Kyaiktiyo. In addition to those I left in my wake as I marched up the mountain, I saw hundreds more making their way down. A few elderly and disabled pilgrims, not to be denied the opportunity to visit this holy site, had hired teams of porters to carry them on stretchers. But the most amazing thing I saw was an amputee on crutches making the climb without any assistance. I tried to fathom the effort and dedication that it must have taken for that man to painstakingly struggle up the steep incline by himself.

Despite the chilly temperatures, many locals were planning to camp out overnight at the top of the mountain. It was going to be a party, judging from the staggering amount of luggage they brought, all of it carried by porters, stacked in long wicker baskets that were strapped to their backs. Even with such heavy loads to shoulder, those porters made the climb up the mountain almost effortlessly. I tell you, it had all the makings of a new Olympic sport.

When I reached the top, crowds were milling about the spacious tiled terrace that leads to several observation points and the Golden Rock itself. A sign at the entrance declared: "Footwearing is Strictly Prohibited on the Precinct Onward." Going barefoot, however, required an observant eye. The betel nut spitters were out in force, making the floor look like a kindergarten art experiment gone awry.

I zigzagged around clusters of pilgrims until I found a set of stairs that led down to an observation platform adjacent to the sacred boulder. Several men and boys were huddled next to the Golden Rock, some touching it reverently and praying, while others affixed more gold leaf to the boulder's surface. Women were noticeable in their absence. Due to strict Buddhist protocol, females are not allowed to approach or touch the rock.

By nightfall, temperatures had dipped considerably, but the number of people arriving had grown, swelling to more than a thousand. Bundled in layers of warm clothing, the worshippers lighted incense and candles, made offerings of food, ate meals together, and snapped photos incessantly. I walked around, passing an occasional foreign tourist with a nod and a smile, and immersed myself in this peaceful gathering of kindred souls.

The serenity and feeling of community that pervaded the mountain-top on that cold December night warmed my own soul and lifted my spirits. Meanwhile, Golden Rock, now bathed in floodlights, with the nearly full moon providing a celestial halo, glowed radiantly in the background.

Getting to Golden Rock

There are no flights to Kyaiktiyo, but you can hire a car from either Yangon or Bago to take you there. From Yangon the trip takes four to five hours. From Bago the journey averages around three hours. There are also direct buses that go to Kinpun (the nearest town to Kyaiktiyo) from Yangon's Aung Mingalar Bus Terminal (Highway Terminal). From the base camp at Kinpun, most people pile into a flatbed truck for the final ascent to the top of the mountain. (For more on walking up, see page 153.) That ride can cost as little as 800 kyat per passenger, or 1,500 kyat for a front seat—if you're really brave!

Ticket tip

The Golden Rock entrance fee for foreigners is $6. You only have to pay this price once. I was able to visit the mountaintop one afternoon and again the next morning using the same ticket.

Golden Rock Hotel

My single room was a bit overpriced by the country's standards, but that was due to the location near the top of the mountain. Staying there saved me time, along with wear and tear on my body, since I didn't have to endure the gut-wrenching truck ride up and down the mountain an additional time. The staff at the hotel was very friendly and the restaurant food was quite good. Depending upon the time of year, room rates are $38 to $46 (single) and $50 to $60 (double).

Kyaiktiyo
(+95-35) 70174
(+95-1) 502-479 (Yangon office)
grtt@goldenrock.com.mm

UMA Spoken English Class

This language school is on the second floor of a building on the right-hand side of a narrow street, just after you have turned off busy Mahabandoola Road. The students and the teacher will be ecstatic to have a foreign guest help them practice speaking English.

129 Seikkanthar St.
Botataung Township
Yangon

Sign of the times

On the bus journey to Kinpun, east of Bago, I looked out the window on the left side and noticed a distinctive shop sign: "Wuthering Heights Café." I wish I could have stopped for a cup of tea and found out who was running this intriguingly named place—out in the middle of nowhere. If you have a chance to stop and check it out, make sure to write about it and post your article on *ThingsAsian*.

www.thingsasian.com

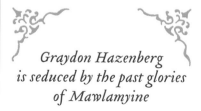

Graydon Hazenberg is seduced by the past glories of Mawlamyine

I didn't know what to expect before I finally made it to Mawlamyine. I was a bit jaded by Myanmar's other "old" cities. All too often any sort of faded colonial charm had disappeared, replaced by nondescript huddles of concrete. But I was immediately captivated when I arrived in the first British capital of Burma, and spent a happy day wandering its streets, soaking up the atmosphere of bygone glory.

Mawlamyine—or Moulmein, as the British called it—has a beautiful setting, located where the Thanlwin, one of Asia's least known great rivers, is joined by its last two major tributaries. The city sprawls along the left bank of a broad estuary, with a spine of hills hemming downtown. A series of grand-looking monasteries crown the ridge, and below the hill, streets run in labyrinthine fashion, providing many an opportunity to get happily lost as you meander along on foot.

I'm far from the first visitor to be intrigued by the setting. Over a century ago, Rudyard Kipling made a brief stop here. Although the poem he wrote is called "Mandalay," the beginning lines are set in Mawlamyine:

> By the old Moulmein Pagoda,
> lookin' eastward at the sea,
> There's a Burma girl a-settin',
> and I know she thinks o' me.

There is still a profusion of colonial-era architecture in Mawlamyine. This may be because the British made the city the capital of Lower Burma from 1827 to 1852, during their piecemeal conquest of the country. Old schools and grand churches of various Christian denominations crumble picturesquely on all sides, while houses and shop buildings seem to date from the days when George Orwell was in town, famously shooting his elephant.

Although there are a few of-ficial "sights" to see, such as the Mon State Museum and some of the monasteries, it is more the city itself, its quiet streets redolent of tropical languor and genteel decay, that captures the attention. The buses make Yangon's look positively modern; Mawlamyine may have the only fleet of wooden municipal buses that you will ever see, and because of the lack of prosperity compared to Yangon, there is little traffic on the streets, making walking a pleasure. Not that many tourists make it down here, and as you stroll around, you will find a lot of friendly waving and smiling and invitations to sit down to tea. Mawlamyine-ites seem pleased to see foreign faces again, recalling those days when many English and Anglo-Burmese retired here.

Unlike Europe, few cities in modernizing Southeast Asia really have much atmosphere or appeal as historic destinations. Luang Prabang in Laos is one, and Mawlamyine another. For a contemplative day or three of walking, sketching, photo-graphing, or sitting beside the Thanlwin while the tide rolls upstream or the fishing boats set out for the day, Mawlamyine deserves a place on your itinerary. As you sit down to dinner one evening, watching the sun set over the river, you might even find yourself accompanied by the spirit of Kipling, as you look eastward at the sea.

Getting to Mawlamyine

Air-conditioned buses travel from Yangon to Mawlamyine. The trip normally takes six to seven hours. The ticket price is 5,000 kyat one way. To assure a seat (and not a standing-room-only spot), it's best to buy your ticket a day in advance. There is also train service, but that journey typically takes an hour or two more than the bus.

Attran Hotel

I like to stay at this hotel right on the riverside. Rates are around $25 to $35 a night, but worth it. It has good views out to the new bridge and the broad estuary. It also has a nice restaurant/terrace outdoors.

Mawlamyine
(+95-32) 25764
attran@baganmail.net.mm

YANGON & SOUTHERN MYANMAR

MANDALAY DIVISION

Serena Bowles bridges cultures in Amarapura

Modern Mandalay is a sprawling, chaotic metropolis where sewers lurk beneath broken paving slabs, waiting to trap the unsuspecting pedestrian. Yearning for more uplifting environs, I arranged to visit the three smaller ancient cities that surround Mandalay: Sagaing, Inwa, and Amarapura.

I enjoyed Sagaing and Inwa, but it was the final destination of Amarapura that most impressed me. This town is the location of U Bein Bridge, said to be the longest teakwood bridge in the world. It is one of the "must see" destinations in Myanmar, especially for the photographically minded traveler.

In 1860, when the royal court abandoned Amarapura in favor of Mandalay as the new capital, U Bein was the mayor. Many different stories surround the bridge, and I was told that on his orders, a thousand teak columns were salvaged from the old palace and used to construct a 1.2-kilometer-long bridge across Lake Taungthaman. It was built without the use of a single nail, and it was pur-

posefully curved to lessen the impact of storms and the annual floodwaters. For nearly a century and a half it has allowed farmers, fishermen, and monks to pass from one shore to the other. It has also enchanted visitors by providing captivating snapshots of everyday life in Myanmar.

I arrived at four in the afternoon, timing my visit to the creaking teakwood structure a bit before sunset. It was late October, the end of the rainy season, and the lake was at its fullest. Enigmatic old trees reached out of flooded fields on either side of the bridge, and clusters of ducks quacked grumpily at each other, climbing onto the occasional patch of mud and preening before returning to the water with a splash. Men and women fished with simple bamboo rods. Some stood knee-deep in shallow water, while others were submerged right up to their necks.

Carefully stepping from plank to plank, I crossed the bridge, while being overtaken by graceful women balancing baskets and other items on their heads. I stopped at one of the five covered rest houses, catching the scent of freshly caught fish frying over small fires. Farther along I passed a bunch of giggling young novice monks, distinctively clad in bright red robes, who were leaning over the side of the bridge to watch the fish feeding from the surface.

An hour later, a delicious golden glow descended with the sun. The evening haze added depth to the surrounding countryside, and distant pagodas punctuated the horizon.

Boys who had been resting in the shade of trees climbed into small boats and began to herd flocks of ducks to their respective homes, creating mobile duck islands that wove between the clumps of reeds. The fishermen prepared to pack up, and dragonflies filled the air. Slowly the sun sank out of sight, leaving behind a colorful sky and irresistible silhouettes on the bridge, soon to be claimed by darkness.

Getting to Amarapura

Amarapura, along with Sagaing and Inwa, which were also ancient capital cities, can be visited as a day trip from Mandalay. Along with my driver and guide, I also stopped off at a monastery and silk weaving factory along the way. Another option is to hire a bicycle, as Amarapura is only ten kilometers from Mandalay. Though you should be prepared for flat tires if you do this, it is cheap and easy to get punctures fixed along the way. Alternately, trishaw drivers are sometimes agreeable to pedaling passengers all the way to the bridge. Such a journey takes considerably more time, and you'll need to compensate your driver accordingly.

Inside angle

The bridge is enjoyable at any hour of the day, but sunrise and sunset are the most atmospheric and picturesque times for photography. For great views,

negotiate a price with one of the boatmen who are apt to follow you as you stroll across.

All-inclusive

To enter Amarapura you are required to show your Mandalay Archaeological Zone ticket ($10), which includes Mandalay Hill and the Mandalay Palace and Fort.

Mick Shippen mingles with the pottery makers of Kyauk Myaung

As an art school graduate and author of a book on ceramics, I always search out the craftsmen in the countries I visit. Of all the pot-making centers I have been to, the villages of Nwe Nyein, Shwe Khun, Shwe Tiek, and Malar—perched high on the western bank of the Ayeyarwady River north of Mandalay—are the most impressive.

As I wandered down the single-track dirt road that connected the villages, I looked out on piles of driftwood, captured from the fast-flowing waters by local fishermen, and set out on the shoreline to dry. Next to this knotted mass of weathered timber, orderly lines of well-bronzed storage pots lay belly-up on a beach of alluvial gold. At anchor were half a dozen wooden cargo vessels stacked to the gills with more of the huge, conical, nut-brown pots, ready to go with the flow as far south as Yangon.

Over time, geography, geology, and history have conspired to make the four villages collectively one of the most inspiring pottery production sites in Southeast Asia. Originally the Shwebo district was populated by the Mon people, known throughout the region for their pot-making skills. During the mid-eighteenth century, the Mon were conquered by Alaungpaya, the Burman king. Many of the captured craftsmen were put to work, and in 1754 the Mon potters were sent to Ma Au village, where they were ordered to produce their glazed pottery.

Several years later, royal consent was given to relocate pottery production to the village of Nwe Nyein, a major source of good quality clay and situated beside the country's major trade artery, the Ayeyarwady. Benefiting from the new location, production was expanded and further pottery villages were established atop the steep riverbank. The four thriving villages are now more commonly known to visitors as Kyauk Myaung, which is in fact a small and bustling market town a few kilometers away. Today, on the land once taken from their forefathers, the descendants of the original Mon captives continue to dig for clay and, with practiced hands, form it into wares, which are exported all over Myanmar.

Taking a sharp turn away from the main road trimmed with shophouses and storerooms, I ducked down a side street with deeply furrowed tracks,

cut by the narrow wheels of bullock carts. The massive thatched-roof pottery sheds were clearly visible, and evidence pointing to the sheer scale of production was everywhere. As I wandered along the well-worn track, carts pulled by draft animals and loaded with oversized storage jars rolled sedately passed me. Clinker, ripped from sagging firebox walls and used to fill potholes in the road, laid the way for a smoother journey.

At the juncture of dusty trails, I stood and watched female workers with baskets of pots daringly balanced upon their heads flit quickly by, leaving only the memory of capacious smiles. Following the natural contours of the undulating terrain, I followed a trail cut through an embankment shored up by walls of broken and distorted pots before turning off into yet another trail that pushed its way between a jumble of workshops. Here I witnessed men shouldering the weight of voluminous unfired jars held firmly in the grasp of a bamboo cradle as they ran toward the darkened opening of a cavernous kiln.

People, their skin and clothes smeared with ocher-colored clay, were continually on the move. Looking down from a hillside onto the angular expanses of thatched roofs, I watched as ephemeral clouds of smoke emerged from stunted red-brick chimneys. The scene was magical, medieval … otherworldly. It was as if the inhabitants of this insular community had themselves emerged from the clay that they command.

Inside the pottery sheds, half-light prevailed. After entering, I had to wait a few moments for my eyes to adjust. The high roofs, low light, and earthen floors of the workspaces provide the shady environment necessary to make pots, and a welcome cool for wanderers like myself. The bulk of production here was of large earthenware storage jars. A common site across Myanmar, the jars sit outside village homes, buried up to the shoulder out of the sun. Although normally used to store rain water, they also function as containers for staples such as *ngapi*, preserved bamboo shoots, mangoes, damsons, and cooking oil.

The Ayeyarwady River remains, as it always has, the main channel of distributing the jars. Traditionally, hundreds of jars were lashed together with bamboo and serving as flotation tanks, they drifted downriver where the raft would be disassembled. Then the pots were loaded onto bullock carts and taken to provincial towns. Although this method of transportation still takes place, it is becoming less common. As speed of distribution increasingly becomes a factor, ferry boats and trucks are taking over.

All over Myanmar, roadside stalls sell these pots. They remain an essential fixture of the country's landscape and a constant reminder for me of these magnificent pot-making villages.

Pottering around

The villages of Nwe Nyein, Shwe Khun, Shwe Tiek, and Malar are situated about 150 kilometers north of Mandalay. The easiest way to reach the villages is by hiring a mini-bus from Mandalay to nearby Kyauk Myaung. The journey takes about three hours.

MANDALAY & CENTRAL MYANMAR

CULTURAL ENCOUNTERS

Taking part in the ethnic traditions of Myanmar

In Myanmar, no matter what the month, it is always time to *pwe*! A *pwe* is a traditional festival, and amongst that general category there are countless themed *pwe*, including celebrations for pagodas, sports, spirit mediums, and rice harvests. Since *pwe* are held during full moon periods, there's not a month of the year without an event of some sort.

Though *pwe* have been going on for centuries, you never know what will happen when you attend one. At a *pwe* in Bagan, Tim Cox finds himself invited backstage by the performers. Lots of singing, dancing, and photo-taking are occurring, but Tim is distracted by one big question: Will he be asked to take to the stage himself? Wyn Tut Tut actually makes it to the edge of the stage at a massive *nat pwe*, or gathering of spirit mediums, in Taungpyone near Mandalay, where she is the guest of a famous transvestite medium.

Whether you're interested in experiencing a *pwe* or any other type of festival, celebration, or performance, you won't have to look hard. The biggest annual event in Myanmar is the *Thingyan* water festival in mid-April. Join Morrison Polkinghorne as he wanders the streets of Mandalay in an effort *not* to get drenched while he soaks up the raucous atmosphere. You can also travel up north near the border of India with Ma Thanegi for the wild and hair-raising New Year's celebration of the legendary Naga tribe. Or drift into the Shan State town of Taunggyi with Anne Marie Power to observe the elaborate preparations for a balloon festival. But these aren't just any old balloons. Fashioned from enormous sheets of traditional paper to resemble animals, some are as tall as three-story buildings.

Another beloved tradition, the ancient art of the puppet play is almost extinct in Myanmar, but thankfully there are several troupes around the country working to keep it alive. When James Spencer visits the impressive Mandalay Marionettes Theatre, he is taken with the unusual music and human impersonations of

Marionette theater in Mandalay

the classic puppets, while Laurie Weed is surprised by some of the more risqué aspects of the show. Never underestimate what a puppet master can accomplish with a few strings! Laurie also precedes the performance with sunset drinks on the river and dinner at the Mandalay night market, turning her evening out into one of Myanmar's most appealing experiences—a full-on cultural immersion.

MANDALAY DIVISION

Morrison Polkinghorne soaks up the New Year in Mandalay

The man standing next to me in the hotel lobby wrung his shirt, a puddle immediately forming on the carpet. He sheepishly looked up and apologized. "You must excuse me. This is our national holiday, and I've been dancing under the water all afternoon."

Welcome to *Thingyan*, Myanmar's annual water festival. As in neighboring Thailand and Laos, this holiday is held throughout the country during the middle of April. With several more months before the monsoon season begins, *Thingyan* offers a reprieve from half a year of relative drought. The cel-

ebrations normally last for three to five days, the number determined by that year's lunar calendar. Most shops are closed and families head home for reunions and worship.

"My name is Maung Maung. I am a film director. I'm very famous," the wet man told me, without an ounce of braggart. "Just ask anyone. They'll know Maung Maung." Then the elevator chimed, and the giant hulk lumbered into the lift for the ascent to dry clothes.

Maung Maung wasn't joking. He is indeed well known around the country, and he is obviously successful, as his choice of hotels that night, the Sedona, is Mandalay's finest, conveniently situated across from the palace compound, right in the middle of the city's largest street party. Specially built for the occasion, a *mantab*, also called a *pandal*, which is part bleacher and part discotheque, blared out music to the premium-paying hotel guests facing the royal moat.

Normally I avoid these watery "New Year" festivities in Southeast Asia. I really don't like unexpected drenchings, and one very memorable year during Thailand's *Songkran*, I even had to replace my soaked passport, ruined in the unbridled merriment. In Thailand, foreigners are prey to the mad frenzy of water pistols, hoses, and even bins of ice water aimed at the unawares.

But in Myanmar, the water festival is more of an optional event. Revelers willingly drench themselves under the *mantab*, and special seats are set up nearby for those who are content to enjoy the celebration dry. *Thingyan* festivities bring out the inner child, and grown men like Maung Maung will suddenly shout like banshees and leap under water streams for hours of frenzied dance. Revelers take turns manning the hoses, joyfully drenching any willing passersby, and no one seems to mind. But there are unexpected exceptions to avoiding participation, and no one is allowed to object.

"Come here, I wish to bless you," an old monk called to me from a decaying pagoda in Sagaing, Myanmar's spiritual center and a former capital, located about twenty kilometers southwest of Mandalay.

The end of the festival was nearing, and I'd largely missed the soakings over the previous three days. Obligingly, I crept up to the monk and proffered my right shoulder, pitifully praying to myself, "Just a little." Two mammoth pails full of cold water followed, and I was drenched. My partner and guide followed suit, all of us quietly thankful for this spiritual cleansing, but inwardly cursing the cool afternoon weather for failing to quickly dry our clothes. It was too

unfair. Just hours ago, I'd been climbing the ruins of earthquake-damaged Mingun Paya in nearby Mingun in scorching heat and would have welcomed a drenching. Now, with late afternoon temperatures dipping, I wasn't so eager.

Then I pictured the bulking frame of Maung Maung, gleefully dancing up a storm, and I saw the drenching for what it was: a blessing for being able to experience this delightful country during its most popular and playful time of the year.

Sedona Hotel Mandalay

The hotel is across the street from the southeast corner of the Mandalay Palace and Fort complex. Priced at over $100 a night, rooms aren't exactly cheap, but ironically provide a good option for travelers who are strapped for cash, since the Sedona Hotel accepts credit cards—a rarity in Myanmar. An excellent buffet breakfast is included in the room rates.

Corner of 26th Street and 66th Street
Mandalay
www.sedonamyanmar.com
(+95-2) 36488

The downside of Thingyan

During this time, it is difficult to get around the country. Buses, trains, and planes are booked solid and are often more expensive than the rest of the year.

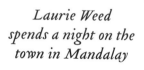

Laurie Weed spends a night on the town in Mandalay

A perfect evening in Mandalay begins just before sundown, on a gentle rise of land to the west of the dusty city, at a place known as the Viewpoint. Don't let the uninspired name or the unassuming eponymous restaurant put you off. This is the Technicolor panorama you've come for, and you won't be disappointed.

The beer at the restaurant isn't very cold, and the food isn't even worth mentioning. Just order something so you can take advantage of the extraordinary vantage point, or treat your trishaw driver to a lukewarm beer while you soak up the atmosphere. As the sun begins to descend, stand near the low wall at the top of the hill and watch the sky spill into the Ayeyarwady River, painting it with streaks of pastel orange, rust, and gold. Below, women in colorful, tightly-wound *longyi* wade waist-deep in swirling, cocoa-brown water, their bare shoulders gleaming. On their heads, they balance baskets of laundry, and on their hips, naked babies, all due for a wash at the end of the day.

Unless you love karaoke in surround sound, you'll want to time your Viewpoint departure just before the last ray of light disappears. Make your way back to central Mandalay and stop at the lively night market, where you can pull up a child-sized stool at one of the busy noodle carts and sample some of the best and spiciest *monhinga* in town, for about 20 cents a bowl. Once you've eaten, wander through the stalls and pick out a *longyi* or two for yourself. If you really want to amuse the locals, try them on.

Now catch a taxi to the Mandalay Marionettes Theatre for the eight thirty show, a mix of traditional dancing, music, and master puppeteering. Your patronage helps to keep folk art traditions alive. Near the end of the show, the upper curtain is raised to reveal the magicians at work, a fascinating display led by revered septuagenarian puppet master, U Pan Aye. Be forewarned that this portion of the evening's entertainment ought to be rated PG. Although most of the bawdier jokes will not be translated into English, there are visuals. Full frontal puppetry? Only in Mandalay.

Sunset views

Ask your trishaw driver to take you to the sunset viewpoint overlooking the river; look out for a big, hand-painted sign that says, "Viewpoint." Plan on about twenty-five minutes to get there from the center of town, depending on traffic and on how tired your driver is after a long day of pedaling.

Mandalay Night Market

Every evening vendors set up along 84th Street between 28th and 29th Streets. The block is closed to motor traffic at sundown. There are a few craft booths for tourists, but this market caters mainly to locals who come to buy street food and cheap housewares and fabrics from China.

Mandalay Marionettes Theatre

For more about puppetry performances here, continue on to the next essay.

James Spencer pulls some strings at a puppet show in Mandalay

The ancient art of the puppet play is almost extinct in Myanmar nowadays, but thankfully there are some troupes in the country working to keep it alive. One of the best performs at the Mandalay Marionettes Theatre, my venue of choice for viewing Myanmar's classical puppetry.

Historically, puppet shows were presented at monthly pagoda festivals, known as *pwe*, and went on for hours, from after dark until just before dawn. Nobody has the patience for such marathons today, neither the performers nor the audience. So shows at Mandalay Marionettes Theatre last for an hour, giving a good overview of the tradition.

The theater is not large, just a long narrow room with rows of chairs for the audience, and a stage and small orchestra pit at one end. The walls are hung with huge marionettes, though these are normally not used in shows. By necessity, the performance puppets are much smaller. Not only do the puppeteers have to hold these heavy wooden figures, but also whirl them round the stage as they fly and dance.

The performance begins with an introductory preamble, and then the orchestra strikes up with drums, gongs, clarinets, and pipes. The music is like nothing I've heard before. I won't try to describe it. Suffice to say that it's not like Chinese music, nor Indian, nor Balinese. According to the country's historians, it's of Thai origin, dating from the Burmese conquest of Thailand in the eighteenth century. But I can't say that it sounds very much like any Thai music I've heard, either.

When the puppets arrive, they descend from above: the *zawgyi*, or magician; the Princess and Prince; the General; and many entertaining others, including elephants, monkeys, demons, gods, goddesses, heroes, and villains. The most complex of the puppets have sixty-four strings. That's sixty-four individual strings, with separate strings for lips, eyebrows, and finger joints, all being controlled by a single man. As you can imagine, it takes many years to learn the skills to master this complex art.

One of the highlights is the part in which a human imitates the movements of the puppet. Accustomed as we are to seeing puppets imitating people, it's a little unnerving to watch the reverse. But such artistry! The dancer's arms seem to rotate in their sockets without the normal constrictions of joints, the head flops as if the strings have suddenly gone slack, and the body jerks convulsively as if some gigantic puppeteer in the sky were twitching at unseen strings.

Two women from Mandalay, Daw Ma Ma Naing and Daw Naing Yee Mar, are the founders and driving force behind the theater. Giving the theater its cachet is an artistic team supervised by U Pan Aye, one of the country's last great master puppeteers; both he and the group's U Shwe Nan Tin were pupils of yet another master puppeteer, Shwe Bo U Thin Maung. Trained by the old specialists, the Mandalay Marionettes Theatre troupe has toured extensively in Europe and North America and is recognized as one of the leading guardians of the art of traditional puppetry.

Mandalay Marionettes Theatre

The theater is located on the street behind the Sedona Hotel, one block from the southeast corner of the Mandalay Palace and Fort. Performances are held nightly, from 8:30 to 9:30 p.m. Tickets are usually available at the door, but the theater is quite small, and you may want to arrive by eight to get a good seat near the front. Tickets are $8, and proceeds support the troupe's other activities, which include an outreach program to re-introduce

the tradition of marionette artistry to villages around the country. Most of the spoken part of the performance is in Burmese, but English-language programs are available. Handmade marionettes, including the large display models, are on sale in the workshop next to the theater.

66th Street (26/27)
Mandalay
(+95-2) 34446
www.mandalaymarionettes.com

Helping out

On Friday afternoons the theater holds English conversation classes for local students. If you would like to assist, contact the theater for details.

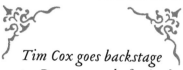

Tim Cox goes backstage at a Bagan pagoda festival

Little do I know, when setting off with my wife to explore more of Bagan's nearly three thousand pagodas, that a few hours later I will be backstage meeting the stars of a *pwe*— a traditional festival. We stumble upon our self-appointed guide while eating a simple noodle soup at a makeshift restaurant. He is all of fifteen years old and thrilled to be the one to bring these exotic, camera-lugging foreigners behind the scenes, to the place where the traveling performers live, sleep, and then undergo a metamorphosis into all manner of characters before heading onto the stage each night.

Although large outdoor *pwe* are held throughout the country, they are most common during full moon periods. Despite, or perhaps because of, the cool December weather, there always seem to be more festivals at this time of year, which is why we choose it to visit. *Pwe* can take over a whole neighborhood, with stages blocking the residential streets. Some have precarious-looking Ferris wheels, and all have numerous food stalls lining the road. This one, at the old Bagan pagoda of Alo Pyi, has just one large bamboo stage, backed by the dusty quarters where the stars make a temporary home. In front of the stage, surrounding the crowd, are stalls selling snacks and treats, teenagers gambling a few cents away at the stands, and plenty of souvenir stalls for locals.

The show finally begins around nine in the evening and carries on into the early morning hours, until nearly sunrise. The spectacle begins with a finely tuned traditional dance; elegantly dressed women in colorful dresses with elongated trains whirl around the stage. The moment they are gone, local pop music blasts from the speakers. Young performers run through squeaky synthesized tunes that sound straight from the 1980s. They are followed by slapstick comedy that largely involves actors running, jumping, and falling about in colorful costumes. Then, around

midnight, a lengthy theater piece begins which is most likely a story from a classic tale like the *Ramayana*. All the while musicians add rousing accompaniment on drums, cymbals, and variations of oboes and flutes. While the epic storytelling may be largely lost on foreign audiences, the presentation of singing, dancing, and comedy knows no borders.

Before, during, and after the show, our host drags us backstage where the performers fall in love with us and our digital cameras. We take numerous photos, and they all ask that we come back with printed copies for them. They also urge us to watch the show from the side of the stage. This may be some kind of honor, but the nagging feeling that any minute we'll be dragged out for some impromptu "audience participation" never goes away. Meanwhile our new friend, the fifteen-year-old guide, borrows one of our cameras to go off exploring. He takes photos of many girls that he says are his girlfriends; most don't seem to know him, but are impressed by his camera and new foreign friends. There are few places in the world where you would give your brand-new camera to a teenage boy whom you've just met and let him run off with it. Here I don't give it a second thought.

Numerous *pwe* troupes operate across Myanmar, making a meager existence from shows that are often performed for free. Poor as they may be, some are megastars in their field. Although the audience never applauds, gifts for performers are common. One male singer at our *pwe* finds himself showered with flowers, a soft drink, a wallet, and ... ahem ... a calculator. One person offers money but it isn't accepted. Perhaps it was too much. Perhaps not enough?

Attending a pwe

Because *pwe* occur during a full moon, chances are good of attending one while you are in Myanmar. Ask your guide or hotel staff about any *pwe* that are being held while you are in town. Taxi drivers, trishaw drivers, and horse cart drivers will also know where to find one.

Bagan's Alo Pyi pwe

Although Alo Pyi is not featured in many guides, it is popular with locals who pay visits for the pagoda's wish-fulfilling powers, along with its well-preserved frescoes. It is situated roughly between the Bagan-Nyaung U and Anawrahta Roads, almost two kilometers northeast of Old Bagan, due east of the Tharaba Gate. The nearest "big" pagoda is Htilominlo Pahto, which is across the road from Upali Thein, another old pagoda with lovely frescoes. There are a few good sunset spots near Alo Pyi; cross the main road and there are a number of smaller pagodas that you can climb for a good view.

Hpone Thant braves a spirited forest near Mount Popa

Just off the road from Mount Popa to Bagan, in the shadows of the mountain, there is a clump of deep green forest. What makes this forest so special is that the local people think the land is guarded by two *nat*, the spirits that are believed to watch over almost everything in Myanmar. These particular *nat* are said to be brother and sister who escaped from the clutches of an evil lord during the Bagan Dynasty in the tenth century.

This forest is heavily wooded, cool and verdant, a sharp contrast to the surrounding hot and dusty central plains. Tall trees normally seen in moist, tropical environments grow in it, as water is plentiful inside the woods. Adding to the unusual landscape are huge, black, igneous rocks strewn around the forest floor, remnants of the enormous eruptions that occurred at Mount Popa, which geologists believe was an active volcano two million years ago.

The people of Myanmar are very superstitious. Even the most sophisticated city dwellers and those with college educations would think twice before offending a *nat*. As for the residents of nearby Zi O village, they dare not take even a small twig from this sacred forest before asking permission from the two guardian spirits. If they wish to use wood from the forest to erect a *pandal* for a ceremony, they must first ask the *nat*. To make such a request, the villager will make a silent or mumbled prayer.

During one of my visits to this forest, the villagers living near the Zi O Monastery showed me a huge neem tree that they say is more than nine hundred years old. They told me that this tree was split in two by enormous elephants that inhabited the area during the Bagan Dynasty. The drooping branches are now supported by concrete pillars, which were erected by the Forest Department to prevent them from breaking off.

Many people from Zi O village use a shortcut through the forest to reach other villages in the vicinity, but as a mark of respect to the *nat*, they always take off their shoes before entering. Deeper inside this wooded area is a small shrine. The villagers regularly bring offerings of flowers and help to keep it clean. They also take care that no angry or harmful words are used inside the sacred forest. I met one local man whose house had recently burnt down for no apparent reason. He attributed the fire to a quarrel he had with his father-in-law in the forest a few days earlier.

It's not only hot tempers that people have to be careful of, though. It is also common practice that young lovers dare not engage in sweet talk inside the forest. It is said the sister *nat* does not like suggestive language.

After hearing so many villagers telling me about the sensitivities of the guardian *nat*, I paid extra attention to what I said or did whenever I visited the forest. I even left an offering of flowers at the shrine the last time I was there. And when a mosquito buzzed around my head, I dared not get angry and try to slap it. Why risk having my house burn down?

Getting to Zi O Thit Hla Forest

If you are coming from Bagan toward Mount Popa by car, turn left off the Bagan-Kyaukpadaung Highway after about twenty-one kilometers, at the sign reading: "Zi O Thit Hla Forest." Follow the dirt track for about eighteen kilometers. You will pass many other villages before you reach Zi O village.

Nat worship and Mount Popa

There are many *nat* shrines on the walkway leading to the top of Mount Popa. During full moon festival times, many pilgrims visit this sacred site. If you visit Mount Popa be prepared to encounter monkeys—hundreds of them—that run around the steps and support beams of the covered stairway. They are normally well-behaved, but avoid teasing or petting them.

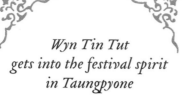

Wyn Tin Tut gets into the festival spirit in Taungpyone

During most of the year, Taungpyone is a quiet town. The shrines at the local pagoda are kept locked, and few worshippers come to visit. But on the day my friends and I arrived, having flown to Mandalay and then hired a van to drive the remaining twenty kilometers, the road was packed with cars and buses on their way to the Taungpyone Festival, the biggest annual event in Myanmar's world of the *nat* and mediums. Beggars lined the route, and revelers threw money to them. Apparently, the pilgrims believe it's never too early to begin the festivities, and during their morning devotional prayers, they were far from silent, exuberantly and noisily teasing friends and strangers alike. It is believed that the spirits like to be made happy, thus all the wild celebrating.

Buddhism is the main religion of Myanmar, but *nat* worship has been part of our culture for centuries. Some believe that the spirits worshipped by animists were once human beings who died violently. The Taungpyone Festival is held in celebration of two such spirit brothers: Min Gyi (Elder Prince) and Min Lay (Younger Prince).

The ancient story goes that they were the sons of a princess who lived in the woods at the foot of Mt. Popa. After a series of tragic events, both young men were executed. Upon hearing the news, their mother died of grief. Subsequently, all three became spirits, and shrines were erected in their honor. The princes' shrine is at Taungpyone, where they died, and their mother, Mai Wunna (also called Popa Mai Daw, or Goddess of Popa), has her shrine at Mount Popa.

According to custom, all of the country's mediums and their followers in Myanmar are compelled to attend the Taungpyone Festival. I have no idea what punishment the fierce spirit brothers would deal out to absentees, and no one wants to take the risk of finding out. Fortunately, the spirits do not mind non-believers like me coming to gape, as long as we refrain from making insulting jokes. My friends, although non-believers themselves, warned me of this rule, as they are fully aware of my smart-alecky mouth.

In recent years, transvestites have nearly taken over Myanmar's medium profession, and it was amazing to see so many of them in Taungpyone, strutting their stuff in full Revlon war paint, their collective perfumes wafting to the skies. As spirit mediums, they can dress up and be as campy as they wish, remaining free from ridicule. Though the majority of Buddhists may not be *nat* worshippers, they, like me, are not going to chance any bad luck by making fun of these followers.

During the first two days of the festival, people pay homage at the shrine, bringing offerings of flowers, scarves, and food to the gilded images of the two spirit brothers. The next two days feature elaborate ceremonies led by the descendents of the original guardians of the shrines. When we arrived, the crowds were so thick that we despaired of even laying eyes on the images, which have been in place since the eleventh century. Fortunately, we were staying with a medium, the distant cousin of one of my friends, and we were allowed to accompany him.

Mediums must show how successful they are in order to attract even more followers, and our host was so prosperous, he could afford to have a large wooden house that he used only during the short celebration season. The preparations he took prior to the ceremony lasted almost an hour, but they were fascinating to watch. A personal beautician took care of his makeup and hair, and another assistant laid out the court costume, which consisted of a white, long-sleeved jacket reaching to the hips and sewn with spangles; a turban covered with expensive orchids, which were carried from Mandalay in an icebox; and tons of glittery jewelry.

He was a magnificent sight as he grandly marched out to greet his wealthy and well-dressed followers. These believers, all dripping with diamonds, proudly followed him, bringing along offerings of soft drinks, cakes, and imported fruits. Our group trailed behind, looking sheepish and most unglamorous in our ordinary clothes.

Since he was a successful medium with a rich and powerful following, my friend's cousin got a slot to perform early in the evening. After the preceding dancer left, quickly appraising our

medium's jewels, it was our turn. The traditional orchestra of drums, gongs, and cymbals played steadily, and we sat or stood on the edge of a carpeted floor while our hero minced over to the images, knelt, and paid obeisance.

As he stood up and began to dance, the music quickened, the thump of the drums and clash of cymbals pumping excitement into our veins. His arms moving in graceful sweeps, a look of enchantment on his face, eyes blissfully closed, he twirled ever faster. My heart pounded as the music hit my eardrums like mallets. The followers threw cash, hoping that would motivate the musicians to play longer. It did. Twenty minutes later, when the music finally ended, the medium gently slowed his dancing, composed his garments, and elegantly walked off stage. We followed, swaying dizzily.

Although there were to be some more rituals the following day, we returned that morning to Mandalay, since the main part of the ceremony, the dancing, was over. Busy with work, we could not party on, much as we would have liked to. On the drive back, my friend relayed a message to us from her medium cousin. The next time we visit, if we want to follow him in the procession, we'd better be wearing silk and diamonds. Apparently we had been a disgrace to him, *not* being draped with expensive jewelry. In that case, I reflected sadly, I would surely not be welcomed backstage at this spirit party of the year anytime soon.

Getting to Taungpyone

Taungpyone village is about twenty kilometers from Mandalay. Most tourists usually stay in Mandalay and drive over for the day. It's possible to rent cars or ride in the popular "share taxis." Rates depend upon the number of passengers. There is also a train running from Mandalay, if you want to celebrate en route with happy mediums.

Taungpyone Festival

The festival lasts for nine days and begins on the eighth Waxing Moon Day of Wagaung. According to the country's lunar calendar, this occurs sometime in August or early September. Shortly after, another annual festival called Yadana Gu is held for Mai Wunna in Amarapura.

SHAN STATE

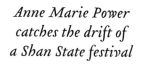

Anne Marie Power catches the drift of a Shan State festival

What motivated me to visit Myanmar for the first time? I can sum it up it one word: balloons.

Officially called *Tazaungdaing*, the Hot Air Balloon Festival is held in Taunggyi during the full moon of *Tazaungmon* (late October/early November). Situated in a beautiful, mountainous region of Myanmar, about thirty kilometers from Inle Lake, this hill town was a popular holiday destination for the country's British community during the first half of the twentieth century, serving as a cool retreat during the hot summer months.

I was introduced to the balloon festival by a well-known papermaker and expert on Asian hand papermaking. I was fascinated by her tales of the festival and its use of huge paper balloons crafted into the shape of various animals. She told me how designing, constructing, transporting, and then flying each enormous but delicate paper artwork is a phenomenal undertaking. A dedicated group of six to ten people might spend up to two weeks to construct a single balloon. Their creation is then carefully folded and transported to the local fairgrounds where, along with many others, it will be launched.

As a keen paper artist, I arrived a week before the start of the festival to watch the balloons being made. Two different types were being assembled for the festival. The balloons for daytime launching were made of sheets of paper glued together to form birds, bears, pigs, cows, fish, ducks, and other animals—all as large as helicopters. Watching the craftspeople at work, I couldn't help but be impressed by their extraordinary dedication. But it was even more thrilling for me to witness these magnificent creations in flight.

Both the day and night launchings were spectacular, but in quite different ways. On the first afternoon of the festival, I followed a group of people to the fairgrounds at the base of Sulamuni Lawka Chantha Pagoda. We were joined by hundreds from the surrounding villages and many foreign tourists. The balloons, about ten in all, were launched individually, or in clusters of two or three. The spectators roared their approval as the balloons rose into the sky. The surreal sight of these animal-shaped creations slowly soaring over the surrounding hills put me in a meditative frame of mind.

The oval-shaped balloons that flew at night were bigger than the daytime balloons —some the size of a three-story building—and were crafted from handmade sheets of Shan *kozo* paper. They were decorated with colored foil papers, along with cellophane containers in which candles were placed. Wooden structures were attached to their bases to hold fireworks.

These gigantic constructions were lit by spotlights and masses of candles. When the balloons ascended into the night, cascades of fireworks spumed from their bases, lighting up the sky. In contrast to the peaceful daytime launchings, the night flights were much more electric. It was somewhat like watching a New Year's Eve fireworks display in the West, with brilliant and dramatic flashes of colored lights.

As each of the magnificent paper balloons slowly drifted skyward, I found myself caught up in the reverential and passionate excitement.

I joined the huge crowd, cheering loudly. Watching the balloons floating higher, I felt my own spirit soar alongside them.

Getting to Taunggyi

Local airlines run daily flights from Yangon to Heho, near Taunggyi and Inle Lake. Taunggyi is thirty-five kilometers east of Heho. For help arranging your trip details, I recommend Cathy at Magado Travel.

www.magadotravel.com

Paradise Hotel

When I stayed at this hotel in Taunggyi, the manager, Soe Soe, and her staff were exceedingly helpful. Soe Soe offered her assistant, Thidar Soe Tint, to serve as my guide. This delightful lady accompanied me, or organized other staff or drivers to take me, to see pagodas and the making and flying of the balloons.

157 Khwanyo Rd.
Taunggyi
(+95-81) 22009, 23586
www.inleparadise.com

Alternative lodging

Taunggyi hotels fill up quickly during *Tazaungdaing*. If you can't find a room in town, or would prefer a quieter alternative, you can stay in Nyaungshwe and take a taxi to and from the festival. The Paradise Hotel group (see above website) also has a hotel there.

EASTERN & NORTHERN MYANMAR

The art of giving

Besides the balloon making and flights, another fascinating aspect of the festival is the communal procession, which features objects that have been donated by the townspeople to local monasteries. The collected items are carefully affixed to large wooden frames, resulting in striking displays of art. These heavily laden frames are then mounted onto trailers for a procession around town. The collection of items I saw being paraded through the streets included household goods such as bowls, plates, towels, brooms, umbrellas, clocks, and bars of soap, as well as bank notes. Upon arrival at a central pagoda, these lovely creations were deconstructed, and the items distributed to the monasteries for the monks to use.

Myriam Grest explores the ethnic villages of Kyaing Tong

One of my favorite places in Myanmar is Kyaing Tong, nestled in the hills of eastern Shan State. When I first traveled there in 2000, I immediately fell in love with the lovely town and its friendly residents. Since then I have returned numerous times, taking walks around town and exploring ethnic villages in the nearby hills.

I am especially captivated by Kyaing Tong's morning market, one of the most colorful and liveliest markets I have seen in all of Asia. This is where members of the area's various hill tribes come to sell their products each morning. The array of merchandise on display is dazzling: produce, bright hill tribe clothing, handmade jewelry, and other local handicrafts. In addition to these items, there is also a lot of general household merchandise imported from Thailand and China. But my favorite corner of the market is the area filled with pottery stalls. This is where I find wonderful pieces made by skillful artisans from the surrounding villages.

During my first visit to Kyaing Tong, I hired a local guide to take me to some of the hill tribe villages. He proved to be invaluable, not only showing me the sights, but giving me a greater understanding of and appreciation for what I was seeing. He had been brought up in a missionary school and could speak the languages of many of the various Shan State ethnic groups. Each of the groups in the area is fiercely proud of its heritage and culture. These tribes do not consider themselves to be Bamar (ethnic Burmese), but instead each identifies with its own ethnicity, wearing a distinctive style of clothing and adhering to its own customs.

During one exploration of the area, I hiked into Pintauk, a village bordered by a craggy mountain range. Walking through lush green forests, I passed a small waterfall and entered a valley of flooded rice fields. It looked as if a huge, green, patchwork blanket were shimmering in the water. White and yellow butterflies showed me the way to nearby Akha villages, where a medicine man invited me into his house. While drinking rice wine, he showed me his collection of roots, with which, he claimed, he had already cured six cases of TB.

One of my favorite excursions is to the Loi village of Wan Nyat, about two hours by car from Kyaing Tong. The teakwood monastery on the outskirts of the village has beautiful carvings on its doors. During one of my visits, a friendly monk proudly showed me his astrological book, which was made of Shan paper. About a two-minute walk from the monastery is the village itself, which mostly consists of very long houses with many families living under one roof. Once children are married, the huts are extended for the new family; hence, the houses become longer and longer. Although many families live together, they cook separately. By counting the number of fireplaces, you can tell how many families are living in one house.

In Wan Nyat, I asked the chief what his people needed most. Not surprisingly, his answer was "money." But I don't like to give money directly, so I made some inquiries and found out that the village only had two cows and one ox. Cattle are very important for the villagers, and many depend on breeding livestock for

their income. So, when I returned to Kyaing Tong, I paid a visit to the local cattle market.

It was fascinating to see how cattle were traded. I met one man who was about to sell his only ox so that he could pay for his seven-year-old son's *Shin Pyu*. This is a ceremony in which young boys are temporarily initiated into local monasteries as novice monks. The man told me that with the money he planned to get from selling his ox he would be able to invite his whole village to the initiation. I asked him if he had another ox, and he said no, only some cows, but they wouldn't bring as much money as the ox. One ox, based on its size, can sell for $300 to $500. The *Shin Pyu* ritual will typically cost a family $100 to $500, depending upon on how elaborate the ceremony or how many people are invited. With the help of my guide, I eventually negotiated to buy six cows at the market and donated them to Wan Nyat village.

My trips to Kyaing Tong and the neighboring hill tribes have left me deeply touched by the warmth of the people I've encountered. When I talk to the villagers and see their humble way of living, it reminds me of the simple but important values in life. They may remain poor, at least by our standards, but even with their lack of material possessions and "creature comforts," these people seem to be more content than most I meet in Western countries. It's such a big difference from the West where we have food and good health and still we want more. As long as the harvest is fine, there is enough food, and nobody in the community is sick, the villagers are satisfied.

Getting to Kyaing Tong
See the fact file on page 32.

Around Kyaing Tong
Due to bumpy road conditions, it is not easy for travelers to visit some of the remote villages. But there are a couple of interesting towns in the area that are accessible by road. About thirty kilometers east of Kyaing Tong is Loi Mwe, a former British colonial hill station. Loi Mwe literally means "misty mountain," and a visit here will tell you why. It is sixteen hundred meters above sea level, and noticeably cooler. North of Kyaing Tong, on the Chinese border, is Mongla. I like to call it the "Tinseltown" of Myanmar because of its many casinos.

Advice on giving
Almost all of the villages need medicine. Some villagers need medication to treat worms and parasites, and many also need milk powder for infants, but it's not a good idea to hand items out directly to the villagers. I give medicine to our guide, so that he can distribute it and explain how to use it.

Ken Merk dances in the streets of Kyaing Tong

During one of my visits to Kyaing Tong, a local friend asked me to accompany him to a dance show ... or something like that. Since he was speaking in a Yunnanese dialect, and I was using broken Mandarin, I couldn't understand what exactly he was inviting me to see. But that's what I enjoy about being only partially fluent in any foreign language. It adds a sense of mystery to the adventure. I figured I'd just follow him and find out what was happening when we got there.

I hopped on the back of his motorbike and we headed toward the vicinity of Naung Tung Lake. After a series of turns and swerving down a few darkened alleys, we arrived at a street party, illuminated only by candles. The festivities were in full swing, with people of all ages and varying ethnic backgrounds eating, drinking, and generally having a good time.

There was also a lot of gambling going on, mostly in the form of card and dice games. One version was played with three large dice, kind of like a local version of craps. Each side of a die had an animal on it, and players bet by putting their money down on corresponding animal squares on the board. If the rolled dice showed the square you selected, you were a winner.

My friend took me over to a nearby street corner where a stage was set up. Some drunken local guys were dancing with a group of pretty young Shan women, all of whom were dressed up for the occasion in colorful traditional outfits along with powdered white faces, bright red lipstick, and lots of eyeliner. If you wanted to get up on stage and dance with them, you had to pay 100 kyat (around 8 cents) for a ticket.

My friend purchased a wad of tickets, handed them over, and a couple of women came to dance with us. They began to move slowly, swaying back and forth, and making graceful circular movements with their hands. Every thirty seconds or so, the matron of the event would click her stopwatch and blow a whistle. At that point the Shan women would rip up one of the tickets from their cache, showering us with the confetti remnants as they continued dancing away.

As we were dancing, I looked out into the crowd—probably close to a hundred people at that point—and saw that some of them were dressed in the garb of neighboring hill tribes, such as the Akha, Lisu, Lahu, and Loi. When I turned back to check on my friend, I found that he was long gone, presumably off to drink some moonshine with his mates.

Everyone in the crowd was pointing, laughing, and clapping along to the music. But I soon realized that much of the attention was being directed at me, the sole Westerner at this affair. I certainly enjoyed the dancing and the spirit of the oc-casion, but I wasn't keen to be the center of attention, so I tried to find a way to ease myself back out of the spotlight just a bit.

You would think my friend would have come back to retrieve me. But no, he apparently had other priorities, which pretty much left me to my own devices. Fortunately, with the number of women now dancing around me and the frequency with which the matron was blowing her whistle, my batch of dance tickets dwindled quickly. And for some crazy reason, the women were a lot less interested in me once I was rendered ticket-less!

The party was memorable, and I can say that in some small way I now know how the hill tribe people feel when tour groups come marching through their villages, staring and snapping pictures of them. This experience was a bit of a role reversal.

The next time you find yourself playing the part of a camera-toting tourist, think about taking a step back and giving the locals a little breathing room. In a similar situation, would you want to have a camera stuck in your face? And as you travel through Myanmar, if by chance you happen to find the tables turned and get caught center stage, just smile and appreciate the irony.

Getting to Kyaing Tong

See the fact file on page 32.

Dancing in the streets

As for the street party, the alleys were dark and the turns were many, so I can't give specific directions. But they are held frequently in town, and if you wish to find one and partake in the festivities, ask your guesthouse proprietor to steer you in the right direction.

KACHIN STATE

Ma Thanegi rings in the New Year Naga style

You haven't seen an awesome New Year celebration until you've experienced the one held in mid-January by the Naga, an ethnic group that lives in northwest Myanmar near the border with India. Some of the Naga tribes have to walk a week or more over mountain ranges to gather at the festival venue, and on the night I attended, in the town of Lahe, some tribes were still arriving after midnight. As their bare feet pounded in dance on the icy ground, and their deep-throated grunts and chants echoed in the surrounding hills, the hairs on my neck rose.

Known for their vibrant costumes, the Naga wear beads of all colors, strings of coral or shell necklaces, tiger claws and fangs, and a most intriguing if bizarre pendant, a

monkey skull with cane woven around it. Their hats of woven cane are decorated with black bear or red-dyed monkey fur, embellished with boars' tusks and hornbill feathers. The headdress of one tribe is the size of a large tray and covered with red seeds. Brass or silver coils are worn as armbands, with the most precious ones made of ivory; they are cut in sections and the arms simply pushed through the center hole. In their pierced ears, the Naga put in anything pretty they can find: tinsel, orchids, cigarette foil, shells, wildflowers, and for the more sedate grandmothers, rods of amber.

All of us visiting the festival were bedded down in a wooden schoolhouse, the rooms emptied of desks. We each had a mattress, pillow, wool blanket, and dark green mosquito net that, since there were no mosquitoes, was more useful for privacy when changing our clothes. At one end of the school were several bathrooms with clean Western-style toilets, built especially for this occasion. Large pots of boiling water were kept for us to mix with cold water, which we could use to take comfy baths. We were grateful not to have to go into the bushes when nature called, or to take dips in icy streams.

Despite these niceties, the accommodation of visitors is not the Naga's concern. They are not simply putting on a show for tourists. Practicing their dances in the mornings and gathering at night to outdo each other in the glow of roaring bonfires on the town's soccer field, the different tribes ignored the audiences altogether, caught up in the intense rhythms of their songs. I felt invisible, a mere moth fluttering around the edges, but I was thrilled to my toes to experience this event.

From one end of the field to the other, piercing cries ripped through the air, as if the Naga were letting fly shards of glass. Their bodies, taut with steely muscles, twisted and turned in the light of the flames, and their heels stamped on the ground, creating a sound like muted thunder. A tribe that had just walked in from over the mountains gathered at the log drum in the traditional ceremonial hall some distance away, and the drumbeats announcing their arrival echoed in the dark hills and valleys beyond the town.

Watching the dancers, I thought about how not so long ago the Naga were headhunting warriors. In the 1940s, after the insistence of succeeding governments, they were forced to give up this practice. Now living in peace among themselves and in accord with nature, they remain proud people who refuse to surrender the rest of their customs.

Celebrating the Naga New Year

The festival I attended was in Lahe, close to the Indian border. Some years the three-day festival is held in Leshi, to the southwest. Both towns are in the northwestern part of the country. A trip to see the celebrations can be arranged only through a licensed tour company in Myanmar, as permission is necessary from the relevant government departments to visit this area; because permits can be expensive and difficult to obtain, you should inquire well in advance of your trip. I was attending the festival at the invitation of Myanmar Bavarian Tours. The owners, Kalaya and Gerald Schreiber, are deeply dedicated to preserving the ethnic culture and ecology of the country. Though the website is in German, the Schreibers speak English.

6 Tayza Rd.
Kyan Khin Su Quarter
Mingaladon Township
Yangon
(+ 95-1) 663-347, 652-191, 721-869
www.myanmar-discovery.com

MAKING FRIENDS

Discovering the country through local hospitality

While you are traveling in Myanmar, it would be difficult *not* to become friends with at least one person you meet. It might be a guide on the street, a monk in a monastery, a helpful hotel worker, a souvenir seller, a trishaw driver, or a person you chat with in a teashop or restaurant. Despite the Orwellian reputation that "Big Brother" is watching you, I've found the people of Myanmar to be incredibly approachable and open to talking with foreigners.

Walking around a new town offers the perfect opportunity to meet locals, and some of these interactions can be unlikely ones. While exploring Yangon one day, Sudah Yehuda Kovesh Shaheb stops at a small watch shop to ask about repairs, a simple encounter that gains him the lasting friendship of the shop's owner. As he walks back to his hotel in Mandalay, Steve Goodman meets a disheveled, betel-nut-chewing cyclist; though suspicious at first, Steve eventually discovers an intelligent, inquisitive individual behind the downtrodden façade. And when Jennifer Gill treks into the hills near Kalaw, what makes the adventure so memorable is her guide, a fatherly (or as Jen might say, "grandmotherly") fellow known as Mr. Chain.

Personal encounters can also be unique to a place. Visitors to Bagan are often overwhelmed by the number of vendors aggressively trying to sell souvenirs around the area's ancient pagodas. In explaining how he deals with these persistent hawkers, Peter J. Walter also reveals how this led his family to become close friends with a couple that sells paintings at a pagoda in Old Bagan. Ken Merk, on the other hand, wants to find a crowd of kids in a Shan State village so that he can give them the photos he took of them three years earlier.

Visiting monasteries offers an excellent opportunity to meet monks and learn more about the lives of these dedicated students of Buddhism. While at a Mandalay monastery, I am invited for breakfast, and although the lines are long, I'm not

surprised. There are twenty-seven hundred hungry monks to feed! And at an unusual-looking monastery on the outskirts of Nyaungshwe, Don Gilliland finds himself returning to chat with the young monks, whose dedication to their studies is matched by their enthusiasm for rubber band wars and air guitar performances on their brooms. As always, every encounter comes with a pleasant surprise in Myanmar.

YANGON DIVISION

Sudah Yehuda Kovesh Shaheb takes his time in Yangon

In Western societies, we have come to regard material possessions as things that are useful when they are functioning, but to be thrown away the moment a mechanism fails. For example, there is little charity felt about our watches. Over the years I have collected my share of watches, most of which have stopped working. But many have sentimental value, and I want to keep them. Some were gifts from grateful patients or friends in other countries. One gold watch belonged to my grandfather.

On a recent trip to Myanmar, I brought some of my old watches with me to see if they could be repaired. While it may seem strange to bring them all this way, in the US or Australia, the cost to get one fixed would be impractical compared to the original price of the watch. I did so because I am fortunate to have become friends with two kind men who run a small watch repair shop in Yangon.

I stumbled upon this particular shop while walking around Yangon's Indian quarter on Anawrahta Road one evening back in 2002. As an anthropologist as well as a doctor, I was excited to be exploring this part of town, where you see ethnic races of many types and most of the shopkeepers are Muslim. As I was passing the watch shop, I noticed one man with a very distinct face; he looked South Indian, like someone from Tamil Nadu.

The man greeted me with a huge smile. I began the conversation by asking him whether he spoke Tamil. He replied that he did. I introduced myself and asked about repairing a watch I had with me that had stopped working. The man, whose name was Vasu, looked at it and determined that it only needed new batteries. Unfortunately, the appropriate batteries were not in stock, but he said he would ask around at some other shops on the street and try to find replacements.

"Please come back tomorrow morning," he said. "We will get the batteries for you."

The next morning, before returning, I went searching for a print shop but got lost. I stopped at another watch shop and asked a man for directions. He was helpful, and as I turned to walk away, I heard someone call to me: "Please come back, sir. We have the batteries for you." It was Vasu. He had been working behind the display case, and I hadn't realized that this was the same shop I had visited the day before. Vasu introduced me to the man who had given me the directions, Yusef, the shop's owner.

While I waited on my watch, I chatted with Yusef. He told me about his children: seven sons and one daughter. "I am sixty-eight," he said, "and my children tell me, 'Retire from business, Father, and spend your time saying prayers in the mosque.' 'No, no, I am not ready for that yet,' I tell them. I am happy that each one of my sons has a different kind of shop all along this street, and I am happy to be near them. And if I don't come to work every day, I would not be happy. I have been looking at watches ever since I was sixteen years old."

During our conversation, I mentioned that I had collected many watches over the years, most of which had stopped working. He suggested that I bring some to him the next time I visited. When I returned to Yangon a few months later I brought four more watches, all needing various types of attention.

The watch shop is truly a hole-in-the-wall operation. Yusef stands inside a small cubicle that is lined with glass cases filled with various watches and other accessories. There is only space for him to sit down on a stool, or he can lean on the glass case that faces the sidewalk. Vasu usually sits on a stool next to a small table right on the sidewalk.

Yusef's professionalism, attention to detail, and vast knowledge of watches has earned him a faithful clientele over the past fifty years— all of it spent in the same spot on Anawrahta Road. Despite the shop's tiny size, it has managed to generate enough income for Yusef to care for his elderly mother, and educate and set up businesses for his children. He was also able to go to Mecca.

During my return trips to Yangon I eventually had all my watches repaired at Yusef's shop. A Swatch that had been in my possession for seven years, but worn very rarely, only needed a new battery. My Casio altimeter, which tells the weather and elevation, was repaired and continues to forecast with greater accuracy than any meteorologist. My cheap Australian souvenir watch, made in China, now has a new strap. I also had an American Indian band, made of heavy silver and with embedded stones. The watch it came with, a Timex, never worked. Even the vendor I originally bought it from told me to get another timepiece, saying that the value was in the silver band. According to Yusef, this Timex was a good make but wasn't working because it had not been used enough.

I had nice conversations with Yusef and Vasu each time I walked past their shop. Very little money passed hands during my visits, but a firm friendship with the two men was established. So much so that on my last visit to Yangon, I was invited to Yusef's house. When I left town, I didn't say goodbye. Instead, I told them it would be *hasta luego*—see you later—until I brought more watches in need of repair, or my soul in need of their company.

Yusef's watch shop

This no-name shop is nothing more than a cubicle with a small work area in the back. In addition to making repairs, Yusef sells watches and accessories such as watchbands and batteries.

Anawrahta Road (near 28th Street) Yangon

Stuart G. Towns seeks shelter with a Yangon monk

I was looking out the window of my plane when a voice announced that we were approaching Yangon Inter-national Airport. As we descended through dark clouds, accompanied by jostling and bumping, my mind was as dark and uneven as the plane ride. I was anxious about what I would find on the ground. How would a Westerner be treated by the infamous military government? Would my every move be watched? Would my travel be restricted? Would I find myself being hassled by the police or army? Would the local people shy away from talking to the foreigner out of fear of being branded troublemakers?

Soon after we landed, my frame of mind improved drastically. I breezed through immigration and customs, and secured a taxi outside with no problems. My taxi driver was a friendly, talkative fellow, who helped put me at ease. I checked into my hotel and immediately headed out to tour the city on foot, despite the threatening storm clouds and my lingering worries.

As it turned out, it was the clouds that I should have been the most anxious about. As I walked through the streets of Yangon, the welcoming smiles of passing strangers made me feel at home. My first impression of the people was that they were shy and reserved, yet very happy that a Westerner like me would want to visit their country. This lifted my spirits, even as the skies above me grew darker.

By the time I reached Sule Paya, a golden pagoda rising from the middle of a traffic circle, the heavens opened up. Seeking shelter, I stepped into the complex of stalls and small shops surrounding the pagoda. As soon as I walked through the entrance, a teenaged burgundy-robed monk smiled and waved to me from a dry spot under the eaves of the roof. The rain was coming down hard now, so I walked over to where he was crouching and sat down with him to wait out the rain.

We introduced ourselves and talked for a few minutes. Ko Yin spoke English quite well, but from the puzzled look on his face when I spoke to him, I could tell that he wasn't accustomed to hearing native English speakers. As we made small talk, I marveled at my first look at the inside of one of this country's Buddhist pagodas. Splashes of color were everywhere—the rich red color of the monk's robe, the ornate gold roof, multi-colored LED halos flashing above the head of every Buddha image, and the reflection of it all in the water running down the polished marble walls, collecting in puddles on the floor.

Eventually, the downpour stopped and Ko Yin told me to follow him around the slick wet walkway that circles the pagoda. Along the way he explained what we were looking at. Hearing him talk about the differences in Buddhist religious theory and the mythology that surrounds Sule Paya and other centuries-old pagodas in Yangon, made it obvious that he was a devoted student of Buddhism.

Ko Yin asked if I wanted to go to another pagoda, located not far away, near the river. He was such a knowledgeable and personable guide that I was more than happy to accept the offer. We crossed the street and wandered through Mahabandoola Park, surrounded by beautiful old colonial-era buildings. Unfortunately, these structures are now slowly crumbling under the combined weight of the rain and grasses that are taking root in the cracks.

The tall, obelisk-shaped Independence Monument sits at the center of the park, and it is here that our conversation turned towards the political. Ko Yin expressed his fervent hope that Myanmar would be a truly free country again someday soon. His father, he said, was a member of an insurgent army that is fighting against the current regime, but Ko Yin had chosen instead to live and study at the safety of a monastery in Yangon.

I was surprised by how readily Ko Yin talked to me about the political situation, and because I was enthralled by his insider's view and what the average person thought, I was more than happy to listen. At the same time it made me very sad that such a passionate, intelligent young man was not allowed to reach his potential and contribute to the prosperity of this beautiful country.

We continued walking for several long blocks, eventually coming to Botataung Paya, situated on the banks of the Yangon River. This pagoda is beautiful, but the most distinctive aspect is its huge, golden *chedi*, which is hollow, enabling visitors to walk through it. The original *chedi* was destroyed by an Allied bomb in 1943, and many antique sculptures and other religious objects were found in the rubble. When it was reconstructed, the builders made a passageway through the *chedi* and housed the artifacts in glass cases along the walls, as if in a museum.

Ko Yin kept up a running narration throughout the walk, pointing out scale models of Indian temples or naming some of the Buddha's disciples who were represented in gold images. He also talked about his own life and his daily routine at a monastery outside of town. "Would you like to visit?" he asked.

But of course!

Soon we were in a small taxi, manufactured many decades ago, riding through the countryside, dodging people, dogs, cows, bicycles, buses, other taxis, and hundreds of potholes. On the way to the monastery, I formed a picture in my mind of what it would look like: a typically grand, Southeast Asian temple surrounded by well-manicured grounds and scores of novice monks studying or doing chores. My imagination did not prepare me for the reality. The monastery consisted of two rundown wooden buildings in the middle of a huge, unkempt lot. Only four monks lived there at the moment. Ko Yin, who was in his late teens, was the youngest, and the eldest was a frail old man who hobbled through the grounds using a walking stick.

We walked to the building farthest in back, where the head monk was resting. He was relatively young, still in his thirties, and as gentle in manner as you would expect a monk

to be. Although he did not speak a word of English, I could tell that he was very happy, if not honored, that I would visit his small monastery. Ko Yin, however, was ready to continue his tour, and we didn't stay long. Soon, we were in a taxi heading toward the other side of Yangon, to a pagoda that he thought I would find more interesting than his monastery. This one, Yele Paya, was indeed unique, if only for its location, perched on a small island in the middle of the Yangon River.

When we arrived at the shore, boats were taking worshippers to the island, but for some reason, Ko Yin couldn't convince any of them to take us. Several boat captains told us that the pagoda was closed. Another said, "This boat no good for foreigner." I tried to assure him that I wasn't expecting luxury. Any boat would suit me fine. Eventually, I realized that what he meant was that these boats were not government certified to carry tourists. After several minutes of negotiation, and waiting another twenty minutes, a "certified" boat appeared and we were ready to go.

By the time we returned from the island pagoda, it was getting dark. We hailed yet another taxi and rode through the dark streets to my hotel. Ko Yin and I said our goodbyes and I gave him some taxi fare for the long ride back to his monastery. As he disappeared from sight, I was surprised at how sad I was to see him go. His honesty and openness, the pride he had in the culture and the history of his country, and his willingness to share his faith with a stranger, made me feel I was leaving behind a close friend. I could only wave goodbye and hope he someday sees the Myanmar of his dreams.

Pagoda hopping

Yangon's Botataung Paya ($2 admission for foreigners) is located at the intersection of Strand Road and Botataung Pagoda Road, next to the Yangon River. Sule Paya is situated in the middle of a traffic circle, connecting Sule Paya Road and Mahabandoola Road in downtown Yangon, directly across the street from Mahabandoola Park. Yele Paya ($1 admission for foreigners), set on a small island in the Yangon River, can be reached from the nearby town of Kyauktan.

MANDALAY DIVISION

Steve Goodman learns a lesson in acceptance in Mandalay

I had just enjoyed a wonderful dinner at a Shan restaurant in Mandalay with a friend, and we were walking back to our hotel, down a dark, unfamiliar street, when a man riding a bicycle approached. Spitting out a spray of red betel nut juice, he hopped off his bike and asked if he could speak with us.

I stopped and sized him up quickly, as one does when approached by a stranger. His bike was old, with dented fenders and flaking paint; as if to match, his clothes were dirty, ill-fitting, and torn. They had obviously been mended multiple times. With a hint of suspicion, I asked him what he wanted to talk about.

"You are native English speakers?" he asked.

I nodded.

"I like to practice my English speaking to native speakers."

Maybe it was because his mouth was stuffed full of betel nut, but the man spoke with an odd, slightly muffled accent, different from the usual, clear diction of most English-speaking locals I had met. I asked him his name. "Sonny Boy," he answered with a smile, revealing a dark red mouth and decayed, blackened teeth, indications of a longtime betel nut chewer.

As we talked and strolled along the road, with Sonny Boy walking his bike alongside us, we gradually dropped our guard. Noticing the Nylon Ice Cream Parlor up ahead, we invited him to join us for dessert. He seemed embarrassed that he wasn't dressed "properly" for the occasion and said he hoped we were not offended to be seen with him. We told him not to worry, and he beamed with joy and accepted our invitation.

As it turned out, once we were seated in the ice cream shop, my American buddy and I were the curiosities to the staff, not Sonny Boy. He was smiling and enjoying our company, and didn't act uncomfortable in the least. He just seemed delighted that we were kind enough to treat him to a cold sweet treat that was, for him, an extravagant luxury.

While sitting in the little open-air ice cream shop, Sonny Boy told us about his life. Now in his mid-thirties, he was an only child and lived at home with his elderly parents. He had earned a university degree in physics, but rather than seek a job in that field, he felt obligated to assist his parents in running their business, a small gas station on the outskirts of Mandalay. He said that he had studied English in school "a little bit, a long time ago," but continued practicing by talking to tourists and religiously listening to BBC World News and Voice of America on an old radio at home in the evenings.

From our conversation, it was obvious that Sonny Boy was a bright fellow. He had a wide range of interests and liked to follow international news and current events. After hearing that I was American, he was full of questions about the US. He also asked me to explain the meanings of an amusing array of slang and euphemistic phrases he had heard. One he was especially unsure about was "once in a blue moon."

During my trip to Myanmar, I found almost everyone to be exceptionally warm, kind, and friendly, and in that respect Sonny Boy was quite typical. But what made our brief conversation so remarkable was the incongruity of his appearance with his genuine and heartfelt intellectual curiosity. Talking to him, I deeply felt both the sadness and loneliness in his life, as well as the great joy he took in simple things like learning what "once in a blue moon" meant. I was also impressed by his dignity, devotion to his parents, and discipline to learn more about the world and other cultures.

After we said our goodbyes, my friend and I admitted to each other that we had both been close to blowing him off when he first approached us. But he was such a lovely, humble, and intelligent man, that we now agreed it was our luck to have met him.

For me, the moral of the story is to simply give people a chance. If you submit to your own insecurities, fears, or jaded-traveler instincts, putting up a protective shell of disinterest or hurrying along your way dismissively, then you may be missing out on some wonderful experiences. Sonny Boy was a good example. Being able to spend time with someone like him, who was so thankful for just a forty-five minute conversation with us, was rewarding, and a good reminder that you can meet the most charming and unforgettable people when you least expect it.

Nylon Ice Cream Parlor
173 83rd St. (25/26)
Mandalay

Impromptu English lessons

At many places around Mandalay, you will often find locals who want to hone their English skills with native speakers. Some English teachers and their pupils hang out in front of the Mandalay Marionettes Theatre before the show each evening. If you arrive a bit early you can have a lovely conversation with people of all ages who will be truly thankful for the time you spend with them. You are also likely to find students near the southeast corner of the Mandalay Palace and Fort complex, across the street from the Sedona Hotel, and at the top of Mandalay Hill. You must have a ticket to the Mandalay Archaeological Zone to climb Mandalay Hill. The ticket price, which includes admission to other popular sites in town, is $10.

Morgan Edwardson breakfasts with 2,700 monks in Mandalay

One of my favorite spots in Mandalay is the "Monk District," a serene neighborhood of shady trees and narrow lanes tucked away in the southwest corner of the city. Here you will find dozens of attractive monasteries and old pagodas, provid-ing a soothing retreat from the harsh features of modern Mandalay.

Shwe In Bin Kyaung, a late-nineteenth-century monastery made entirely of teak, is one of the highlights in this area. No matter where your gaze rests—doorways, windows, walls, ceilings, rooftops—you will see intricately carved teakwood figures adorning the small but exquisite building. In contrast, only a few hundred meters down the road, over a small bridge that crosses a narrow canal, is Mandalay's largest monastery, Ma Soe Yein Nu Kyaung, home to more than twenty-seven hundred monks. During my cycling expeditions around the city, I often stop there to chat with the friendly, inquisitive monks that wander the sprawling, tree-lined compound.

During one such visit, I was talking with a trio of students when I noticed a group of men (local gents, as opposed to monks) cooking in huge pots and woks near the canal. One of the students told me that this crew was preparing food for the monastery's breakfast the following morning. Sensing my curiosity about such a massive feast, he invited me to return the next day and witness the ritual for myself.

The only problem with experiencing this morning extravaganza—and watching breakfast being served to twenty-seven hundred monks certainly qualifies as such—was getting up early enough to see it all begin. Monks don't sleep in, so this meant I needed to get to the monastery before six if I wanted to catch the main feature. Predictably, I was groggy

MANDALAY & CENTRAL MYANMAR

when my alarm went off at five the next morning, but I managed to crawl out of bed, take a quick shower, and hop on my rented bicycle for the pre-dawn ride. Due to the dearth of streetlights in Mandalay, I brought along a flashlight, hoping it would ensure that I didn't collide with any stealth trishaws en route.

When I wheeled through the gates of the monastery, I was pleasantly surprised to find my monk friend there waiting for me, his perpetual smile in place. He escorted me to an area behind one of the buildings where meals were being efficiently dished out by a crew of volunteers. After receiving their food, the monks walked silently to an adjacent building and then marched up a set of stairs to a huge hall where they ate their meal.

Meanwhile, more lines of monks waited patiently outside. Because of the large number of monks in residence—let me repeat, more than twenty-seven hundred—it obviously took more than a few minutes to feed everyone. The food distribution required two complete shifts, the first one starting at five thirty, which were broken down into smaller units of monks. No matter where I looked, there appeared to be groups of monks in motion: turning corners, lining up in formation, marching forward fifteen meters and then halting again. Stop. Go. Wait. Such maneuvering required a coordinator, usually a senior monk, who nodded when it was time for a group to move forward to the next waiting point.

Looking around, I realized that I was the only Westerner in attendance. I asked the monk if it was okay to take photos and he nodded. After I had snapped some shots, one of the volunteers who had been distributing food came over and introduced himself. He was a very nice gentleman in his seventies, and spoke English well. After talking for a few minutes, he invited me upstairs to meet a group of senior monks.

I certainly wasn't going to turn down such an opportunity, so I followed him up to the second floor where five older monks were seated in large, ornate chairs. I watched as the monks led prayers and bestowed blessings upon members of the community who had donated various items. People such as these often donate money or food to local monasteries in order to make merit. After that little ceremony was finished, I was ready to head back to my hotel, but the volunteer insisted that I join him and the monks for breakfast, a lavish spread of curries, vegetables, fruit, and de rigueur pots of tea.

Thankfully, I managed to get through the meal without spilling anything or committing any embarrassing cultural blunders. I thanked everyone for the hospitality and walked back outside to retrieve my bike. As I was leaving, another volunteer motioned me over to his truck and handed me a big bag of oranges. I accepted the gift, thanked the man, and stuffed the oranges into my backpack.

I was tickled by such a nice gesture of hospitality, but honestly, what was I going to do with so many oranges? There must have been a dozen or more in the bag. Besides, I was already stuffed, and I had a teashop visit planned that morning. Twenty minutes later, I found the perfect solution.

As I was cycling back toward my hotel, I spotted five novice monks making alms rounds on the street. I parked my bike and walked over to greet them with a hearty "*mingala-ba*." Taking the bulging bag out of my backpack, I rationed out the bounty, placing two oranges in each monk's alms bowl.

What a fine way to make merit on another glorious day in Myanmar.

Ma Soe Yein Nu Kyaung

The monastery is located south of Shwe In Bin Kyaung, across the bridge over Thinga Yarzar Canal. The first breakfast shift starts at around 5:30 a.m.

89th Street (37/38)
Mandalay

Renting a bike

I rented my bike from Mr. Htoo's stand on 83rd Street, the same block inhabited by the popular Nylon Ice Cream Parlor (see page 94). The rental rate was 1,000 kyat for a full day.

Peter J. Walter is befriended at a Bagan temple

It was late afternoon, the sun was setting low in the sky, and I had just arrived in Bagan, a city renowned for its thousands of ancient religious monuments. I was eager to escape the confines of the car and explore the vast expanse of sun-drenched pagodas that swept majestically across the horizon.

After securing a rental bicycle, I clumsily rode along sandy trails until arriving at the entrance of an interesting-looking pagoda called Minyeingon—not the largest in the area, but one that later became my favorite for viewing sunrises and sunsets. Inside, the air was damp and smelled strongly of bat guano. With my flashlight, I peered around the dark interior, stopping to reflect on the peaceful expression of the enormous Buddha figure seated in the center of the pagoda. The cool, tranquil atmosphere was inviting after a long day of traveling, but I remembered the fading sunlight and looked around for a way to the top for a better view.

Locating a low staircase on one side, I began my ascent. A soft, gentle voice called out, "Mind your head," to warn me of the large, dusty bricks looming above my hunched shoulders. The owner of the mysterious voice produced a beam of light from above to illuminate my path and guide me through the narrow passage.

Emerging onto the lower roof, I saw all around me pagodas of various sizes and shapes stretched across the plain. The gentle sunlight blanketed everything with a golden hue and cast long, spiky shadows behind the pagodas. Once outside, I could finally make out the face behind the helpful voice: a young lady smiling warmly as if she were welcoming me to her own personal pagoda. She introduced herself as Ma Aung, and nodded toward the external stairs that led still farther up the structure.

I noticed several other tourists camped out on the upper ledge above me enjoying the view. Below, a few smiling vendors, who hoped to sell their wares, patiently waited for them to descend. I climbed as high as I could go, breathing in the fresh air and relishing my first taste of Bagan's splendor. In front of me stretched the seemingly endless plain, while behind, the Ayeyarwady River flowed south towards Yangon.

After enjoying the panorama and snapping some pictures, I went back down for a look at the paintings and other handicrafts offered by the vendors. I chatted with the group for awhile, learning that Ma Aung and her fiancé, Koko, regularly worked here at Minyeingon. Koko painted and made crafts, while Ma Aung came to the pagoda every day at sunrise and sunset, the best times to

catch the small flow of tourists, who mostly came for the glorious views.

Koko and Ma Aung told me that they planned to get married soon, move into a small bungalow in a nearby village, and continue with their daily commute to Minyeingon. They seemed to have a pleasant and peaceful life, but with many other vendors as competition, and a limited pool of tourists, it must have been a difficult way to make a living.

During that trip and over the course of several more I took with friends and family, I have become close with some of the Bagan vendors and learned a bit more about their lives. A few have very kindly invited me to their villages and homes, providing drinks and food despite limited means. They have taught me little things about the Burmese language, the history of Bagan, and provided some suggestions on good places to eat.

Not all the vendors share the warmth and friendliness of Ma Aung and Koko, however, and sometimes the commercial persistence of unrelenting sales pitches can distract from the tranquility of the place. But it's important to remember that these people are just trying to eke out a living from tourists. On the whole, I've found that with a little firm insistence—and lots of smiles—that it's possible to be left alone to enjoy the sights on my own terms.

Since I started traveling to Bagan with my wife and our two young children, we have become good friends with Koko and Ma Aung. They have always been incredibly accommodating in helping get our kids, as well as me and my wife, up and down the steep pagoda steps safely. During the last night of our most recent visit, Koko surprised us by bringing hundreds of candles, which he lit and placed along the side of the rooftop ledge after dark. The candlelight cloaked the temple in a beautiful glow, giving us and those looking on from below an unforgettable view of its profile.

Ma Aung, Koko, and other local residents are blessed in many ways to have been born in a part of the world that is so special and beautiful. And I feel blessed to have the chance to know such lovely people, whose warmth continues to beckon us back to Bagan.

Minyeingon Pagoda

The pagoda is located just south of Old Bagan, off the main paved road that leads to the Bagan Thande Hotel. It is across the street from the Archaeological Museum.

www.hotelbaganthande.com

Renting bikes

Bicycle rental rates vary, depending upon where you stay. For example, prices are generally cheaper in Nyaung U (a few kilometers north of Old Bagan) than in New Bagan. Prices normally range from 1,500 to 2,500 kyat for a full day.

Morgan Edwardson doesn't run away from the market in Pyin U Lwin

I met Sheila near the peas and carrots.

It was a cold January morning, and I had just wolfed down a hot bowl of spicy noodles at a stall in Pyin U Lwin's Shan Market. My belly full, I was aimlessly wandering the colorful aisles of the fruit and vegetable section, soaking up the atmosphere and taking photos, when an old woman approached me.

"Good morning! How are you?" she exclaimed in flawless English, reaching out to shake my hand, as if I were some long lost friend. "Happy New Year! Better late than never!"

With that last declaration, I almost burst out laughing. Who was this funny local lady with the perfect language skills?

She told me her name was Sheila. She was in her seventies and a lifelong resident of Pyin U Lwin, although she still called the town by its colonial name, Maymyo. A few minutes into our conversation, she remarked that she could use a bit of money to buy some food and medicine. She seemed sincere, plus I liked the old gal, so I forked over a combination of kyat and dollars and wished her well.

I thought that would be the end of our meeting and was ready to say goodbye, but Sheila had other ideas. She insisted on guiding me around the rest of the market and over to a nearby Chinese temple. "Oh, you must see it," she urged. "It's very close to here."

First, though, she insisted that we stop for tea. As we waited to cross the busy main road, she grabbed my arm and issued a warning. "Be careful, these cars will knock you down and run away!" Thankfully, we made it across the street without getting flattened and found a small teashop nearby.

We had cups of hot tea, sweetened with condensed milk, and munched on tasty cinnamon rolls. I was getting ready to pay for our snacks when Sheila peeled out some of the bank notes I had given her earlier and took care of the bill. Later, walking down the road, she stopped and bought me a bag of Shan sweets, telling me to keep them for later when I was hungry.

As we were approaching the Chinese temple, Sheila advised me to watch my belongings while in town. "You have to be careful. If you leave your bag on the ground, they'll take it and run away." On the subject of buying from markets in Pyin U Lwin, she had additional advice. "You have to watch them. If you buy something for 300 kyat and give them a 1,000 kyat note, they will take your change and run away." If what Sheila was saying was true, there were a lot of shifty people in this town who were keen to do bad things and head for the hills.

Fortunately, that didn't turn out to be the case. Nothing alarming happened during my stay in Pyin U Lwin, and I found the people there to be just as friendly and polite as anywhere else I visited in Myanmar. If you visit the town's Shan Market early one morning, don't be surprised if you are given an enthusiastic greeting by one very sweet old lady. Word of advice: If she invites you for tea, whatever you do ... don't run away.

Getting to Pyin U Lwin

Share taxi prices from Mandalay can vary. I paid 6,000 kyat for one of the coveted front seats. Spots in the back, which you can expect to share with two or three other passengers, are a bit cheaper. The ride usually takes about two hours. You can show up at the share taxi stand in Mandalay on the day you want to buy your ticket, or book your seat the day before. In the latter case, you can arrange for the taxi to pick you up at your hotel. The share taxi stand is at the corner of 27th and 83rd Streets.

About Pyin U Lwin

The former British hill station once known as Maymyo is located about seventy kilometers from Mandalay. It is a scenic and charming town: mountains in the distance and stately old Tudor-style homes gracing the tree-lined streets. The historic Candacraig Manor/Thiri Myaing Hotel (mentioned in Paul Theroux's *The Great Railway Bazaar,* as well as *Ghost Train to the Eastern*

Star, in which he revisits the haunts featured in the first book) is one of several colonial-era mansions now functioning as hotels. The sprawling National Kandawgyi Gardens is the town's biggest attraction. Due to its elevated location, Pyin U Lwin is cooler during Myanmar's hot summer months and positively frigid in January, which is when I made my visit.

www.pyinoolwin.info

Shan Market

This market is located just south of the roundabout at the intersection of Circular Road and Mandalay-Lashio Road, the town's main drag, also known as Main Road.

Circular Road Teashop

This shop is on the northeast corner of the aforementioned roundabout, in a row of shops on the right-hand side of Circular Road, if you are facing north.

The Chinese Temple (Cantonese Temple)

This temple is on the first "big road" past the teashop heading north on Circular Road. Take a right and you will find it across the street from the Aung Chantha Pagoda.

SHAN STATE

James Spencer hangs out on the riverfront in Hsipaw

A friend in Australia told me about a woman he met on a flight from Yangon to Bangkok. The woman seemed like your normal middle-aged tourist, nothing remarkable, the sort you see down at the local Kmart on a Saturday morning buying warm socks for winter. She was obviously Australian, the accent a dead giveaway. They got to talking, and my friend asked the woman, Maureen, where she lived, expecting her to be from some suburb of Sydney.

"Hsipaw," Maureen replied. Seeing the confused look on my friend's face, she explained. "I live in Burma and run a café in a town called Hsipaw."

Six months later I arrived in Hsipaw, wanting to visit the Shan State town for many reasons, not least of which was to meet Maureen at her Black House Café. Hsipaw also interested me for historical reasons. Until the early 1960s, the town had its own resident Shan Saopha (prince) and Austrian-born Mahadevi (princess), and the last king of Burma, Thibaw, had taken his name from the town (the Shan word Hsipaw is pronounced "Thibaw" in Burmese).

EASTERN & NORTHEASTERN MYANMAR

Nowadays it is famous among backpackers who take advantage of the town's location for treks to scenic hill tribe villages in the area.

I did all the things a traveler is supposed to do in Hsipaw. I slept at Mr. Charles's guesthouse. I visited Mr. Food and Mr. Book (the first runs a restaurant, the second a bookshop). I went to the ex-*Saopha*'s ex-palace. I watched a demonstration of how corn is popped by hand at the popcorn factory. I toured a shrine where offerings were being made to the *nat*. I walked to Five Buddha Hill one day and Nine Buddha Hill the next, where I watched the sunset. I even took a morning excursion, billed as a trek, to a waterfall and some villages on the outskirts of town. But most notably, I met Maureen at the Black House Café.

The café occupies a hundred-year-old teakwood building down on the banks of Dokhtawady River. There is a sign out the front saying, "This Is a Café." I found Maureen to be much like the typical Aussie housewife my friend had described, friendly and talkative, but perhaps a touch more eccentric than most.

I spent most of the afternoon on the terrace. Another Aussie and his girlfriend came in around sunset, and Maureen decided to close up shop and have dinner outside. We purchased food from Mr. Food and beer from the market. It was a full moon that night, and as we sat and talked and watched the moon rise over the river and the distant Shan hills, Maureen told us the story of how she ended up in Hsipaw.

She had been living in a little country town in Victoria, but had a falling out with the president of the Ladies' Lawn Bowling Club, which as close to a *Mahadevi* as you can get in rural Australia. The Lady President told Maureen that she should treat the Lady President with more deference, and Maureen called the Lady President something very unladylike, which more or less ended Maureen's chances of getting another game at the Bowling Club.

"Well, I'd visited Burma before, and I'd made friends in Hsipaw, and I liked it," said Maureen, "so I thought about it a bit and decided why not live here for a bit. I've never regretted it. Never thought about going back to Victoria."

Besides attracting tourists, Maureen's café is popular with at least two locals. "There's this couple, they come once a week, on separate motorbikes," Maureen told us. "He comes from one direction, she comes from the other direction. They meet here, they have a cappuccino, and then they get back on their motorbikes and off they go again, him in the one direction, her in the other. Why? I've never asked. I reckon their parents maybe don't approve, you know, like Romeo and Juliet. But you never ask those questions, do you?"

There is another reason Maureen wound up in Hsipaw. "In Australia in one day I'll meet fifty people and they'll all be the same person; here, I meet fifty people and they're all different!"

While she was speaking for herself, she also spoke for travelers like me. This is the reason we come to Myanmar. Yes, the sights are wonderful, but it's the people—even unlikely ex-pats like Maureen—that make this country so enticing.

Getting to Hsipaw

Most travelers reach Hsipaw from Mandalay or Pyin U Lwin. This journey can be done by bus, share taxi, or train. The taxi ride from Mandalay can take four to six hours, while a train journey, although very scenic, is considerably slower, taking ten hours or more.

Black House Café

The café is located in "downtown" Hsipaw, on the banks of the Dokhtawady River, just north of the central market. It's not hard to find. Getting lost in Hsipaw would take rare talent. It offers a variety of coffee—espresso, flat white, short black, you name it—all made from locally grown beans. You can enjoy your coffee inside, or have it served on a terrace overlooking the river at the back of the building. The café is open daily, though the hours change frequently.

Jennifer Gill is spirited away in the hills outside Kalaw

I'm usually not a breakfast eater. On most mornings, coffee and cigarettes suffice for the first couple hours of the day. But the complimentary breakfast in Myanmar's hotels and guesthouses, if anything, gets you up. It's hard to turn down free food.

At the Golden Kalaw Inn, as I examine the odd burn patterns on my cold white toast, a round-faced man with a belly to match enters the dining room and starts passing out bottles of water. Mr. Chain is fifty-six years old, wears army-issued shoes that resemble Converse All-Stars, and carries a brightly colored children's rucksack. He is the understanding father, the favorite uncle, the doting grandparent—a natural caregiver—and he will be our group's trekking guide for the next two days as we hike into the hills and minority villages that fringe the quiet town of Kalaw in Shan State.

While I thought I might lose a kilo or so on this thirty-kilometer hike, at every rest stop Mr. Chain pulls more food out of his seemingly bottomless pack: oranges, cookies, crackers. He is like an Italian-Jewish grandmother. "Eat, eat," he constantly urges. If he had added, "You're getting fat!" I would swear he was possessed by my Grandma Bess.

Around midday we stop in a village, and Mr. Chain takes over the dirt-floored wooden shack of a small monastery, complete with wood-burning fire, and cooks lunch for us. Fatigued after five hours of walking, we enthusiastically eat our noodle soup, rice, avocado with lemon and salt, and peanut brittle. Mr. Chain then lays out pillows for us in the meditation hall. "Sleep now. The sun is strong." We do as we're told.

Even in the late afternoon, the sun and dust suck the fluid from our bodies. While the group audibly gulps down water out of large bottles, Mr. Chain sips from his itsy-bitsy flask. He's like a camel. When we question his stamina, he proudly asserts, "If I hadn't given up cigarettes, I'd be dead by now." I have no idea how this relates, but I am not about to question this man's pearls of wisdom.

That he loves his job is obvious. He is a knowledgeable and compassionate storyteller and teacher. With pride and nostalgia he tells of a time when the hills were covered in trees. He talks about farmers, their crops and harvest seasons. He explains the hunting method of a group of men we see on the hillside across the valley. After the hunters form a vertical line down the slope and make yelping sounds to scare animals away from them, their prey then runs toward another group lying in wait.

As we enter each village, he describes the habits and customs of the inhabitants. The Palaung cut down their trees for firewood and never eat vegetables, and for fear of malaria, they live near the tops of the mountains where water is scarce. The Danu, on the other hand, use trees for shade and controlling water flow. Their living conditions are visibly better than that of the Palaung. They grow vegetables. Their children are clean.

In one Palaung village, multiple families live in "longhouses," which are just what they sound like. Mr. Chain relates an amusing story about one such abode where the children of the different families didn't get along. To solve the problem, the inhabitants cut out the middle section of the structure to create two individual homes. Not the most

effective way to teach the youngsters how to share, but who am I to judge?

As we reach the Viewpoint Tea House where we will be spending the night, Mr. Chain asks me how I'm doing.

"Tired, but good," I reply.

Then he adds, matter-of-factly, "You have big body, but you walk very good."

Turns out the spirit of my Grandma Bess is in there after all.

Finding Mr. Chain

I met Tin Maung Chain through the Golden Kalaw Inn, which helps travelers book local treks.

Nat Sin Road
Kalaw
(+95-81) 50311

Taking the trek

The cost of my two-day trek was $7 per day. This included water (though you should bring extra bottles), four meals, snacks, and one night's accommodation. As always, prices are negotiable and dependant on the size of your group, the duration of the trek, and whether it is one way or round trip.

Don Gilliland sweeps through a monastery near Nyaungshwe

My taxi bounced down the rutted road toward Nyaungshwe, green mountains rising in the east, the famous waters of Inle Lake only a few kilometers to the south. Looking out to the right, I noticed a small monastery.

The old teakwood building stood about three meters off the ground, supported by large wooden posts, but what especially struck me were the windows: enormous, oval-shaped portals that looked as if they could easily accommodate my six-foot frame. Several young novice monks leaned out, their red robes providing a sharp contrast to the sun-baked brown wood, as my taxi hurtled past. As the monastery disappeared from view, I promised myself I would come back and take some photos. Several hours later, I did just that.

Dating back to the nineteenth century, Shwe Yan Pyay Kyaung is located about a kilometer north of Nyaungshwe, which made for an easy excursion by bicycle. On that afternoon of my first visit, I found a group of novice monks sweeping the grounds. At least that's what they were supposed to be doing.

One youngster had dropped his broom and was kicking around an empty plastic bag, trying to keep it suspended in the air. Another was playing air guitar with his broom. "Purple Haze," anyone? Yet another monk had finished cleaning cobwebs from a teakwood post and was now using his broom to take a poke at one of his buddies, a boy who was leaning out a window and shooting rubber bands down at the broom crew.

I took some photos of the slacker sweepers, along with a few shots of a trio of monks standing near one of the big windows. In between clicks, one of the smiling window monks motioned for me to come up and talk. After taking my shoes off, I climbed a wooden stairway up to the main *vihara* (sanctuary). My chat with the one monk soon drew a trickle of other curious monks. They were gracious hosts, encouraging me to walk around the monastery and ask questions.

Like most monks I had met in Myanmar, they welcomed the chance to practice their English, plus they wanted to know more about me, where I lived, and what I did. I had studied Burmese prior to this trip, trying to build an arsenal of useful words and phrases. I always welcomed "monk sessions" such as these as an opportunity to speak Burmese and inquire about the language, much as the monks worked on their English by speaking with tourists. The novices here were helpful, patiently answering my endless questions and correcting my pronunciation whenever I butchered a phrase.

One of thirty monks in residence, a fourteen-year-old from Taunggyi told me that he had been studying at Shwe Yan Pyay Kyaung for the past three years. When he turned eighteen, and was no longer a novice, he planned on moving to a larger monastery in his hometown, remaining a monk there indefinitely. He and the other novices studied the Pali language and Buddhist texts for most of the morning and afternoon. After studies were over, they swept the monastery grounds and did other chores. When they had free time in the evenings, another boy confided with a giggle, he and his friends sometimes watched TV or listened to music. Oh, the decadence!

I had such a good time talking to these monks that I made three more visits during my stay in Nyaungshwe. On my last day in town, I went on an early morning shopping spree at the local market, buying various items to give them: a couple kilos of oranges, soap, pens, and notebooks. I also considered getting some shampoo, until I realized that was something the shaved-head fellows probably didn't need.

When I arrived that afternoon, some novices were engaged in their usual playful sweeping maneuvers, while a few others were perched next to the monastery windows, posing for more camera-toting tourists. Like the famous leg-rowing fishermen on nearby Inle Lake, I suspect that these monks have become accustomed to being the subject of photographs and take it all in stride.

The novices accepted my gifts with smiles and bilingual thanks, and before I left, they also had a present for me: a bamboo tube packed with some sticky rice. It was a nice gesture from a nice bunch of young monks. So what if they were a little lax when it came to sweeping up.

Shwe Yan Pyay Kyaung

The monastery—known as Shwe Yaunghwe Kyaung in the Shan language—is located about one kilometer north of Nyaungshwe on the main road that leads to the junction for Taunggyi and the airport in Heho. The best time to visit

the monks is when they are not studying: from 11 a.m. to noon, and usually after 5 p.m., though sometimes the studies continue until 6 p.m. or later. Air guitar performances are held at random hours.

Ken Merk reminisces in a Loi village outside Kyaing Tong

My wife and I have had the opportunity to visit Myanmar's Shan State on several occasions. In my opinion, there is nowhere else in the world where you can find such a fascinating diversity of ethnic groups in one area. You only need to make one quick visit to the morning market in Kyaing Tong to see an example of what I mean. There, along with a few Western tourists, are Burmese, Chinese, Shan, and a colorful mixture of other hill tribe people, all wandering around, shopping, and socializing.

On one recent trip, we made a return visit to the Loi village of Wan Seng. This small hill tribe village, located north of Kyaing Tong, consists of about half a dozen thatched communal houses and a small Buddhist monastery. The houses, which are similar to tribal longhouses in Borneo, have groups of up to six families living together in them. This is quite different from the living arrangements of the other hill tribes in this area—such as the Akha, Lisu, and Lahu—who tend to build individual huts for each family.

Since the opportunity to re-visit a remote hill tribe village doesn't come up every day, I thought that it might be fun to print out pictures of the kids we had encountered on our previous trip and pass them out—that is, if we could find them. Upon our arrival, with photographs in hand, I walked around from hut to hut, looking for the children.

My first attempts to identify kids were not successful, so I decided to walk over to the village monastery. I approached a group of novice monks who were milling around outside. After a few hand gestures, they understood what I wanted. As we started sorting through the pictures together, I discovered that three of the children we had photographed were now among these monks.

One of the boys had been only about five or six years old when I had taken a photo of him carrying around his little sister strapped to his back—babysitting duties start at an early age in these parts. I never would have recognized him, but fortunately, he picked himself out of the photos. What a difference a few years make. On that previous trip, he was a grubby little guy with tattered clothes, but now, three years later, we found a handsome boy with a shaved head, wearing the flowing robes of a Buddhist monk.

Wan Seng village is isolated, and the conditions are quite rustic. Dirt paths lead between the huts, which don't have any electricity or running water. It's definitely not the kind of place where the local residents would have access to a one-hour photo processing lab. So I expect that the kids here have few, if any, photos from their childhood.

It was obvious that the monks really got a kick out of seeing the pictures I had brought of them and their friends when they were younger. They were all gesturing at the images, snickering, and teasing one another.

This village doesn't get many foreign visitors, and despite the obvious language barrier and children's initial shyness, passing out the photos turned out to be a great way to break the ice and bridge cultures. It also provided me with an opportunity to snap a few more pictures of the same kids as they reacted to seeing photos of their younger selves.

While I've always found that visiting Myanmar is a great experience, to be able to come back and share something personal with the local children made it even more rewarding. And I'm sure that I will receive a cordial welcome on any future return visits to Wan Seng, with my album of village photos in hand.

Getting to Kyaing Tong
See fact file on page 32.

Visiting Wan Seng
Wan Seng is one of two Loi (Lwe) villages that are about a two-hour ride north of Kyaing Tong, along the road to Mengla. (For more about the second village, see page 81.) Once you reach the dirt turnoff for these two villages, it is about a four-hour round-trip hike along a dirt path to Wan Seng. Permits are needed to visit this area. These can be obtained from local travel agents (see page 267).

EASTERN & NORTHEASTERN MYANMAR

Retail Therapy

An insiders' primer to boutiques and markets

When I think of shopping in Myanmar, I immediately visualize the vibrant local markets. The splashes of color and symphony of merchandise always captivate me. The most famous market in the country is Yangon's historic Bogyoke Aung San Market. One morning I roamed its aisles before purchasing a trio of charming handmade puppets for my nieces back in the States. After I paid the shopkeeper, she started fanning the shelves of merchandise with the bank notes I had given her. "Lucky money!" she explained with a big smile. As I was later to learn, this is a custom at shops and markets all over Myanmar. The proceeds from the first sale of the day are deemed lucky and are ceremoniously fanned over the merchandise.

Bogyoke Aung San, or Scott's Market as it's sometimes still known, is also the most popular stop for tourists looking for souvenirs, clothing, or handicrafts. But don't limit yourself to browsing the busy ground floor aisles. Whenever possible, stick with the locals, like Ma Thanegi, who one day unexpectedly discovers an entire world of boutiques and tailor shops virtually unknown to foreigners—up on Bogyoke's second floor.

If you want an authentic immersion into a traditional market, you won't find escalators and air-conditioned comfort, but you will encounter a lively tapestry of local life that hasn't changed much in decades. When Guillaume Rebiere follows the path, and scent, to Yangon's bustling Hledan Market, he is mesmerized by an atmosphere that seems suspended in another era. And when Mick Shippen explores the morning market in the central Myanmar town of Pyinmana, he is intoxicated by pink-robed nuns, cheroot-smoking vendors, and townsfolk going about their business with captivating grace.

Besides large markets such as Scott's, Yangon also has many interesting specialty shops, which this chapter invites you to peruse. Along with his penchant for traditional venues, Guillaume also appreciates some of the city's upscale furniture

Woman tending her shop in Taunggyi

and handicraft boutiques, and Caroline Nixon is enchanted by the artistry of a local glass factory. As for Don Gilliland, his simple quest (or so he thinks when he starts out) to find some local music turns into a farcical afternoon of "touring" guitar and stereo shops before finally achieving his goal.

Whether you're searching for a perfect gift, as Don does in the lacquerware shops of Bagan, or a memorable painting by a local artist, which Gill Pattison guides you to in Yangon, you are sure to find a treasure or two. And while you're welcome to bargain, try to be playful about the process. Remember, vendors need to feed their families far more than you need a good deal. And you never know when a chance interaction with a shopkeeper or street hawker will turn into one of the most memorable experiences of your trip.

Yangon Division

Gill Pattison paints a picture of Yangon's art world

Stretching my neck back, I looked up to locate the ninth floor of an old Yangon building that housed a talented artist I had been looking for. It was hot, and I could feel the sweat dripping down my spine. "You don't have to come up," I told Samuel, my driver.

"You never know what we'll see up there," he laughed, climbing up the betel-nut-juice-splattered stairway.

I trailed behind, wondering—as I had more than once—why I thought that opening an art gallery in Yangon would be a good idea, and why so many artists lived on the top floors of decrepit buildings.

Tracking down Myanmar's best artists took me to corners of the city I would never have seen otherwise and offered me a glimpse into the lives of ordinary folk; the ones I visited just happened to have extraordinary creative talent. The trek was not always rewarding. Sometimes the artwork turned out to be slapdash and derivative. But this day, which began with an ascent to Zaw Zaw Aung's studio, has since stuck in my memory as the one with surprise treasures at every stop.

After passing seventeen doorways with collections of flip-flops outside, we finally reached Zaw Zaw Aung's apartment. Opening the door with a sympathetic smile, he revealed a high-ceilinged studio, packed full of paintings in various stages of completion. There was also a dusty collection of antiquities from Myanmar, his other passion.

Zaw Zaw Aung painted monks, and although all of Myanmar's artists can paint monks, these were unlike any I had seen before. For a start, he sometimes depicted the front view, a rarity in local art. Beautiful, watchful faces, with eyes that regarded you calmly, if somewhat skeptically. He placed the photorealistic religious figures in bright-yellow pointillist fields, giving the paintings an edgy, contemporary feel. I knew I wanted these wonders for my gallery, and we quickly worked out the deal. But I could not tarry. That morning I had three other artists I wanted to see.

Next stop was Kyee Myintt Saw, who lived near the Yangon River. Directions to his place had included an olfactory element: "Turn left when you smell the fish market." Soon Samuel and I were peering through wire netting windows into tiny houses adjoining the market, scanning for any evidence of a painter's craft. Outside one house, an elderly gent, as thin and wrinkled as a dried tobacco leaf, hailed us. It was Kyee Myintt Saw himself. He led us to his home and studio, where two large canvases on easels dominated the small room. One was a vibrant market scene bursting with life and color. To achieve a textured effect, he applied the finishing touches to the impasto with a hair comb.

Apart from his masterly brushwork, Kyee Myintt Saw's special talent is conveying the quality of light and shade over scenes of everyday life. He told me he was working on a series about the night market as well, and with a flourish he produced a finished work from the back room. Just as he was pulling off the protective paper, someone on the street outside passed by the house with a laden trolley, and a powerful whiff of fish filled the room. Even now, I swear that I smell fish each time I look at one of his stunning paintings.

From the fish market, we headed to the northern suburbs to find Zaw Win Pe. The roads became progressively worse until they were nothing more than rutted paths. Zaw Win Pe was waiting for us outside his house, but I hardly registered his smile and greeting. I was transfixed by the huge painting on an easel beside him, a piece that seemed to glow and shimmer in the sun. It was a semi-abstract landscape of hills and fields, painted with a broad palette of intense colors. Painting with a knife, he built up textured layers, which gave the work a startling clarity and depth. I could envision these blasts of color on the walls of the new gallery, and we quickly agreed on three paintings that I could take to start.

My final find of the day was to meet Ma Nann Nann, a female artist whose cool, elegant creations in black and gold pay homage to her deeply felt Buddhism. She lived in a small housing development a few kilometers north of the city. We got lost several times in the maze of look-alike lanes but finally located the house number. After climbing yet more stairs, we were welcomed into her flat. We contemplated the tranquil beauty of her paintings while she tended to her new baby.

Although an accomplished figurative artist, Ma Nann Nann's current work is largely abstract. With her use of gold leaf squares and a white crescent representing her meditation seat, she references the devotional aspects of Buddhism. While the inspiration for the works is very specific to Myanmar, I reckoned that the sophisticated style would strike a chord with the visitors to my gallery.

This is how I spend many days in my efforts to track down the country's best contemporary artists. Other trips take me farther afield to Mandalay and Mingun, where I have fond memories of negotiating with one artist, along with eight puppies, in the shade of the giant cracked pagoda. The journey to find the artists and learn something of their hopes and dreams has proved just as satisfying as showing the art to an appreciative audience. If you too want to see their work, you can climb up to the studios, slosh through the fish markets, and get lost behind the teashops. Or you can view the results of such adventures at the River Gallery, all under one roof.

River Gallery

The Strand Hotel Annex
92 Strand Rd.
Dagon Township
Yangon
(+95-1) 243-377/8/9, ext. 1821
www.rivergallerymyanmar.com

Caroline Nixon
shops for glass goodies in Yangon

With half a day to spare in Yangon, I decided to visit the Na Gar Glass Factory on the north side of the city. I hired a taxi, assuming the driver would know the way. He didn't. After several wrong turns, and stopping to make phone calls to get directions, we finally drew up outside the "factory"—a wooden shack hidden down a small lane in an overgrown, jungle-like garden. My fear that I had arrived in the wrong place was allayed as I walked through the gate and down a narrow path, lined with seemingly discarded heaps of multi-colored glass objects.

I was greeted by the owner, a charming, giggling man who spoke excellent English. He offered me a tour of the premises, followed by demonstrations of the glass-blowing process. Everything at Na Gar is entirely handmade by a team of skilled workers and apprentices. These artisans scoop up globules of molten glass on the ends of rods, and then blow, twist, and otherwise coax them into complex shapes. It was fascinating to watch, but the heat from the furnaces proved too much for me, and I had to step away after a few minutes.

Leaving the workshop, I was led to the showroom, a dusty area with an ancient display cabinet. After browsing for some time, I settled on a set of unusual wine glasses, charmed by their smoky burgundy color, the numerous small bubbles flecking the glass, and the slightly wonky rims.

After I made my selection, the assistants went off to find a set for me in the stockroom. In fact, this was not a room at all, but more outdoor jungle-garden space where glasses were stacked in huge piles, covered with dust, cobwebs, and leaves. Although there was apparently no order to these piles, the staff knew exactly where to find just what they were looking for. After a quick polish with a duster, the glasses were produced in pristine condition and carefully packed in a box. They also threw in a little something extra for free: a perfectly crafted clove of garlic, full of bubbles and texture, made as a practice piece by one of the apprentices.

Na Gar Glass Factory

This factory produced the glass eyes for the huge reclining Buddha at Chaukhtatgyi Pagoda in Yangon. It also supplies glass items to many restaurants in Myanmar and further afield. To get there, it's a good idea to have someone at your hotel, or your taxi driver, phone the factory for directions, as it's quite hard to find.

152 Yawgi Kyaung St. (near Insein Road)
Hlaing Township
Yangon
(+95-1) 526-053

Guillaume Rebiere peruses the handicraft shops of Yangon

Yangon doesn't have the exciting array of modern shopping centers that you'll find in Bangkok or Singapore. Instead, most shopping is confined to traditional markets such as the famous Bogyoke Market, a spot that is usually on the itinerary of every tourist who visits the city. But that's not the only place in town where you can find high-quality products and handicrafts at reasonable prices. While living here, I've discovered some delightful shops that sell fabrics, teakwood furniture, bronze carvings, and other handmade items.

Among the many places for teak furniture, Innerspace is my favorite. It stocks innovative, modern, and

YANGON & SOUTHERN MYANMAR

stylish items, as well as a variety of decorative objects. Moreover, the quality of everything it carries is outstanding. Along with the wide range of furniture, offerings are as diverse as clocks, wooden board games, mirrors, and picture frames—much easier to transport home at the end of your trip.

The shop is owned by a very nice Burmese-Swiss couple with a flair for design. They have created interiors for several local homes and businesses, and they made the striking spiral teakwood stairway in Yangon's 50th Street Bar & Grill. One day, I showed up at the shop with drafts of a china cabinet and some dinner chairs I wanted made. In less than two weeks, the customized furniture was produced, and the cost was remarkably reasonable. If your airplane baggage allowance is limited, Innerspace can arrange to have your purchases shipped overseas. I've used this service for items such as beds, cupboards, and coffee tables, and nothing has ever cracked or shown signs of damage.

Another favorite of mine, Augustine's Antiques, is a place that seems to have been untouched by the passing of time. Whenever I visit, I find myself transported back to the colonial era. The shop feels like an old bazaar. Everything is haphazardly stacked in piles, and there's not much order to the sea of merchandise. But as you explore, you might find all types of treasures, including antique clocks or furniture, traditional Karen bronze drums, brass and copperware

bowls, or carved wooden figures. It's getting more difficult to find genuine antiques here, but everything in stock is of high quality.

Violet Fashion is a small boutique that sells handmade Kachin fabrics, such as silk and cotton, by the meter. The colors and designs are some of the most beautiful I have seen in Yangon, and the quality is excellent. The bright, warm tones especially complement teak. My wife and I have had tablecloths, napkins, and curtains made here, all of which bring an exotic touch of Myanmar into our home. We have also ordered custom-tailored clothing (both Western and local designs are available) at reasonable prices.

Even if you aren't in the market for a picture frame or a new blouse, I still recommend visiting these shops, especially Augustine's Antiques for the ambience. Personally, I enjoy simply soaking up the atmosphere and seeing craftsmen working with the same tools and techniques that they have been using for centuries.

Augustine's Antiques

23A Attiyar St. (Thirimingalar Street)
Kamayut Township
Yangon
(+95-1) 705-969, 504-290, 504-409
www.augustinesouvenir.com
nbawga@myanmar.com.mm

Innerspace

The shop is located next to the Alliance Française de Rangoun (French Cultural Centre). The time it takes to complete special furniture orders depends on several factors: the kind of wood you want (it might have to be specially ordered); the design (the more complicated, the longer it takes); and time for the varnish to dry (during the rainy season it usually takes longer).

290 Pyay Rd.
Sanchaung Township
Yangon
(+95-1) 536-966

Violet Fashion

Pearl Centre is located opposite the popular Mr. Guitar Bar, at the corner of Kaba Aye Pagoda Road and Saya San Road.

Pearl Centre, First Floor
Saya San Road
Bahan Township
Yangon

Shopping advice

If you buy products such as gems, marble, or teakwood, make sure you get all the necessary receipts from the store where you made your purchase. Taking items such as these out of the country is subject to authorization and declaration at customs. All of the shops listed here can ship your purchases overseas and can help you with customs paperwork. If they don't have their own shipping departments, they will use a local shipping company with whom they have a contract.

Don Gilliland searches for local music in Yangon

I was walking down Bogyoke Aung San Road late one morning when I found myself shadowed by a small boy selling postcards. After listening to his eloquent spiel, I had to break the news to him that I wasn't interested in purchasing any of his fine products. But, like most salesmen the world over, he was persistent and quickly resumed his pitch. Though I was amused by his effort, I felt the need to stop him before he got his hopes up. I turned to face the youngster, smiled, and repeated that I really and truly did not want to buy any postcards. Have a nice day ... see ya!

The boy shrugged off my rejection good naturedly, a big grin never leaving his face. But instead of retreating into the shadows or rushing off to look for other potential customers, he kept following me as I took my long strides down the street. I wasn't particularly annoyed, but puzzled why he was still tailing me. Did I look like an easy mark?

While I was waiting to cross a busy intersection, the boy, still hot on my heels, introduced himself as Win Ko Ko, blurting out the words as if he was extremely proud of the name. I told him my name and asked how old he was. "One three," he replied.

It took me a moment to understand what that meant. He was thirteen.

We attempted more conversation, but his limited English skills weren't up to the task of understanding much of anything I was asking, so our chat soon fizzled out. But he was such a pleasant kid, tagging along behind me, that I started to feel sorry for him. Looking at his skinny frame, I figured he could use a good meal—or three—and I asked him if he wanted to grab a bite to eat at a nearby Shan noodle shop I had visited the day before. He nixed that idea, suggesting instead a street-side curry place only a block away.

After our lunch, where we both devoured very tasty dishes of chicken curry and Star Cola, I asked Win Ko Ko if he could help me find some music CDs. I'm a big music junkie, and whenever I visit a foreign country, I like to buy a few discs of the local tunes. I explained that I wanted some acoustic guitar music, preferably akin to folk or country, but with a local twist. Even something Shan would do.

Win Ko Ko looked absolutely bewildered by my request. As my Burmese language skills were almost nonexistent, I mimed playing a guitar to illustrate what I wanted. He nodded and led me down a few streets until we came to a guitar shop. Close, I told him, but not quite what I had in mind.

I said "CD" again and this time mimed listening to music. Win Ko Ko nodded again. The next shop we visited sold Discman players and other stereo equipment. Well, we're getting warmer, I thought, trying to remain optimistic. I patiently explained my request again, trying to make him understand that I wanted to buy a CD, but not a VCD or DVD. No pretty videos or karaoke melodrama. Just the tunes, please.

Finally, at the fourth place we visited, a shop called Pearl, I found a good selection of music for sale. The next obstacle was choosing something remotely interesting to buy. The clerk recommended a few titles: a concert recording from a band called Iron Cross and a CD by an eyeglasses-wearing guitar player named Sai Hti Saing. I took her advice and bought them both.

While not the folk style I was looking for, the Iron Cross album, *Acoustics,* celebrating the band's fifteenth anniversary, turned out to be pretty darn good. The band may be called Iron Cross, but there is nothing remotely "metal" about their sound. These talented musicians stick to a melodic pop-rock groove, with vocals handled by several of the band members. Along with what I assume are some original compositions, the group performs covers in Burmese of Dan Fogelberg's "Leader of the Band" and "One" by the Bee Gees. The more I listen to it, the more I like it. Some of the songs really stick in your head. Iron Cross is perhaps Myanmar's most popular band, and it's highly likely you will hear one of their CDs, or see one of their DVDs, as you are traveling around the country. These guys rule!

As for the Sai Hti Saing disc (I can't tell you the name of the specific album, but he has released several), it is also quite good. The music gets a bit too saccharine in spots for my tastes, but I like his voice a lot.

Outside, purchases in hand, I bid goodbye to Win Ko Ko, handing him a wad of kyat notes for his time and efforts. He seemed pleased with the remuneration and thanked me. I watched him shuffle down the street, postcards in hand, a big grin on his face. I'm sure that the next time crazy tourists ask where to buy CDs, he'll know where to take them straightaway—too bad, since they'll miss the entertaining shopping tour in the process.

Pearl VCD Production and Distribution

151 Anawrahta Rd.
(35/Mahabandoola)
Kyauktada Township
Yangon
(+95-1) 249-362

Man Thiri Music Production

This is another good shop for local music CDs, cassettes, and VCDs. It also has a large selection of titles, and the staff is very helpful. This company also has a well-stocked branch in Mandalay on 26th Street between 82nd and 83rd Streets.

72 Anawrahta Rd. (40/Bo Aung Kyaw)
Kyauktada Township
Yangon
(+95-1) 252-903, 241-700, 705-458

Bogyoke Aung San Market

Located in the far west wing of the market, CD II shop has an excellent choice of CDs, VCDs, and cassettes. As in most shops in Myanmar, you can listen before you buy.

Online shopping

CDs by musicians from Myanmar can be found through various Internet sites, including:

http://shwemyanmar.net/catalog

Shanachie Entertainment

This label in the US has released several interesting traditional music albums as part of their "Burma Music" series. Check with online dealers or retail music shops for availability.

www.shanachie.com

Ma Thanegi sneaks upstairs at Yangon's Bogyoke Market

When I was a child, I often went to Bogyoke Aung San Market with my mother, tagging along when she shopped for silks, clutching at her *longyi* and bored out of my mind. As I grew older, the market was where my friends and I would sneak away from Methodist English High School, which is now called Dagon State High School No. 1. The school was only a block away, and when the teachers had meetings, they left us in the care of student monitors who could not stop us from crawling through a hole in the fence and skipping away to the market, where all we could actually afford to buy were jelly-lemonade drinks. Later, when I was in university, I would meet my boyfriend under the market's big clock. We ate noodles in the large canteen before going to the cinema across the street.

Built by the colonial British, this huge market has been a fixture in Yangon since 1928. It was named Scott's Market after Sir James George Scott, a famous administrator during the late 1800s. After the country became independent in 1948, the name was changed to honor General Aung San (*bogyoke* means "general"). The sprawling ground floor offers products such as silks, crafts, velvet slippers, imported fabrics, hand-woven cottons, and silk-and-cotton mixes in shimmering colors. There are also tailoring shops where you can have clothing sewn to order in a day or two, though tailors don't make Western-style suits like in Bangkok.

Despite my familiarity with the market, it was not until recently, many decades after my first visit, that I ever thought to wander upstairs. In fact, I had no idea there were any shops on the upper floor. But while I was shopping with a friend one day, she took me to see her tailor. Upon venturing up the stairs in the front of the market, I was surprised to see an entire

corridor lined with curtain material by the bolt and several tailor shops. While my friend looked through pattern books and got measured, I explored the rest of the floor.

The first shop I discovered was Yoyamay, which means "traditional maiden." Its small showroom is filled with old and new textiles, jewelry, and folk art from the many ethnic groups of Myanmar. Among its treasures are accessories and beads from the Naga tribes, intricately hand-woven textiles from the Chin Hills, pretty Kachin fabrics, and Akha costumes embellished with beads, Job's Tears, and silver coins. I really wanted to buy a necklace of woven orchid fibers, which held a monkey skull pendant. I thought what fun it would be to make my friends recoil in horror when I turned up wearing it. But knowing they would probably never speak to me again if I did so, I reluctantly put it down.

Located next to Yoyamay was what looked like, to me, a small museum. Heritage Gallery has superb old lacquerware, exquisite *objets d'art*, and coins from the ancient Pyu civilization. The owner has written a book about his personal collection of rare coins, but unfortunately he keeps his treasures locked away in a safe at home and refuses to sell any of them.

Now, as an adult of mature years, I am more interested in antiques than finding the right lipstick color. Still, whenever I stroll in this sprawling Oriental bazaar, I catch glimpses of a sulky little child tugging at her mother's *longyi*, a bunch of giggling schoolgirls counting their meager coins, and a shy young woman holding hands with a tall young man.

Bogyoke Aung San Market

Bogyoke Aung San Road (Shwedagon Pagoda/Sule Paya)
Pabedan Township
Yangon
Tuesday through Sunday (closed Mondays and public and Buddhist holidays)

Within Bogyoke Aung San Market

Heritage Gallery

Use the stairs built into the walls on either side of the clock tower at the front of the market. The shop lies around the corner at the end of the open corridor to the left of the clock.

#21, Upper Floor
thantunmimi@mptmail.net.mm

Yoyamay

#20, Upper Floor
yoyamay@mail4U.com.mm

Guillaume Rebiere floats through a tourist-free Yangon market

Locals in Yangon have told me that Hledan Market is one of the busiest markets in town, and it sure feels that way as I walk toward the entrance, carried inside by the buzzing crowd. It is only six in the morning, but it already looks like rush hour at a subway station in New York.

This is a part of town where few foreigners venture. Unlike at the tourist-friendly Bogyoke Market, I don't see any souvenirs for sale here, and nobody comes up to me and asks, "Hello, change money?" No, this is not the sort of place I expect to find big buses spewing out loads of camera-toting tourists. Hledan Market is where the locals go to buy food and other items they use in their everyday lives.

Near the entrance, on the left, rows of flower and fruit vendors are lined up like a colorful invitation to come inside. But this initial refreshment does not last, as I reach the section that is dedicated to fish and meat. The aroma here is not so genial. It certainly is authentic though.

Amongst swarms of flies buzzing in the dim light, I step over streams of bile and blood to get a closer glimpse of the butchers. They sit behind piles of ribs and internal organs, busily chopping and cutting. In another aisle, one offering in particular catches my olfactory attention: the famous local specialty known as ngapi. A paste made with fermented fish or shrimp, ngapi is used as a condiment with many local dishes such as curries. I would buy some if I were more adventurous and not afraid of carrying the odor around with me the rest of the day.

After a few minutes of wandering, I feel an overwhelming need for fresh air and step outside for a quick stroll. Then I go back in and take the stairs to the upper floor to look around at the silk, cotton, satin, and handmade fabrics. Local women buy these materials to make dresses and *longyi*. This is a joyful and colorful part of the market, a good place to experience the cool rhythm of a Yangon day. The wide, un-cluttered aisles and tranquil calm provide a striking contrast to the frenzied activity I have just seen downstairs.

Outside, in an alley behind this main building, I find a cluttered area that looks more like a traditional vil-lage market: no roof, no stands, and no order or organization of any kind. This is where people from the coun-tryside come to sell their products. Most of this merchandise is sold from baskets or on blankets thrown down on the dusty ground, which turns to mud when it rains. Piles of mangoes, papayas, guavas, and jackfruit are displayed on mats, their skins glisten-ing with honey-colored juices under the morning sun. Merchants call out to passing shoppers, shouting out the prices of their goods. I ask one vendor for a discount on some okra, and we playfully bargain until agree-ing on a price.

As I wander, I find myself floating along with the flow of people moving up and down the narrow alley. Colors, fragrances, and sounds are all sewn together into a patchwork. The street is framed by some of the city's last traditional wooden houses. Old men rest on rails of elegantly carved

balconies, smoking cheroots in the shadow of their teakwood decks. Time seems to have been suspended in this neighborhood, as if nothing had changed much since Orwell and Kipling visited Burma so many decades ago.

Hledan Market

The market is located near the intersection of Insein Road and University Road. Make sure to arrive early so you don't miss all the activity of Yangon residents starting their day.

Hledan Road
Kamayut Township
Yangon

Julie Faulk prays to the souvenir gods in Yangon

"No madam, it 'tis not possible," the man softly murmured in a British-Burmese accent.

Oh dear Souvenir God in heaven, did he just say it is not possible? After traversing the world and buying every gaudy, kitschy souvenir imaginable—from tin Eiffel Tower earrings to a Pope soap-on-a-rope—I was com-mitted to never spending another dime on cheap, mass-produced souvenirs that would eventually be added to yet another landfill.

This time I was in search of the most superb of souvenirs. The souvenir that surely would maintain its uniqueness throughout my lifetime. The one souvenir that I was sure would most likely not eventually be on sale at the local Pier 1 store. A trishaw.

Trishaws are common forms of transportation throughout Myanmar. The trishaw driver pedals an ordinary bicycle that is attached, via a sturdy, iron frame, to a wooden seat in which the passenger rides. The whole contraption somewhat resembles a motorcycle with sidecar.

Riding in a trishaw may have been an everyday activity, but what was not possible, according to my hotel concierge, was the purchasing and exporting of one—even though his assumption of impossibility was based only on the fact that he had never heard of it being done before. That was precisely why I wanted one. As I stood in front of Mr. Not Possible, a higher sense of commitment to obtaining this "souvenir" grew in me, and I had a visceral response that I can only equate to a natural high.

"Of course it is possible!" I exclaimed.

"No," he repeated even more gently than before. "It 'tis not possible."

Flippantly, I said, "Let's just ask one of the trishaw drivers how much he will sell his trishaw for."

Turns out this inquiry was tantamount to asking a driver to sell a member of his own family. My offer was flatly rejected. This left me with the option of having to buy one "off the rack," so to speak.

After big smiles and gentle encouragement on my part, the concierge finally agreed to make a few phone calls and see if any master welders had any trishaws in stock. We paid a visit to one workshop where we discovered that a ready-made trishaw was not available. If I really wanted one, I was firmly told, I would need to have it made to order. The problem was that I was scheduled to leave in about forty-eight hours, and it would take a minimum of five or six days to have a master welder bang one out.

"As you can see madam, it 'tis not possible," the concierge told me once again. With that declaration he walked outside and plunked himself into a trishaw, leaving me sitting in the dark interior of the tiny, cramped workshop, where the smell of iron and oil permeated the air.

Over the course of the next twenty minutes, the concierge would periodically get out of the trishaw, walk into the workshop, and beckon me, trying in vain to get me to leave. I would give him a big toothy smile, and just wave and wave, not saying a word.

Eventually he returned to the shop and spoke at length to the master welder, as I sat there hoping that my gentle reluctance to accept "It 'tis not possible" would prevail. Finally, he sighed, turned to me, and said, "The master welder will work for the next twenty-four hours straight to make you a trishaw. But you must understand that it will cost you ..." He paused for gravity. "Seventy US dollars!"

The master welder did indeed work through the night and produced for me a beautiful, sturdy, and unique souvenir. Upon arrival at the workshop to pick it up, I asked if I could take a picture of the weary master welder. "Wait," his wife said as she whipped a comb out of her pocket. She licked it, ran it through her husband's hair, and clucked at him to stand up straight. As he posed for the picture he wearily murmured, "Congratulations, congratulations."

Purchasing a trishaw

If you decide to buy a trishaw frame, know that it takes a huge commitment with much suffering to get it home. It is made of thick iron and weighs more than thirty-six kilograms (eighty pounds). The seat weighs about half that and has to be purchased separately at a furniture store. While the master welder did his best to wrap the frame in a large rice sack, it was still difficult to carry through the various airports that I passed through. To give you an idea of the size, someone asked me if it was a bear trap, and another person asked if it was a plow. Because DHL quoted me $900 to ship the trishaw from Myanmar, I chose to hand carry it. I bought my trishaw frame a few years back. Post-9/11 regulations may restrict such an item as a carry-on or checked luggage, so check with your airline beforehand.

Meeting a master welder

My trishaw was made by Win Myint Baytway.

90 Myaungyi St.
Pazundaung Township
Yangon

Mother Land Inn 2

This is the hotel where my "trishaw broker" worked; it's a popular place, and someone here will surely be able to help you if you decide to purchase a trishaw.

433 Lower Pazundaung Rd.
Pazundaung Township
Yangon
(+95-1) 291-343
www.myanmarmotherlandinn.com

MANDALAY DIVISION

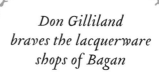

Don Gilliland braves the lacquerware shops of Bagan

"Would you like to see my auntie's lacquerware shop?" the boy asked me. He was one of several kids following me down New Bagan's main street, a dusty thoroughfare interspersed with small teashops, guesthouses, restaurants, and the occasional horse cart parked in the shade of a tall tree.

In the Bagan area, in towns like Myinkaba, Nyaung U, and New Bagan, you'll find places selling beautifully crafted lacquerware items on almost every inhabited block. It seemed as if all the postcard-peddling kids that I met also doubled as sales agents for an "auntie" who owned one of these shops. Not surprisingly, the kids were all eager to show me around, practically salivating at the prospect of getting a commission. But as someone who hates to buy souvenirs (I think my last such purchase was a pair of Elvis nail clippers that I bought across the street from Graceland in 1991), I couldn't muster up the enthusiasm for a tour of lacquerware boutiques.

I felt like telling these kids that I had no desire whatsoever to visit any shops, that in fact I'd rather suffer through the ordeal of listening to a George W. Bush speech, but wanting to be polite and agreeable in this foreign town, I refrained from making any such snide remarks, and just nodded my head and said, "Sure, lead the way."

Other than trying to get their sales commissions, the kids were not pests whatsoever. In fact, they proved to be delightful and helpful companions, genuinely trying to make certain that my stay in town was as comfortable and *pyaw dey* (happy) as possible. I had to keep from laughing when they introduced themselves. Everyone had a nickname that sounded as if the parents had been stuttering: Maung Maung, Tun Tun, Nine Nine, Min Min, Zin Zin, Kyaw Kyaw. Nine Nine had the best English skills of the bunch. He told me that he preferred being called Ninety-Nine "because it's easy for foreigners to remember, and my grandfather said it would bring me good luck."

I was hoping that Ninety-Nine's presence would bring *me* good luck, because I actually did have a shopping need: finding a gift for my parents. Their fiftieth wedding anniversary was coming up in a few months, and I wanted to get them a nice present from Myanmar.

Ninety-Nine and his buddies led me down the town's narrow side streets to a couple of lacquerware shops. I poked around inside each place, admiring coaster sets, bowls, and platters. It all looked lovely, and none of it was expensive, but I wasn't moved to buy anything.

Farther up the road, Ninety-Nine pointed out another auntie-owned shop, a place called Royal Myanmar Handicrafts.

"Is this one good?" I asked.

"Yes, very good," was his predictable answer.

I entered somewhat reluctantly, but was immediately impressed by what I saw. The small shop was attractively decorated and the merchandise displayed in a well-organized and easy to browse manner. Along with a variety of necklaces and bracelets made of jade, stone, and crystal, there were some cute stone and jade animals, such as turtles, fish, and ducks. In addition to that lot were framed embossed pictures (gold, silver, or bronze) of Burmese dancers and scenes of village life.

Khin Hnynn Aye, the personable woman who managed the shop, spoke excellent English and politely answered my questions about the merchandise. She never once tried any hard-sell tactics or pressured me to buy anything. For tourists in a foreign country like Myanmar, that's a restraint you learn to appreciate.

I scanned the shelves, hoping something would jump out at me and scream, "This is it, buy me!" Amazingly, that's about what happened. As I browsed, my eye kept wandering back to one of the embossed pictures on the shelf. It depicted a couple riding a bullock cart past a pagoda, the woman holding a large umbrella to shade her from the sun. On the back was a notation: "He and she join hands in hands, riding a fine cart to let all relations view that they are ever together."

"Please wrap it up," I asked Khin Hnynn Aye. "This will make a perfect anniversary gift."

Royal Myanmar Handicrafts

This shop is located near the corner of 5th Street directly opposite the dirt road that leads to the Thazin Garden Hotel.

Main Road
New Bagan
(+95-9) 200-2762

Guided tours

Young Mr. Ninety-Nine should not be too hard to find in New Bagan. Everyone in town seems to know him. Just ask around for "Ninety-Nine," and he will soon appear. He is usually hanging out in front of the NK Betelnut Hotel on the Main Road selling postcards and other souvenirs. If you are looking for a cheerful young guide during your horse cart tour of local pagodas, take him, or one of his friends, along for the ride.

*Mick Shippen
savors Pyinmana's
poetry in motion*

With self-importance, imbued by wordsmiths past, the road to Mandalay elbows its way north toward parched environs. Pyinmana marks the halfway point of the journey from Yangon, a cursory left-hand turnoff serving as an inadequate acknowledgment to its existence. The town's terse response is revealed in translation: *Py-in-ma-na* means "do not take rest here." To heed such words, however, would be a mistake.

Walking down the broad streets of this central Myanmar backwater, I was unsure if I was witness to decay or rejuvenation. Islands of creased and crumbling asphalt pushed their way up through the tender, salmon-pink earth, as if the healing of a wound had begun. Old teakwood shophouses leaned against their concrete counterparts, seemingly propping up the featureless modern creations. Languid avenues stretched forward as horse-drawn carts rolled over them, the sound of gently falling hooves keeping the beat of a different era, occasionally obscured by the wasp-like drone of a passing motorcycle.

Stepping onto the home turf of trishaw drivers, I deflected their relentless calls with a nod, a smile, and a backhand wave. Leaving them with no opportunity to respond, I slipped down a darkened alleyway and out of earshot. As I emerged on the edge of the morning market, the contrast in atmosphere was immediate.

Since daybreak the area had become a canvas stretched across narrow dirt roads, brushed with strokes of violent color reminiscent of Gauguin's palette. Squatting among nests of verdant produce, traders drew crowds as eager for gossip as they were for a good deal. Down one street, shallow bamboo baskets lay stippled with red and orange tomatoes, each one calling out for attention. Down the next, a miniature landscape of rice mountains brought to mind images of cooler climes, while the pure white lilies placed at their summit expressed exquisite attention to detail.

With every glance or tentative inquiry, I was greeted with a generous smile and a handful of playful words. Each woman's face, cheeks washed with pale yellow *thanaka* paste, radiated a mesmerizing glow—circles of pure light illuminating sun-blessed skin. Fresh flowers tucked into coils of woven hair recalled yet more sketches of Gauguin. Tripods of bamboo, from which hung the traders' scales, cleanly dissected space.

On a daily basis, the inhabitants of outlying villages sit in the market and dole out some sales patter, weigh up the competition, and throw in a little something extra for good measure. Stopped in my tracks by a powerful aroma, I stood and watched as one of these street vendors went through the ritual process of choosing a durian for a customer. Selecting a piece of fruit, his fingertips defying the armored exterior, he pulled it suffocatingly close to his face. Eyes closed and inhaling deeply, he responded to its pungency with a knowing smile, found the weak spot, carefully inserted a slender blade, and broke the seal. With its defenses breached, the durian yielded to further pressure, eventually cracking to reveal its treasure—two golden pillows of succulent flesh.

The atmosphere of the market was intoxicating. While holding slender green cheroots, the lips of young women offered thick, smoky smiles, and old ladies dispensed "cure-all" herbal remedies. A raucous laugh revealed a flash of silver teeth, proving that in Pyinmana it really does pay to put your money where your mouth is. As barrow boys raised a sweat wheeling around wooden barrels of cool drinking water, others sought the welcome shade cast by groves of oversized umbrellas. The townsfolk went about their business in the market with a captivating grace and an intriguing economy of movement.

Away from the market lines, Buddhist nuns exchanged blessings for a few grains of dry rice. Wrapped in pale pink robes, the shaven-headed girls walked in single file collecting daily contributions from the faithful.

MANDALAY & CENTRAL MYANMAR

Pausing for a moment to watch, I was greeted with a sweet rhythmic roll of words, barely above a whisper: "Please give a donation to the Lord Buddha." Obliging, I was rewarded with a heavenly smile.

The whole of Pyinmana seems to move with that same sweet, rhythmic roll. Here, a stone's throw from the road to Mandalay, among the pockets of color and calm, a small market town is poetry in motion.

Aureum Palace Hotel & Resort

At the time of publication, the only hotel in Pyinmana that we are aware of that is authorized to take foreign tourists is the Aureum. Prices for deluxe rooms are $65.

Inquiries and reservations should be made through the Yangon head office so guests can be met at the airport or railway station. One other possibility mentioned by travel agents is the Royal Kumudra Hotel, but this could not be confirmed. Another hotel that previously did accept foreigners, but now does not, (though it may again, who knows?) is the Phoenix Hotel. The Aureum Palace head office is located in Yangon.

41 Shwe Taung Gyar Rd.
Ground Floor
Bahan Township
Yangon
(+95-1) 513-300, 502-649
(+95-67) 414-108 (in Pyinmana)
sales-aureum@myanmar.com.mm

Traditional marionette in Bago

SECRET GARDENS

Where to hide away from the touring masses

Although it is one of the least touristed countries in Asia, Myanmar still has its crowds, especially in the big cities. Fortunately, you don't have to step too far off the beaten tourist path to find a little peace and quiet. It could be a secluded beach, quiet forest stream, or rural path that skirts a radiantly green rice field. Even in the major cities like Yangon and Mandalay, if you venture a few short blocks off the main roads you will find yourself immersed in an entirely different world. Finding your own secret garden is as easy as following your instincts—or a group of village children.

One of my favorite refuges in Yangon is Happy World, an amusement park with swimming pools. Proof that you can get away from it all even amidst crowds, it's a great place to mingle with locals and cool off from the intense heat. For a calmer experience, Linda Hall hides away at the Savoy Hotel's happy hour, where she treats herself to complimentary snacks and the elegant colonial atmosphere. Equal parts Happy World-refreshing and Savoy Hotel-relaxing is Marydee Nyquist's favorite escape: Fancy House Beauty Salon, where she basks in beauty treatments, massages, and the warmth of the staff.

Those who travel to Mandalay should visit the three nearby ancient cities: Amarapura, Sagaing, and Inwa. But for a real treat, slip away to Paleik. Hit the Snake Temple, where locals flock to see the daily feeding of three Burmese pythons, then take a short walk to one of Sandra Gerrits' favorite places in Myanmar, a tranquil park of ancient *stupas*. Like many of the destinations in this chapter, this refuge rarely sees tourists.

There is no more classic getaway than a beach, and Myanmar has some excellent ones. By comparing Chaungtha and Ngwe Saung, a pair of laid-back and upscale beach towns, respectively, James Spencer reveals that sometimes peace is found in a happy medium—in this case the motorcycle ride between the two. Farther up the coast Laurie Weed visits Ngapali Beach, where

Woman selling fresh flowers in Yangon

winding down includes turning cartwheels on the shoreline and playing sand tag with the vendors.

Myanmar also has no end of wilderness areas, and though you are liable to encounter plenty of tourists in and around Inle Lake, you can avoid the crowds by heading for the south end and the enchanting village of Sagar. Framed by a range of forested mountains, it is home to an atmospheric complex of old pagodas and *stupas*. Not many travelers venture beyond the suggestions in their guidebooks, but Caroline Nixon finds the effort worthwhile, both here and at remote Indawgyi Lake, where she tours pagoda ruins, visits with monks, and happens upon a group of "working" elephants.

Little known to the outside world is Myanmar's diversity. This is something you will quickly realize in your search for secret gardens. Whether you join Sandra Gerrits at a Vipassana meditation retreat in Mandalay or follow Roger Lee Huang to a "traditional house" in Pindaya, hideaways both classic and eccentric await your discovery.

YANGON DIVISION

Marydee Nyquist gets fancy at a Yangon salon

During the eleven years that I lived in Yangon, Fancy House became very much a part of my life. It is different from other local hair salons I visited. Not only is it a genuinely welcoming place, but it is spotlessly clean and unpretentious, and most importantly, it has twenty-four hour electricity—a rarity in Yangon.

Agnes Lim, the owner, is a haircutter extraordinaire. I met her several years ago through mutual Hong Kong friends, and after my first haircut from her, I felt as if I had received manna from above. Agnes is one of a handful of Asian stylists who truly know how to work with Western hair, especially the extra fine kind that I have. When traveling in the US, I am constantly asked who cuts my hair. Stylists often run their fingers through it to determine how the unique style that Agnes gave me was achieved.

Agnes is originally from Hong Kong, where she was well known for her two salons and the award-winning hairstyle shows she produced. Then she and her husband relocated to Yangon and became involved in garment manufacturing. However, she never lost her love for hair styling and continued to practice by inviting friends to her home salon. When trade embargoes were placed on products from Myanmar in the 1990s, garment production essentially moved to neighboring countries. But when one door closes, another opens. Agnes and Frank decided to open Fancy House so that she could return to her first love. After just six months in business, it was one of the most popular salons in Yangon.

Fancy House occupies a large, two-story house, situated behind a gated wall on one of Yangon's broad, tree-lined avenues. Upon entering, you are greeted by smiling young women. The entire staff makes me feel as though I am an honored guest, or a family member returning home for tea and a chat. The styling rooms are well lit, colorful, and offer comfortable seating at each station. The manicure/pedicure/foot massage rooms (all with adjoining bathrooms) are furnished with large, deep couches and ottomans. If you wish, lights will be dimmed and soothing music played.

One of the best-kept secrets in the city is the fantastic shampoo experience that Fancy House offers. After I am served fragrant Chinese tea, the shampoo girl escorts me to a comfy chair. While I recline, she gently massages my scalp. Then the shampoo starts. As she scrubs, I slip deeper into a relaxed, blissful state. After rinsing and then a repeat of the process, conditioner is applied and the real scalp and neck massage begins. The process can take from fifteen to thirty minutes. If you doze off, as I often do, you are likely to enjoy a longer experience, since the shampooer does not want to abruptly interrupt your altered state. Shampoo is followed by the service of your choice: haircut, blow dry, perm, or coloring.

To continue the relaxation and rejuvenation, I usually add a foot massage when I visit. One blissful hour (which also includes head, neck, and shoulders) costs less than $3. For maximum relaxation, have the foot massage done first, and then the shampoo. Though if time does not permit, you can have both services simultaneously. Manicures and pedicures are two more of my Fancy House indulgences. In addition, body massage and treatments for women only are available on the second floor.

When I lived in Yangon, I frequented Fancy House two to three times a week. It wasn't only for the excellent services, but because it offered a respite from the daily stress of city living. It was my place to chill out and totally relax, as well as be pampered in a warm, welcoming environment. After a hard day of work—or at the very least, some strenuous shopping or sightseeing—a rejuvenating shampoo or foot massage is always in order.

Fancy House

A haircut by Agnes costs about $12. The price is much less if the cut is by one of her staff, all of whom have been trained by Agnes. She is also a specialist in color and continues to perfect her expertise by attending color and stylist workshops worldwide. The salon is located within walking distance of the Sedona Hotel. It is closed on Mondays.

3C Thitsar St.
Yankin Township
Yangon
(+95-1) 578-931, 704-533, 662-636

Linda Hall spends a happy hour at Yangon's Savoy Hotel

When I first moved to Yangon, I lived at the Winner Inn, just down the street from the Savoy Hotel. A staff member there told me about the Savoy's happy hour specials. From six until eight each evening, drinks are half price and free appetizers are served in the Captain's Bar. The moment I walked through the door, I felt as if I had been transported back to the British colonial era of old Burma, surrounded by an air of elegance, opulence, and serenity.

With room rates of more than $100 per night, the Savoy is one of Yangon's more upscale hotels, so you might assume that drinks in the bar will also come at a high price. As I was pleased to find out, that wasn't the case. During my stay in

Yangon, I usually frequented happy hour twice a week. I enjoyed sitting by the window where I had prime views of colorful street life passing by: barefoot children in hot pursuit of foreigners leaving the hotel, hoping to receive some "money present"; pedestrians clad in *longyi*; skinny men pedaling trishaws; and wealthy locals driving luxury automobiles with tinted windows.

The cozy bar is tastefully furnished with teakwood floors, huge wicker chairs complete with comfy cushions, and pictures of old Rangoon street scenes. In one corner sits a grand piano, though more for decoration than entertainment. I've only seen a couple customers daringly tickle the ivories. Although richly decorated, the room avoids being formal or snobby. I liked to take my shoes off and relax with a book and a drink. The servers, dressed in beautiful silk *longyi* of deep green, dark blue, or rich brown, were always friendly and attentive.

There is an extensive selection of CDs that customers are welcome to look through for making requests, but no matter what kind of music played—rock, R&B, or jazz—it never got so loud that conversation was difficult. The low decibel levels also came in handy, as sometimes I found myself eavesdropping on conversations at adjacent tables.

Many of the regulars at the Savoy's happy hour are long-time residents of Yangon who own their own companies or are employed by large corporations. I occasionally overheard tales involving large sums of money,

or griping about the "extra expenses" of doing business in Myanmar. I learned a lot about the country by listening to these conversations, and sometimes I took a break from my reading and joined them.

Besides the atmosphere, one of my favorite things about this happy hour are the free appetizers. The selection varies but usually includes small slices of homemade pizza, hard boiled eggs, ham, cheese on toast, and other delicate nibbles.

If you're staying at the Savoy, or find yourself in the northern part of town, check out the happy hour one night. Order your half-priced drink, sample a crab puff, sit back, relax, and spend some time soaking up Yangon life, past and present.

Savoy Hotel

When I first started going to the Savoy's happy hour, the price of a drink also allowed you to use the pool. However, after a change of management, non-guests now have to spend $6 in food or beverage in order to swim in the pool. (For more on where to swim in Yangon, continue on to the next essay.) If you just want to sit by the poolside, which is illuminated by hundreds of votive candles at night, and enjoy your food and drinks without swimming, you do not need to pay the pool fee. Happy hour in the Captain's Bar is from 6 to 8 p.m. After happy hour every Wednesday there is live music from eight until midnight.

129 Dhammazedi Rd.
Bahan Township
Yangon
(+95-1) 526-289/298/305
www.savoy-myanmar.com

Winner Inn

This is an inexpensive alternative ($15 to $20) to the Savoy Hotel. I particularly like its location. It is not downtown, and by just walking off the main street, I felt as if I were in a village. The hotel has a small garden which is nice for relaxing in the early evening. Some nights I would have my dinner there.

42 Thanlwin Rd.
Bahan Township
Yangon
(+95-1) 535-205, 524-387, 503-734, 525-931
www.winnerinnmyanmar.com

Morgan Edwardson beats the heat in Yangon

Where do you go in Yangon when you are exhausted from visiting pagodas and dripping with sweat from the oppressive heat? My usual solution is to visit a local amusement park called Happy World and relax in one of the swimming pools.

Happy World offers the usual battery of thrills, including a haunted house, bumper car rides, merry-go-rounds, roller coaster (don't get your hopes up, it's tiny), and lots of kiosks selling snacks and soft drinks. But the main draw for me is the two large swimming pools. In the pool farthest from the slides, there is more than enough room, and usually enough water, to swim a few laps and float around without bumping into hordes of other swimmers. It's the daredevil dudes who use the big slide in the other pool that you have to watch out for. Some of them run down the slide and take flying head-first leaps, skidding to a stop perilously close to the concrete edge. I wouldn't be surprised if there are a few missing teeth decorating the bottom of that pool.

Another compelling reason to go to Happy World is simply to people watch. You can call me a voyeur, but I love observing the locals cutting loose and having a good time with their friends and families. If nothing else, visiting the park offers me a different perspective of life in Yangon, something I wouldn't see while confined to a tour bus or taking pagoda junkets amongst a stew of other foreign tourists.

On one of my Happy World outings, a friend who was visiting from overseas accompanied me. Being the only foreigners at the park that day, we garnered our fair share of attention. Wall to wall smiles, a few giggles, and lots greetings along the lines of "Hello!" and "What's your name?" followed us wherever we walked, or swam.

Near one of the large pools was a group of about twenty young men celebrating. What they were celebrating wasn't clear to me, but they were definitely having a grand time, hooting and hollering and jumping around as if they had just won the World Cup. Meanwhile, the elderly park photographer was patiently attempting to get this rowdy bunch to sit still long enough to take a few photos. After a couple of minutes of stops and starts, he somehow got them all into a manageable formation and snapped away.

Later, the photographer wandered over to chat with us. Like many people I met in Myanmar, he was polite and inquisitive, and had teeth stained red from chewing betel nut. My friend and I decided to throw some extra business his way and had him take a couple photos of us. That went well enough, but it started a chain reaction of curious kids who all wanted their photo taken with us too.

Step right up and pose with the freaky foreigners!

So, this is what fame is like, huh? We humored a few of the little munchkins before announcing that we had to break things up and return to our hotel. Otherwise, I think we would have remained at Happy World posing until well past sundown.

Happy World

Tell the taxi driver that you are going to the Happy World at "Pyi Thu Yin Pyin." Otherwise, you could be taken to one of the other two Happy Worlds, neither of which has swimming pools. And once at the park, be prepared for

lots of people wanting to talk to you. I've been there four times and have yet to see another foreigner. You *will* be the center of attention.

People's Park
Dhammazedi Road (near U Wizara Road)
Dagon Township
Yangon

People's Park

The entrance fee to the park is $1 for foreigners. However, if you use the Dhammazedi Road entrance, you will not have to pay. There is an additional charge for foreigners to use the swimming pool. One time I was asked to pay $3 and another time I only had to pay 1,000 kyat. Maybe it was because I spoke Burmese to the ticket taker that second time! If you don't have dollars on you, they will accept the equivalent in kyat.

Yangon Swimming Club

Another swimming option is the very nice Olympic-sized pool at the Yangon Swimming Club (also called the National Swimming Pool). It costs $3 for a foreigner to use the pool. Some days you have to share it with local swim teams, but the pool is so huge, there is room enough for everyone.

U Wizara Road (next to the Olympic Hotel)
Dagon Township
Yangon

AYEYARWADY DIVISION

James Spencer blazes trails between Chaungtha and Ngwe Saung

My two favorite beach getaways in Myanmar are Chaungtha and Ngwe Saung, although apart from both possessing wide stretches of sand, they have nothing in common. At the unashamedly upmarket Ngwe Saung, there is a beautiful white shoreline, and the swimming is excellent. Chaungtha, by contrast, is a blue-collar beach where the Myanmar middle classes go on long weekends. Little kids sell fried fish and prawns on sticks, giggling teenagers play unorganized sports, and at night there are bonfires and parties on the sand.

Although these two destinations lie only a few kilometers apart, there is no road directly connecting them, thus keeping them relatively isolated from one another. But I found a way to combine these very different experiences into one weekend break from Yangon. The solution is what I like to call the "Beach Motorbike Express."

From Chaungtha, I made arrangements with Nyan, a room attendant at the Shwe Hin Tha Hotel who doubles as a motorbike taxi driver, to take me to Ngwe Saung. He was ready at six in the morning, as we needed an early start. Two hours and three rivers lie between the two beaches. The first river is on the edge of Chaungtha village. When we arrived at the ferry—a canoe with an outboard motor—it was full to the gunwales with ladies on their way to market, but there was a plank amidships, and Nyan and the ferryman manhandled the motorbike aboard.

Roads and streets ended on the far side of that first river. From here onwards it was all beach, freedom, and exhilaration. For kilometer after kilometer we rode with the Indian Ocean on one side and coconut trees and rice fields on the other. Hordes of big red crabs scattered in front of us, and in places the sand was carpeted with shells.

If I had to be Robinson Crusoe for a day, this is the type of place I'd choose. Not a soul was in sight, except once when we went too far and missed the turnoff to the next ferry, and an old man appeared from nowhere, pointing out the right track. "You should have turned left at the second coconut tree, after the water buffalo."

At the next river, the peace was broken. The ferryman apparently felt his passengers would appreciate some local pop songs while waiting and had set up a loudspeaker on a pole. The music was more than just loud. It was purgatory. Nyan, though, grinned. "Good music!" The third ferry took us away from the shore and onto the road to Ngwe Saung.

Eventually, Nyan dropped me off at the Myanmar Treasure Resort, and I spent the next few hours amidst meticulously manicured lawns and gardens. There was an excellent restaurant, and I enjoyed expensive drinks by the huge swimming pool. Beyond the resort property was the beach, where thatched umbrellas dotted the white sands.

While it was pleasant, I felt that something was lacking. Then I figured it out. There wasn't a beach vendor or kid with fried fish-on-a-stick in sight. Still, I had to admit, the solitude was nice. And when the afternoon was over, I was thoroughly relaxed and ready for the Beach Bike Express back to the lively enticements of Chaungtha.

Getting to the beaches

All the big resorts at Ngwe Saung and the Hotel Max Chaungtha Beach provide air-conditioned transport from Yangon. Alternatively, take the public bus from the western bus station (Aung Mingalar, past the airport). From Yangon, the bus trip to Chaungtha takes four to five hours. Once in either Chaungtha or Ngwe Saung, the ride described here is by far the fastest and most convenient way of getting from one beach to the other, as well as being an enjoyable adventure in itself. Hotels in Chaungtha can arrange rental motorbikes, with drivers, for one or two days—prices vary with the time of year. The trip is not advisable during the monsoon season. Resorts in Ngwe Saung are less accustomed to guests making their own excursions, but should be able to help if asked.

Staying in Chaungtha

Hotel Max Chaungtha Beach

More upscale than Shwe Hin Tha Hotel and its backpacker-friendly counterparts, Hotel Max Chaungtha Beach offers villa accommodations on the beach.

Chaungtha Beach
Chaungtha Village
(+95-42) 24966/77
(+95-1) 524-016, 500-123, 513-009, 723-067 (Yangon office)
www.hotelmaxchaungtha.com

Shwe Hin Tha Hotel

Simple, clean, inexpensive, and friendly.

Chaungtha Beach
Chaungtha Village
(+95-42) 24098
(+95-1) 650 588 (Yangon office)

Staying in Ngwe Saung

Myanmar Treasure Resort

Ngwe Saung Beach
Ngwe Saung Village
(+95-1) 503-831/832/842/843
(Yangon office)
www.myanmartreasurebeach.com

Blazing trails

A foreign ex-pat living in Yangon begged me not to write about my motorbike express experience. "You'll ruin it. There'll be trail bikes roaring up and down the beach fifty times a day, and then they build a road, and it'll be lost." Perhaps that will happen. But if so, Nyan and his mates who provide the transportation will be glad to get the extra income.

RAKHAING STATE

Laurie Weed joins the games at Ngapali Beach

Though it's not exactly a secret, Ngapali's uncrowded, low-key, and pristine stretch of white sand does seem to still be awaiting discovery. For now, you can run from your bungalow straight into the Bay of Bengal—and even turn a few cartwheels on the way—without colliding with any other sun worshippers.

A few resorts dot the main beach, with choices ranging from the funky, friendly Linn Thar Oo Lodge to the ultra-luxe Amata Resort & Spa. Wherever you stay, the goofy fake pirate ship in front of the Amata is the place to watch the sun set behind a mini-parade of ox carts and fishing boats, all returning from a day in the sun.

After a couple of Mandalay Rum Sours, pry yourself off the beach and wander to one of the inexpensive seafood shacks on the main road. All offer fresh fish, squid, and prawns. Another good option is the family-owned Brilliance, which serves basics

with notable flair, and makes a mean avocado salad in season to boot.

Not yet overrun by vendors and tourist shops stuffed with lacquerware, Ngapali has all the right ingredients for an idyllic beach break. But I didn't fall head over heels for it until a handful of young knickknack vendors lured me from my sunset stroll, not with the usual cries of "Hello! You buy?" but the much more enticing "Hello! You play?" as they beckoned passersby to join a rousing game of sand tag.

So far, there are no discos or beach bars, aside from the pirate ship, which empties out after dark. Should you become bored with the perfect sand, lapping waves, super-sized lobsters, and crystalline water, there are a few nice local folks selling boat trips, complete with fishing and snorkeling gear. Or wander south along the shore to the nearby Rakhaing village, where you can watch fishermen haul the day's catch off the boats the old-fashioned way, driving ox-drawn wagons through the surf.

If you hang around for a while, you might even leave with more than just a few pleasant memories: perhaps a handful of pretty seashells or limp wildflowers, gifts from curious children bold enough to approach the strangers relaxing in their midst.

Getting to Ngapali Beach

Daily flights leave from Yangon to Thandwe Airport (forty-five minutes each way), or from the Bagan and Heho airports (usually via Yangon) a few times each week.

Tiny Thandwe airfield is less than a ten-minute drive from the beach. Most hotels offer free shuttles, and a few private taxis hang around the airport to pick up stragglers. It's also possible to reach Ngapali Beach by road, but the journey can be a long one, especially if taken on one of the prone-to-break-downs provincial buses. Depending upon the route taken, a journey by bus or private taxi/car can take twelve to seventeen hours.

Linn Thar Oo Lodge

Along with motel-style rooms, this privately owned guesthouse offers beachfront bungalows with small private verandas and summer-camp décor. The bungalows are popular, especially during high season. The staff is courteous and helpful, and rates ($8 to $40) include a buffet breakfast. Reservations recommended.

Ngapali Beach
Thandwe
(+95-1) 652-346/353 Ext. 232/233
(Yangon office)
www.linntharoo-ngapali.com

Amata Resort & Spa

West Horse Race Course Street and Sayar San Street (Yangon office)
Yankin Township
Yangon
(+95 1) 542-535, 544-736
www.amataresortnspa.com

Brilliance Seafood Restaurant

Located at the north end of a cluster of small, casual seafood shacks on the main road (Airport Road) near Best Friends restaurant, and within easy walking distance of the beach, the inexpensive Brilliance shines with great food, generous portions, and personable, quicker-than-average service. It is owned and operated by an affable local family. During the high season, it is open daily for lunch and dinner. Avoid the cocktails, which all seem to be kerosene based.

MANDALAY DIVISION

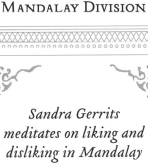

Sandra Gerrits meditates on liking and disliking in Mandalay

While I was in Hsipaw I met a Spanish tourist who was planning to take a ten-day Vipassana meditation retreat in Mandalay. I casually asked what the retreat was all about. I wasn't thinking seriously about going at that point, but thought it might be something that I'd try someday.

The man, I will call him Mr. Spain, gave me a basic rundown and said that I was welcome to join him. I thought about it some more. I didn't have a fixed ticket out of the country, and my schedule was flexible, so we called the meditation center and found out that there was still space available for the session he was going to attend. Suddenly, someday had arrived.

From Mandalay we boarded a truck that took us to the meditation facility on the outskirts of the city. Meditation courses are quite popular in Asia, so I had assumed there would be a few Westerners at this retreat. But upon arrival I found out that we were the only non-locals in attendance. Mr. Spain, who has olive-colored skin and is fairly short, blended in much easier than I did with my blond hair, green eyes, and relatively tall frame. I towered over most of the 130 other participants.

Everyone had to stay at the meditation center during the ten-day course, but I was one of the lucky few to get my own cabin. Instead of the standard bamboo mat, the staff brought me a thin mattress to sleep on, something I thought wasn't that necessary, but for which I was very grateful later on. We couldn't keep any books, paper, or writing material with us during the retreat, so I had to hand in my faithful diary and anything else that was considered a possible distraction.

Men and women were separated for the full ten days, and we weren't allowed to speak with other students for nine of those days. That might sound like a hardship, but the students were extremely dedicated, and I found it easy to follow their

example. We had two vegetarian meals each morning at six thirty and eleven. The kitchen staff gave me extra fruit at each meal and some fellow students took it upon themselves to bring me tiny cups of Chinese tea afterwards. Later, when we were allowed to talk, one of the women told me they were all so happy to have me at the retreat that this was a way of expressing their joy.

At first the regimen was quite daunting: eleven hours of meditation each day, with an extra hour scheduled in the evening for further instruction. We had to be up at 4 a.m. but usually I was already awake. At 3:45 the adjacent monastery rang a gong and the monks started their chanting. Believe it or not, I didn't mind waking to that at all. On the contrary, I found it calming, almost refreshing. Even now, living in my Yangon neighborhood, it's thrilling to hear the wake-up sound of a gong from the nearby monastery.

After four days of sitting cross-legged, I ached all over and felt as if I didn't know how to sit anymore. Luckily my teacher was sympathetic and I was allowed to sit with my back against the wall. Such joy! At least until we got further into the program, because after three days we began our "intensifier." These were hour-long segments, three times a day, where we could not open our eyes (doable), not open our hands (quite a bit more effort), and not move our legs (excruciatingly painful).

Gradually, I got used to the rhythm of the program and felt that I was making progress in understanding the relationship between mind and body. The instructors told us that letting go was the main goal of our meditation—to reach a place where we did not like or dislike, but were free from those feelings and desires.

It was something I could completely agree with concerning dislikes, wants, and needs. But I had a very hard time letting go of likes. I like liking too much! Not that it's easy to keep thoughts of what you like in mind when your leg is aching so badly that all you can think about is the moment when you will be able to stretch it out—which is actually what you are supposed to be doing, accepting the pain as something that will pass and letting go of your dislike of that pain.

I was doing okay until we neared the end of the program, when I encountered one slight problem. Returning to my cabin following an afternoon break, I found a huge spider near the door, just outside the gap underneath the cabin. Buddhists, of course, aren't allowed to kill any living thing, but in my case that wouldn't have happened anyway since there was no way I was getting remotely close to that beast! But what was I going to do? I'm afraid of spiders to begin with, and this one was way out of proportion for my comfort.

When I went to bed that night, I tucked my mosquito net closely around me, with more care than normal. The next day, when I saw the spider again, I didn't freak out. Apparently, I was learning something.

Rather than stressing over it, I was able to let that spider live under my cabin, understanding that the best thing was to leave it alone.

The retreat was an interesting experience, but when it was over, I wasn't sure if it was something I would do again. More than a year later, I have decided I will definitely go back. Many of the things I learned I now use every day. If I get angry, I calm down more quickly than before. I am also more relaxed about things when they don't go the way I expect them to. And although I'm still afraid of spiders, I discovered during the retreat that my mind was capable of refocusing itself. I could let go of my fears, and I must say, I liked that very much.

Mandalay Vipassana Meditation Centre

Yaytagun Hill
Mandalay
(+95-02) 39694
www.mandala.dhamma.org

Learning about Vipassana

For information on the techniques and traditions of Vipassana, go to the following website.

www.dhamma.org

MANDALAY & CENTRAL MYANMAR

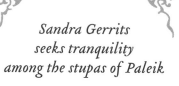

MANDALAY & CENTRAL MYANMAR

Sandra Gerrits
seeks tranquility
among the stupas of Paleik

Paleik is one of my favorite places in all of Myanmar. Even though it's only twenty kilometers from Mandalay, very few tourists go there. And when they do, they usually make a brief visit to the Snake Pagoda (Yadana Labamuni Hsu-taungpye Paya) before continuing to the more famous sites in the neighboring towns of Inwa and Sagaing.

What most visitors to Paleik don't realize is just a few hundred meters from the Snake Pagoda there is a small park spilling over with ancient *stupas* and pagodas. The ruins are packed so tightly together that it looks as if someone tried to cram all of the smaller Bagan monuments into an area about one square kilometer in size.

The first time I visited the Paleik ruins, it felt as if I were in some sort of Indiana Jones movie, stumbling around and finding incredible hidden treasures around every corner. None has had any restoration work done to it, and many are still covered with vines and other foliage, giving the place an overgrown, jungle vibe. With nobody else wandering around, except for a few villagers and monks, it always feels as if I am one of the first Westerners to discover this place.

Sometimes, when the monks aren't busy, they will invite me to drink tea with them in one of the colonial-style buildings that they have converted into monasteries. The last time I was there, a monk told me that in the past year he had seen about twenty tourists at the ruins. Considering this was my fourth visit in a year, and on two previous occasions I had taken other people with me, that meant that only around a dozen others had been.

Visiting the ruins gives you a fantastic overview of the different architecture styles that have been used during the past several centuries in Myanmar. Not a single one of the more than three hundred structures, most dating back to the eighteenth century, looks the same. After four visits, I can still find something new: a well-preserved Buddha figure hidden high up in one of the *stupas*; a lion-guardian almost entirely covered by the encroaching jungle; a carved, mask-like face on one of the ruins; or a gateway I haven't walked through yet.

Apart from the fact that it is so interesting to explore the ruins and take awesome photographs, I love the immensely peaceful feeling that this area gives me. Paleik is one of the most tranquil places I know of in Myanmar. But I have a more personal reason for treasuring its ruins. In front of one of the *stupas*, my Burmese fiancé kissed me for the first time! Even though I can never repeat that special moment, Paleik remains a magical place for me.

Local lore

According to legend, the first of the enormous pythons to take up residence at the Snake Pagoda slithered in from the surrounding countryside back in the 1970s. In the beginning, the monks would take the snakes back into the jungle, but each time they returned, finding a comfortable spot next to the pagoda's large Buddha statue. Eventually the monks decided that it would be best to leave the snakes alone, believing that they might be incarnations of previous monks who lived at the pagoda. I learned that the original snakes died several years ago, but new snakes, donated by faithful followers, have taken their place. One of them is usually curled up around the head of the Buddha statue. Every morning the pagoda is packed with tourists from around Myanmar who come to see the daily feeding of the three resident pythons. They are quite an impressive sight, but even more enjoyable for me is watching the locals and their reaction to them.

SHAN STATE

Caroline Nixon retreats to deserted ruins at Inle Lake

It's six in the morning, and already Inle Lake is coming to life. From my room overhanging the water's edge, I wake to the sound of puttering motors as small boats set off on their way to market. I've spent the night in this hotel, built on stilts near the southern tip of the lake, to be near today's destination, Sagar.

The boat that will take me is already waiting, the driver and guide shivering in the chill of the misty dawn, despite being wrapped in blankets. As we set off my heart lifts in anticipation. What little I have gleaned about Sagar suggests it will have all the components that add up to a perfect day: remoteness, beautiful scenery, and unspoiled pagodas.

We head toward the southernmost part of the lake, glimpsing the old pagodas of Taungto village, still swathed in mist. Soon the wide open waters of the lake narrow into the Belu Chaung, which translates as "Ogre River." My eyes drink in the scenery: a narrow fertile plain backed by purple, forested mountains. Occasionally, we pass small villages and see women washing clothes or bathing, men cutting bamboo from luxuriant thickets, and children herding water buffalo. I spy an old water wheel whose clay pots scoop up river water, which is used to irrigate the surrounding fields.

The three-hour boat trip is over too soon, though my disappointment is eclipsed by the excitement of a glimpse of Sagar's pagoda complex off to our right side. A jumble of tiled rooftops and whitewashed *stupas* seem to float on the water, while a staircase leading up from the river, flanked by lions, beckons me to come explore. First, though, we veer left to Sagar village.

Mooring the boat, we follow a path by a narrow stream, past dilapidated *stupas* to a large wooden monastery. Above us, the smiling face of a young novice monk, his head covered in dust and cobwebs, appears from a hatch in the pagoda roof, quickly followed by a large bamboo basket on a rope. In preparation for a festival later in the week, gilded antique Buddha images and lacquer vessels are being brought down from the pagoda roof, where they are usually hidden away.

We stroll around the village awhile, encountering a school in a garden of sunflowers, full of laughing children; a large seated Buddha in a roofless brick enclosure; and a small boy, his head shaven apart from a topknot, being led by a hairy, wolf-like dog, three times his size. Back on the boat, we cross the river to the Takhaung Mwedaw Pagoda complex. Two newly painted *Chinthe* (a mythical half-lion, half-dragon figure) guard the steps leading up to a modern pagoda, but it is the old complex next door that we have come to see.

The kingdom of Sagar dates back to the 1600s, and all that remains of it now are its pagodas and *stupas*. The pagodas have a clay brick core that is covered with stucco and ornamentation, and topped by elaborate *hti*, which are umbrella-like, metal filigree pinnacles. Scattered around the grounds, the *stupas* resemble those of the better-known nearby sites of Indein and Kakku, but they are different in that they are totally unrestored, retaining a mellow patina which I much prefer, and giving the site a somewhat haunting and mysterious air. Many of these crumbling edifices still contain Buddha images of various styles.

Though I don't want to leave this magical place, the time comes for the long boat trip back to my hotel. As we cruise away from Sagar, I crane my neck for one last glimpse, until a bend in the river finally obscures it from view.

Touring Sagar

Sagar has only been open to tourists since 2003. It's compulsory to have a permit ($6) and guide (fixed price: $15). Also, foreign tourists visiting Nyaungshwe and Inle Lake must pay an additional $3 fee. For the permit and guide, inquire at the tourist office near the boat dock in Nyaungshwe, or at one of the larger hotels in town. Alternately, some agents in Yangon can arrange everything in advance for you, but expect the prices to be higher. A boat from Nyaungshwe will be at least $40 (not including guide and permit). I recommend taking a packed lunch and good flashlight for exploring the pagodas.

Where to stay

The most common base for exploring Sagar is the town of Nyaungshwe, but I found that it makes the most sense to stay at one of the hotel complexes built on stilts on the southern part of the lake. Although this is a more expensive option, it will save you at least an hour on the boat trip, giving you more time at the pagodas. Our trip was arranged by the Shwe Inn Tha Floating Resort, a pleasant collection of bamboo huts built over the water with comfy beds and clean bathrooms. Though it's quite isolated—there's no strolling into town from here—it's very peaceful ... until a boat goes roaring by!

www.myanmar-inleshweinntha-floatinghotel.com
(+95-81) 22077

Roger Lee Huang chills out at a traditional house in Pindaya

I woke up on a freezing cold January morning, temporarily confused by my unfamiliar surroundings. Looking around the room, I saw a machete hanging on the bamboo wall, a Burmese farmer's hat, a Shan paper umbrella, and *thanaka* cosmetics arranged on a dressing table.

The chill was a complete contrast to the heat and dust of tourist-busy Bagan, where I had been the day before. Nestled under layers of heavy blankets, behind a thin veil of mosquito netting, I waited until the morning sun softly brightened the room, taking the edge off the brisk air, before I got out of bed.

My girlfriend and I were staying in a Traditional House at the Conqueror Resort Hotel in the sleepy Shan State town of Pindaya. After days of sensory overload, soaking up ancient pagodas and Buddha statues around Mandalay and Bagan, Pindaya's slow pace was a relaxing alternative. It offered relative isolation from other tourists, and for road-weary travelers such as ourselves, it was an excellent place to wind down from the heavily trafficked circuit for a day or two.

Pindaya boasts one main attraction: the natural limestone caves where the reputedly more than eight thousand Buddha statues easily outnumber the curious visitors and worshippers. Little did I know that I would find peace and tranquility, not in this cave packed with replicas of the Lord Buddha, but during our night at the Conqueror.

Initially, I wasn't convinced of the appeal of the resort. When we arrived, the lobby seemed dull and lifeless. Nothing stood out, even though the design is supposed to be based on traditional "Shan palatial style." I also wasn't impressed when the receptionist informed us we were booked into one of the property's Traditional Houses for the night.

Lying next to the hills leading to Shwe Oo Min Cave, the Conqueror's location offers guests the chance to take a number of hikes around the area. While it was not exactly a trek to our Traditional House, it was far enough from the lobby that it seemed quite isolated from the other guest rooms. As we walked, we had the feeling of being in a remote rural community.

Noticing my surprise as we reached our destination, the porter grinned and gave a nod, confirming that we were at the right place. Our pleasant surprise of a "guest room" was in fact a modest bamboo-thatched house built on stilts in the style of the Danu tribe. It had its own vegetable garden, porch with bamboo seats, and even a cockerel roaming around the grounds.

Because I am not one to renounce all creature comforts, I was happy that some of the more non-traditional, luxury amenities of a hotel were retained: electric lights, a mini-fridge, satellite television, and most important of all, a clean, Western-style en suite bathroom—the only non-traditional room in the house—concealed behind a bamboo door. The Traditional House is as good as it gets for short-term visitors to Myanmar who want a taste of village life without having to rough it.

Still, as much as I appreciated such concessions to a traveler's "needs," the real treasure of this place for me was the sitting room with floor cushions and a traditional fire-heated stove, complete with iron kettle. Sitting by that fire with my girlfriend, smoking a cheroot and drinking Shan tea, this "authentic" night at a Danu village provided just the break we needed before getting back on the tourist track.

Getting to Pindaya

Pindaya is located about thirty-five kilometers from Kalaw, a popular hill station town in Shan State. By car, the trip takes about ninety minutes. Some tourists also make a day trip to Pindaya from Nyaungshwe (near Inle Lake), a journey closer to three hours. It's possible to reach Pindaya by bus from both towns, but this can be long and uncomfortable. Most tourists rent taxis for the trip.

Conqueror Resort Hotel

In addition to a few Traditional Houses, the hotel offers one junior suite and superior rooms. Reservations for a Traditional House are recommended. It can get rather cold from November through February in Shan State. If you come at this time of year, bring warm clothing to sleep in. Heaters can be requested at reception.

Shwe Oo Min Pagoda Road
Pindaya
(+95-1) 448-1211
(+95-1) 256-623 (Yangon office)

Touring Pindaya

Besides the Shwe Oo Min Caves (entrance fee is $3 for foreigners), there are several traditional Shan paper workshops in town. Pindaya is famous for its paper parasols, made from mulberry bark with handles intricately carved from bamboo. A free tour is given for visitors, and Shan umbrellas, papers, and fans are sold at reasonable prices.

Dining with a view

The Green Tea Restaurant offers a great view of Boutalake Lake. It is one of the main restaurants catering to tourists, serving a wide range of reasonably priced Western and Asian food, as well as traditional Danu dishes. The fresh strawberry milkshake is a must.

www.greenteapindaya.com

Dining close to home

In the evening, check out the small restaurant/bar just across from the hotel. By night our hotel's breakfast waiter was a fire-throwing maverick, toying with fire and sword

play. As well, traditional musicians provided accompaniment for shy girls performing Shan songs and dances. During happy hour, $1 will buy you a whisky or vodka cocktail, along with tea and snacks.

KACHIN STATE

Caroline Nixon lucks upon the elephants of Indawgyi Lake

While being one of Myanmar's main tourist magnets, Inle Lake is not the country's largest body of water. That honor goes to beautiful and remote Indawgyi, located far in the north of the country and only recently opened to foreign travelers. Getting there takes time and tenacity, but as I discovered, the effort is well rewarded.

I arrived in Lonton, the largest village on the shores of the lake, just as the sun was setting. Lonton is basically a one-street town with a row of simple wooden houses, a small run-down pagoda, and a military base perched on the hill above. There are numerous little jetties right on the water, from which people fish, bathe, wash their clothes, or simply sit and chat.

At a rustic restaurant next to my guesthouse, as I dined on fried noodles and rather warm beer, my gaze fell on Indawgyi, its calm stretch of implausibly blue water spreading out before me. In the distance, a pagoda glowed in the last rays of the sun. The restaurant's friendly manager, Mimi, declared that she would love to accompany me on my boat trip the next day, so we made arrangements to meet at dawn.

I woke to the sound of water lapping at the shore, and the distant cries of fishermen. Over a fine breakfast of fried eggs on cake and good strong coffee, I watched the mist lifting from the water, revealing mountains on the horizon. The lake was flat as we set off in a small motor boat to our first destination, Indawgyi Pagoda.

From a distance it appeared to float on the water, shimmering in the morning sun. As we got closer, its shabby concrete reality was revealed. Despite its lack of architectural merit, it is an important place of pilgrimage and the site of a large festival every February.

Stopping off at a number of small villages on the more populated western shore, we inquired about the working elephants that were supposedly based nearby. Alas, we were told they were currently deep in the forest, engaged in logging activities. But there was plenty more of interest to see in the area, including simple wooden houses and more old pagodas.

I was resigned to not seeing any elephants that day, but while taking tea with an elderly monk in one of the pagodas, I heard tinkling bells and shuffling noises. I looked up, blinked, and rubbed my eyes: walking past the window were eight of the great gray creatures. Saying

a hasty goodbye to the monk, I caught up with the elephants just as they were led into an enclosure. I watched as their saddles of plaited water reed were removed and their backs painted with an herbal mixture that toughens the skin.

After lunch we returned home by the swampy and much less populated eastern shore, disturbing several herds of basking water buffalo. It was on this part of the trip that Indawgyi's vast variety of bird life was revealed. I'm not normally interested in ornithology, but in this case I wished I had a field guide in order to identify all the colorful birds, the likes of which I had never seen before. One that particularly intrigued me was about the size of a partridge, jet black with bright, almost luminous red feet. It was able to hop about on the half-submerged lily pads, giving an eerie impression of being able to walk on water.

As we made our way back to Lonton, a large flock of seagulls followed the boat, a stunning sight against the vivid blue sky. Mimi fed them, throwing little pieces of rice cake into the air. She said that this would bring luck. I hoped that meant I would return to Indawgyi one day.

Visiting Indawgyi Lake

The easiest jumping off point for Lonton, which is right on the lake, is the town of Myitkyina, which itself makes a delightful base for a few days. From here, an early morning train leaves for Hopin, taking about five hours. Tickets can be bought in advance, but your "reserved" seat may turn out to be a fantasy on this packed train. A pickup bound for Lonton waits for the train at Hopin, though this may be full too, in which case your only other option is a motorbike taxi. The rough, sandy road to Indawgyi is a glorious rural feast for the eyes. As you reach the top of the mountain pass, there are stupendous views of the lake. But if you've had to take the motorbike option, you will miss all this as your eyes will be tightly shut against the dust, and you'll be hanging on for dear life. Expect a couple of lengthy security checks in Hopin, as they see few foreigners here. The same pickup returns from Lonton to Hopin in the morning, from where you can retrace your steps to Myitkyina.

Exploring the lake

You need a motorboat to explore the large lake. The manager of the local Lonton guesthouse seems to have a monopoly on providing these, and charges a whopping and not negotiable $45 for a full day or $30 for a half-day trip along the west coast only. Locals will paddle you around the environs of the village in a canoe at sunset. The cost for a one-hour canoe tour is 1,000 kyat.

Where to stay

Lonton's only guesthouse ($15 per night) is a delight, surrounded by a picket fence and approached by a raised causeway with lotus ponds on either side. There is a large

breezy sitting room, a veranda with unobstructed views of the lake, and three small simple rooms with mosquito nets and private bathrooms. The manager will bring hot water to wash with—you will probably want this, as it gets pretty chilly at night. A generous breakfast is served, and tea and fruit are available all the time on the veranda. The generator runs for a few hours in the evening, but a good flashlight is a must. Though Indawgyi does not get a lot of visitors, there is a chance the guesthouse will be full when you arrive. I heard from one traveler in such an instance who was put up at another guesthouse not normally used for foreigners. Also, the guesthouse has a large sitting area where one could spread mats or sleeping bags in a pinch.

Dining out

There are a handful of simple eating houses in the village. The only one with an English-speaking staff is right next to the guesthouse. The menu is limited, but the service is friendly. As well, Nyaum Pin village at the northern tip of the lake has a couple of small restaurants.

INTO THE WILD

Outdoor experiences for adventurous travelers

Besides its popular attractions like pagoda complexes and festivals, Myanmar has a surprising number of enticing options for adventurers. For those who like to explore, it offers pristine forests, rivers, beaches, and islands that have been seen by only a handful of foreign travelers over the years. Many of these destinations are not easy to get to, and access to some areas requires obtaining special permits, but the effort you put in will be more than rewarded.

In the past two decades the Myanmar Ministry of Forestry has opened fifteen sites around the country for ecotourism activities, including several national parks. When Hpone Thant visits the Alaungdaw Kathapa National Forest, he emerges from his tent one morning to a "wild awakening." Was it or was it not a tiger that traipsed through his camp during the night? David Allardice pays a brief visit to the national park at Mount Hkakaborazi during the pioneering rafting journey that he and his team make in the northernmost part of the country. In between navigating ferocious rapids, he meets perplexed locals who wonder what in the heck these crazy foreigners are doing.

On a much more placid river expedition, Hpone Thant has the good fortune to observe the dolphins in the Ayeyarwady River and the unique interactive relationship that they have shared with local fishermen for centuries. And as Mick Shippen heads upstream for a glimpse of life on the banks of the Sittaung River, he socializes with friendly villagers and impresses the village headman by sampling some of the local chew.

On the southern coast, the Myeik Archipelago is distinguished by its undisturbed coastline and hundreds of uninhabited islands. Graydon Hazenberg travels there to soak up the awesome scenery and blissful solitude, making time for diving and boat trips as well. During one memorable outing, he encounters a group of Moken sea gypsies who remind him how truly untouched by the outside world the region is.

Fisherman on Inle Lake

Though many excursions in this chapter require long journeys to remote destinations, others are a mere car ride away. Just outside of Pyin U Lwin, Jennifer Gill takes an overloaded jeep to the Anisakan waterfall. Adding to the experience is a very dexterous, *very* pregnant soft drink vendor who helps Jennifer climb the steepest parts of the hill to the falls. You will also find popular day hikes and trekking opportunities in other regions, particularly in and around the Shan State towns of Kalaw, Nyaungshwe, Hsipaw, and Kyaing Tong. But a lesser known spot for hiking is Kinpun, which serves as a base camp for travelers visiting Golden Rock. By letting her sense of adventure be her guide, Linda Hall finds numerous trails in the nearby woods, encountering monasteries, isolated villages, plenty of silence, and a proud squirrel hunter.

Along with the great natural treasures of the interior, it's possible to enjoy some of the most beautiful wilderness areas by simply stepping from one country into the next. As Peter J. Walter samples various towns near the Thai border, not only does he have the chance to enter the country from a variety of new places, he savors the experience of crossing cultural borders, as well. Whether we're in the middle of a forest or the middle of a city, aren't those the magical moments of travel that remain with us long after we've returned home?

Mon State

XXXXXXXXXXXXXXXXXXXXXXXXXXXXXXX
ooooooooooooooooooooooooooooooo

Linda Hall hikes Kinpun's winding forest trails

The tiny town of Kinpun isn't on the itinerary of most tourists. If known at all, it's usually due to its proximity to Kyaiktiyo, the famous mountaintop shrine which is also called Golden Rock. For those travelers like me who don't want to splurge on one of the expensive hotels on top of the mountain, staying in Kinpun is a much cheaper option.

That said, Kinpun is more than just an inexpensive overnight crash pad for the jaunt to Golden Rock. This friendly little town also serves as a convenient base for hikes, offering the adventurous visitor a window into local life in this picturesque rural area. In fact, on my first visit to Kinpun I did not even go to Golden Rock. Instead, a friend and I went on long daily walks around town and into the surrounding hills. Branching off the main road that leads to the hallowed rock, there are many small trails, and we would just choose one and follow it, never knowing what we might see that day.

Some days, we walked for five or six hours, and other days we took it easy and went for shorter strolls. But every time we went somewhere, it was an adventure: finding a new village, a tranquil monastery, or a stream for swimming. The small footpaths that weave into the surrounding countryside also offer endless opportunities to witness the daily life of the local people. On one of our hikes, we encountered a village man on the trail. He was wearing a leather pouch filled with squirrels that he had killed with his slingshot. He was very proud of his bounty, happily showing us his catch and posing for photos.

Nearly all tourists who go to see Golden Rock make the trip up the mountain by a truck "taxi." It's possible, though, to walk the entire way from Kinpun via a seldom-traveled trail. Depending on your walking speed, the journey of about eleven kilometers can take anywhere from four to six hours. The villages along this trail used to rely on tourists, mainly people from around Myanmar making pilgrimages, for their livelihood, but now that most visitors take the truck, this trail is rarely used. As a result, the local residents have lost a valuable source of income, and many have moved away, giving the villages an almost deserted feel.

One afternoon, a friend and I walked on this trail for several hours. For thirty-minute stretches and sometimes even longer, we wouldn't see another person until we came upon a small village; people were sitting outside their homes, cleaning rice, cooking in large pots over open fires, or grilling small fish. They were always friendly, but seemed surprised to see a couple of foreigners hiking up the trail. Children would either hide behind their parents or stare at us. I gave out some little stickers, which was a good ice breaker, but it was impossible to give them to just a few children. Once I pulled out my collection, dozens of kids would materialize, all wanting one.

Later, we discovered a beautiful stream. A couple of young boys were swimming while their mother was doing the laundry nearby. As the family was getting ready to leave, I decided to give them some of the bananas I had brought. The only problem was that I was on the opposite side of the stream. I had to carefully climb over a bunch of slippery rocks in order to get closer to where the woman was standing.

Seeing me waving the bananas, she walked towards me, balancing a large wicker basket filled with wet clothes on her head and holding one of her children by the hand. I kept leaning closer, trying to spare her from having to move around the rocks, but she amazed me with her agility. Walking with the grace of a ballet dancer, she leaned over to take the bananas from me, never once having to catch her balance or let go of her child. The heavy basket on her head barely tilted, yet I nearly fell into the water with nothing but the weight of the bananas in my hand.

After hours of walking in the hills each day, my body was pummeled but my spirits were high. It felt like coming home when I returned to

my bungalow at the Sea Sar Guest House. Dusk was my favorite time to sit outside on the porch (after applying mosquito repellent). The town gradually grew quiet as neighborhood kids stopped playing and went inside to sleep. I'd sit there with a cold beer and reflect on the day's sights and encounters with the locals, staring at the stars, serenaded by a chorus of frogs.

Picking up the trail

The beauty of the trails is that they are everywhere. You can just pick one and follow it. These are not nature trails designed for tourists, but are made by the locals to get to their villages or to a stream. It is simply a matter of being adventurous and taking a chance. There are many trails leading to the stream I found. Just choose any off the left-hand side of the road heading toward Golden Rock. As you walk toward the stream, you will pass through small settlements of thatched houses. In the dry season, when the water level is low, it's easy to cross over and connect to a trail on the other side. Don't forget to bring extra bottles of drinking water as you won't find any shops or vendors along the way.

Where to stay

Whenever I go to Kinpun I always stay at the Sea Sar Guest House. It's a comfortable place with good food and the prices are reasonable. Bungalows, as well as small rooms, are set around spacious grounds of trees and large fan palms. Each bungalow is airy and light with many windows and a porch with chairs and a table. The rooms and bungalows are clean but very basic—no hot water or air conditioning. The restaurant offers a variety of local dishes including tea leaf and pennywort salads. The bus from Yangon to Kinpun stops right in front of Sea Sar, a restaurant which is in front of the guesthouse. If you get off the bus and can't find Sea Sar, it is because you are asleep.

Taking responsibility

The young men who work at the guesthouse make only about ten dollars per month, and live a long way from their home villages. I always give them tips for doing extra errands, such as running to a nearby store for a bottle of beer, or getting me a bus ticket at the local price rather than the slightly inflated tourist price. When a friend and I arrived late one evening, we were tired, hungry, and thirsty. The kitchen had closed, but the guys working there agreed to cook dinner just for us. One even went to a shop to get us a bottle of Tiger beer. If there was any change we always told them to keep it. And if you have any extra clothes, shoes, or books, consider donating those to the guesthouse. They will be put to good use by the employees.

Getting to Golden Rock

Kinpun is the point where most tourists catch a shuttle truck for the death-defying ride up the mountain to see Golden Rock. The truck that's used is an aging model with very narrow benches for passengers to sit on, leaving only a hair's width of space between rows. If you are a normal-sized Westerner, your knees will be brushing up against your chin once you are seated. The truck doesn't depart until all seats are filled, which means every effort is made to cram in as many people as possible—and then cram in even more! Just when you think there is no possibility of getting another person aboard, a few more will push their way on, and finally the truck begins its reckless trip up the mountain. For more on Golden Rock and getting to Kinpun, go to page 57.

TANINTHARYI DIVISION

Graydon Hazenberg drifts through the Myeik Archipelago

I always fly south from Yangon with my nose pressed to the window. Below, hundreds of islands cling to a four-hundred-kilometer stretch of Myanmar's Andaman Sea coastline, ranging from Lampi Island—a national park of virgin tropical forests, wild elephants, and the odd tiger—to tiny offshore rocks, the eroded vestiges of vanished mountain ranges.

The fabled Myeik Archipelago is mostly limestone, which is why it is still largely uninhabited. Rising steeply from azure waters, the islands resemble the famous pinnacles in Vietnam's Halong Bay and Thailand's Phang Nga Province. Under their lush forest cover, they have poor, thin soils unsuitable for farming, and the limestone does not hold enough water to last the duration of the long dry season.

Historically only the *Salone*, also called Sea Gypsies or *Moken*, have been able to eke a living out of the unforgiving surroundings, migrating from island to island in their tiny houseboats in search of shellfish, sea cucumbers, and sea urchins. The area was long closed to tourism, but now that it has been re-opened, visitors can see the rich natural bounty of the islands and their offshore coral reefs in an almost undisturbed form, an appealing contrast to the heavily developed coastlines of Thailand and Malaysia.

During my first trip to the archipelago in December, I joined a live-aboard dive boat, the *Faah Yai*, and traveled to ten different locations during an eight-day cruise. I grew accustomed to seeing White-bellied Sea Eagles and Brahminy Kites wheeling effortlessly overhead in the breeze, swooping to pluck fish

from the waves. I learned to read the treacherous currents that surge between islands, bringing much-needed nutrients for the fish, but capable of sweeping puny divers far off course. I marveled at the pristine coral we saw in most places, heavily populated by colorful reef fish and tiny, iridescent nudibranchs.

Larger sea life came in from the deep for takeout meals on the reefs, as schools of tuna, jack, and barracuda flashed by us like silvery missiles, scattering their prey in all directions. We followed octopi, cuttlefish, and sea snakes on their hunting and mating rounds, and kept a wary eye out for the poisonous but exquisitely camouflaged scorpionfish, which lay in profusion on every available coral surface. Huge eagle rays and blotched rays rose effortlessly from the sand at our approach and disappeared with a few flaps of their massive "wings." I swam into caves and through submerged tunnels that ran right through islands, looking for giant lobsters and sleeping sharks.

By the time the trip was over, I was tired but elated. My only complaint was visibility, which was less than I had expected. Recent storms had stirred up sediment and turned a few sites into pea soup. I was told it was a little too early in the season for optimum diving conditions. January and February provide more consistently clear water.

In mid-March, I had the opportunity to return to the area for a few days, staying this time at the Myanmar Andaman Resort. The resort lies in a stunning location on a deep inlet at the foot of the mountain that crowns McLeod Island. Tasteful bungalows are separated from each other in forest glades around the central building, making for some of the most peaceful surroundings in the country. After sampling the numerous activities on offer by the resort's SEAL Asia office, sleep was always easy to come by. Every night I fell asleep to the sound of waves lapping at the shore, and awoke at dawn to birdsong.

The rare Wreathed Hornbills that flapped ponderously overhead attested to the island's good cover of primary forest, and the remote coves and cliffs of McLeod seemed made for exploring by sea kayak. I went beachcombing on the powdery white sand, marveling at the prodigious numbers of hermit crabs. One day I jumped aboard SEAL's catamaran and sailed out to a rarity in the region, a basaltic island, to snorkel and scramble over the imposing boulders. The waters appeared clearer than they had been in December, and provided some of the best snorkeling I've experienced anywhere.

Before dawn on my last day, I clambered up the mountain summit and surveyed the surrounding islands. They looked like green droplets on the azure surface of the Andaman Sea. On my descent through the jungle, surrounded by gargantuan tree trunks soaring skyward like a natural Gothic cathedral, I watched the hornbills flying by and realized how fortunate I was to have another opportunity to explore this vast and diverse region.

If you're very lucky, you may encounter, as I did, one of the few groups of Moken who have avoided being settled in squalid towns, and still practice their nomadic hunter-gatherer existence. Traveling with other tourists in a speedboat one day, I spotted one of their boats, with its distinctive low-slung living cabin, put in next to a remote beach. We veered over to say hello. Ranging in age from ten to seventy, they were boiling up sea cucumbers over an open fire, and they greeted us with dignified friendliness.

Their bodies spoke of the rigors of life as a sea gypsy. Cataracts clouded the eyes of some, a consequence of the unremitting glare of the sun, while their feet bore scars from coral cuts. A doctor in our group disinfected a septic foot wound on the group's patriarch, and dispensed a course of malaria pills. As I returned to our hyper-modern speedboat, I was humbled by the Moken's toughness of body and spirit. Their weather-beaten faces and dilapidated boats brought home how hard it can be to wring a living out of this tropical "paradise," reminding me of the importance of not taking for granted the beauty of this magical island world.

Getting to the Myeik Archipelago

While you can fly in from Yangon, the route most tourists take to the Myeik (or Mergui) Archipelago is through Thailand, crossing from Ranong to Kawthaung, your starting point for a week or so on a live-aboard boat or for the trip to the Myanmar Andaman Resort on McLeod Island. To be able to dive in the restricted border area, arriving passengers are charged $120 per person at the Myanmar checkpoint at the Kawthaung Jetty. Unlike with most land crossings, visitors who arrive at Kawthaung with a visa can stay in Myanmar the standard twenty-eight days. Those wishing to continue to Yangon have to pay an additional $50 per person.

Faah Yai

A week on this live-aboard boat will set you back $1,400 or more, including four dives a day and all your food. The boat is hired out through numerous companies, but I recommend going directly through Michael Burckhardt at Scuba Quest.

(66-86) 952-0772 (Thailand)
www.scuba-quest.de
info@scuba-quest.de

Myanmar Andaman Resort

A week at the resort in high season will likely cost $800 or more. The resort is reached by a nearly two-hour speedboat trip to Kawthaung. Contact information for the resort's offices in Yangon and Kawthaung is available on the website.

Khayinkwa Island
Myeik Archipelago
Tanintharyi Division
(+95-1) 333-1884/5/6
www.myanmarandamanresort.com

Alternative accommodations

If you're stuck in Kawthaung for the night, try staying at the Andaman Club Resort, five minutes from downtown by boat on Thahtay Kyun Island. In low season, it's almost the same price as staying at the dismal hotels in town, and it's infinitely nicer.

www.andamanclub.com

MANDALAY DIVISION

Hpone Thant interacts with wild river dolphins near Mandalay

When I first saw the dolphins, I was onboard a riverboat on the Ayeyarwady, accompanying a group of travelers from Mandalay to the village of Mingun, just eleven kilometers upriver. The Ayeyarwady is the main artery of commerce for the towns and villages situated along its banks, and on this particular day it was busy with traffic: large barges carrying logs or huge earthen jars, small canoes plying between the many fishing villages, and tourist boats with some passengers riding "upper class" ... on the roof!

To the east I could see the blue landscape of the Shan Plateau and to the west the Mingun Hills. Farther away were the outcrops of the Sagyin Hills, where Mandalay gets its supply of marble that is sculpted into Buddha statues. The Ayeyarwady is vast here, especially during the monsoon season, muddy with silt carried from upstream. But this is life-giving loam, and it will settle down and form fertile sandbars on which many cash crops are cultivated.

We were just half an hour into our trip when two wild dolphins snorted their way up the river. I glimpsed their grayish tails and blowholes when they surfaced to breathe, but otherwise it was difficult to get a clear look at them in the muddy water, so far from our boat. When I asked the captain about them, he explained the unique relationship between local fisherman and these wild dolphins, which are native to Myanmar and found only in this part of the Ayeyarwady.

The fishermen from the villages near Mingun use a technique where they tap on the sides of their canoes with wooden mallets. When the dolphins hear the taps, they surface. Somehow understanding that the fishermen will not harm them, the dolphins help scout for schools of fish and show the fishermen where to steer by waving their flukes (tails). After gathering the fish into a tight formation, the dolphins slap their flukes on the surface of the water, signaling to the fishermen that it is time to cast their nets. They will only approach the fishermen's canoes, the captain told me, and never motor-boats. Though intrigued, I did not have a chance to see a demonstration of this fishing practice that day.

Back in Yangon, where I live, I came across an article in the local English-language newspaper about a professor in India who had received a grant from the Whale and Dolphin Conservation Society (WDCS) to study Ganges River Dolphins. This prompted me to write about the dolphin fishing method that the captain had told me about. I sent my piece to a friend in London, with a request to forward it to the society. It drew the attention of WDCS's Brian Smith, who traveled to Myanmar specifically to observe interactive fishing on the Ayeyarwady River.

I accompanied Brian to a village near Mingun, where we interviewed the fishermen about the technique. Later, we paddled into the river for a demonstration. Disappointingly, we didn't see any dolphins at all that afternoon or the following day. Brian was starting to make fun of me, and I was getting anxious. It was close to the time for us to return to Mandalay and take a flight back to Yangon; what must I do to convince this scientist that these dolphins behaved as I claimed?

In an inspired act of desperation, I stuck a 1,000 kyat note at the bow of the canoe and announced

MANDALAY & CENTRAL MYANMAR

that it would serve as a reward for the person who could conjure up a dolphin. No sooner had I done that than a couple of dolphins appeared. I watched in fascination as the fishermen demonstrated their method—with the dolphins' cooperation, of course. Brian changed his plan and decided to stay an extra night in the village so he could observe the dolphins again the following day. I wished I could have stayed too, but work in Yangon beckoned.

Even though I had to return before Brian, I left with the satisfaction that I had finally seen this remarkable fishing technique with my own eyes. More importantly, I was comforted by the knowledge that in these fast-paced modern times, the fishermen are able to continue their unique and environmentally friendly way of living in harmony with the dolphins of the Ayeyarwady River.

Hiring a boat

From Mayanchan Jetty at the western end of Mayanchan Road in Mandalay, visitors can hire a boat to travel upriver to the fishing villages near Mingun. (See recommended travel agencies on page 267.) Prices are negotiable, but depending on your budget, it may not be economical for an individual or couple to hire a private boat. You will need several passengers to make it reasonable. In addition to the passenger boat, you must also rent one canoe—with a minimum of two

fishermen—to get to the area where the dolphins are found.

Though the government has developed interactive fishing as an ecotourism attraction and a portion of the river has been set aside to help preserve this unique tradition, please be aware that the dolphins are wild and nobody can guarantee that they will appear or cooperate with the fishermen at any given time. At least two nights should be set aside for this trip. You are not allowed to sleep in the villages, but you can sleep on the boat. Also, in accordance with Buddhist protocol, women are not allowed to ride in the "upper class" on boat roofs; some boats may allow foreign women to ride in such areas, but it is strongly discouraged.

Side trip to Mingun

Mingun itself makes for an interesting visit. This small river town, which is about a one-hour boat ride from Mandalay, is home to the famous Mingun Paya. When construction began on this pagoda in 1790, it was expected to reach 150 meters in height, but work was halted thirty years later when King Bodawpaya, who had been supervising the project, died. At that point the pagoda was only about 30 percent finished. In 1838 a devastating earthquake caused extensive damage, and the pagoda has been sitting in its cracked, unfinished state since then. Visitors are allowed to climb to the top of the structure, which provides gorgeous views of the river and surrounding countryside.

Mingun also is home to several active monasteries, the distinctive Hsinbyume Pagoda, and the old Mingun Bell, said to be the largest uncracked bell in the world. Also be sure to visit the Mingun Home for the Aged, directly across the road from the bell, and introduce yourself to Thwe Thwe Aye, the personable, English-speaking head nurse who takes care of the patients. Donations of cash or medication (hypertension medicine is in big demand) are greatly appreciated.

Jennifer Gill falls for an oasis outside Pyin U Lwin

I am standing on a metal grill welded to the back of an old jeep, which is carrying far too many people: ten inside and seven alongside me. As I lean into the curves of the road, I think about whom I will use to break my fall if the jeep tips over.

I am on my way to the Anisakan Falls' stop, about a fifteen-minute ride from Pyin U Lwin. There are no signs or distinguishing landmarks to guide us. Instead, my companions and I simply repeat "Anisakan" to our fellow passengers, and eventually someone gives us the nod and points down a dirt road.

As we head along a dusty path, a group of local women with cylindrical coolers on their backs joins us. We exchange friendly smiles and attempt small talk. It is a gradual half-hour descent to the falls, and the women warn us to be careful and walk "slowly, slowly." One of the women is eight months pregnant, and yet she flits down the naturally worn steps. At the especially steep sections, she takes my hand and acts as a brace. I try to refuse her assistance. Surely I can get down a hill without the help of a flip-flop-wearing pregnant woman.

"It's okay, it's okay," I assure her, but she won't relent. How can you argue with someone in her third trimester?

When we reach the falls, the women bring out sodas for sale. This bursts the illusion that their coolers are filled with picnic supplies, and that the ladies are here for an afternoon of leisure. While I could easily feel used, and that we are now indebted to them for their attention, I choose to believe that their concern for our well-being is genuine and not a sales ploy. It is too beautiful a day, and too beautiful a place, for those kinds of jaded-traveler emotions.

The chalky, light-blue pool of water, the highway roar of the falls, and the cool of the mist floating out of the basin are satisfying, and so I touch each can of the cheap, local brands, searching for the coldest beverage of the lot, and happily hand over the cost, about 75 cents. Duty done, I roll up my pant legs and dip my feet into the chilled waters. I lift my face to the sun, letting the sweat gradually dry from my skin.

On an adjacent rock, a youth group is holding some kind of event. I can tell it's a youth group by the speeches and "Kumbaya"-type songs. Boys in *longyi* traverse the opaque pool in inner tubes, while girls, fully covered in jeans and long-sleeved shirts, shriek wildly as they splash handfuls of water on one another.

After we've had time to enjoy the soothing atmosphere of the water-fall, the soda women lead us back up the hill, this time taking a more precipitous but direct route. When we stop to catch our breath, they fan us with large leaves taken from the ground. My friends and I are all very uncomfortable being tended by "the natives" and beg them to stop.

Back at the top, our unsolicited guides sit down and wait for their next potential group of customers to arrive. It turns out their workday is not over. But they don't ask us for money. And we don't offer. Both are of our parties are content with "thank you" and "goodbye."

Getting to the falls

The jeep stand for rides to Ani-sakan is across the street from the movie theater in Pyin U Lwin. It's about two blocks south of the main road, just before the central market. Just say "Anisakan" and you will be put into the right car. The price is 500 kyat per person. For the return trip, stand on the side of the road and wait for any local public transport. Stick out your hand and someone will pick you up. Hiring your own taxi is another option, but the cost may be 10,000 kyat or more. At the falls, women should cover themselves adequately for swimming. For more on Pyin U Lwin, go to page 99.

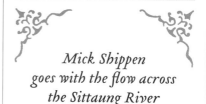

Mick Shippen goes with the flow across the Sittaung River

The track was beaten. So well beaten, in fact, that just beyond the village boundary it became virtually impassable by car. Forced to con-tinue on foot, my progress involved picking a cautious path along the edge of a waterlogged trail. With my gaze cast downward, my attention was focused solely on putting one foot tentatively in front of the other, until I came face to face with the Sittaung River.

It was impossible for me to move on without first allowing the eye to follow the river's course and the mind to con-template its power. Cutting through a flat, green landscape, the brown and swirling waters seemed to underline their undeniable ability to deliver mixed blessings. The river sustains the local community, but it also has the power to destroy, as witnessed by the inevitable annual floods.

Nets cast hopefully into the muddied waters pulled their catch gasping to the surface, while fields of sugarcane, flourishing on the flood plains, nodded approvingly in the warm breeze. At a confluence of rivers, a couple of ramshackle bamboo huts masqueraded as a ferry terminal. Middle-aged men lay grounded, unable or unwilling to be diverted from the demanding task of chewing the fat and sipping the local brew. At the river's edge, one of three huge, teak-hulled boats promised to carry me upstream.

Once I was on board the ferry, the quiet yielded to a violent outburst of raw energy as the diesel engine kicked in and the ferryman headed for deeper water, struggling as he did so to turn the boat in the direction of Swar Yarma village. The approach to the village shoreline was a cautious one. Bordered by high sandy banks and a fringe of coconut palms, mud flats stretched out in a wide arc, trapping fish in the shallows and threatening the boat with a similar fate.

Clambering up the steep riverbank, I was greeted with a mixture of surprise and genuine curiosity. It was clear that it was not every day that a Westerner washed up on these shores. On a bench in front of the local store, however, U Aung Kyaing, the village headman, remained impassive. With well-practiced fingers, he sat preparing betel nut, the contents brushed with lime and wrapped neatly in a fresh leaf. Only the occasional cursory sideways glance seemed to acknowledge my presence.

I approached and sat opposite him in the shade cast by a roof dressed with dried teak tree leaves. A welcome was extended in the form of a small emerald green packet pushed into the palm of my hand. Accepting the "local chew" drew an appreciative nod from U Aung Kyaing.

As headman, U Aung Kyaing also carries the somewhat cumbersome title "President of the Peace and Development Council," and like most others in the community, he is a subsistence farmer. His meager income is generated from working an acre of sugarcane, two of paddy, and another of pulses, such as soybeans and lentils.

Life moves forward at a leisurely pace, always a little work to be done, but always time to sit and talk as well. Among the stilted houses and gardens, the people's wealth is tangible, free of affectation, uncluttered by desire. If there is any threat to this life here, it comes from the river and the annual flood. With homes raised on wooden pilings and boats hewn from local timber, the community plays a waiting game, and every time they overcome the temporary hardship.

From the safety of a window, an old man looked down on me, unruffled by the vulgarity of my intrusive camera lens. Backing away, I was captured by a group of small children who tailed me with the persistence I deserved and a good humor that I welcomed. Their every joyful step was punctuated by the bouncing rhythm of the local tongue—music to my ears, needing no translation. Followed to the edge of the village, I stopped at the beginning of a wooden walkway that stretched across luminescent rice fields to the foot of hills flattened by clouds.

Outside every village home, water jars sat sweating, the liquid within slowly leaching through the porous earthenware bodies. Evaporating on the surface, this small sacrifice ensured the liquid inside remained cool for the thirsty passersby even on the hottest of days. With my cup overflowing, I took my fill and took my leave of Swar Yarma. As the boat pulled away from the shore and cut through the restless waters of the Sittaung River, I was showered with waves and smiles as the entire village stood on the riverbank and watched my departure.

Getting to Swar Yarma

Swar Yarma is located in Mandalay Division. To visit the area it is best to base yourself out of Pyinmana (see page 124). Any journey to Swar Yarma will involve considerable effort as it is an extremely rural area. Having a guide will be essential. If you can organize a lift from Pyinmana to the Sittaung River (about forty minutes), you will then have to walk along the riverbank for a few kilometers until you meet a tributary where boats to Swar Yarma are available. Fares for boat rides along the river are negotiable. Make sure to agree on the fare with your boat driver prior to departure.

SAGAING DIVISION

Hpone Thant tells tiger tales in Alaungdaw Kathapa National Park

A few years ago, I accompanied a group doing a flora and fauna survey in the Alaungdaw Kathapa National Park, located between the foothills of the Pondaung-Ponnya mountain range and the Chindwin River. Our team was composed of members of the Scientific Exploration Society (SES) from the United Kingdom, as well local conservationists and forestry officials.

After four days of steady marching deep inside the forest, we were all near exhaustion. We struck camp for the night, and shortly after dinner, tired and heavy with food, we soon fell asleep. A big bonfire roared in the center of the camp, and only the forest ranger on guard duty stayed up to keep watch.

Being this deep in the forest, I was sensitive to every noise that I heard, especially on nights like this when it was pitch black beyond the fire. At times there were so many sounds coming from the forest that my imagination conjured up the worst. Bamboo limbs rubbing against each other in the wind seemed like human screeches. Despite how spooky it all was, I managed to get some sleep.

I was awakened at dawn the next morning by a forest ranger. Poking his head inside my tent, he announced, "Sir, I think a tiger approached our camp last night."

There were still cobwebs inside my brain, and he had to repeat himself before the information sank in. It seems that the ranger on watch had heard the call of a *hgnet ngu* bird during the night. According to jungle lore, this bird always accompanies the tiger on its hunt, scouting ahead for possible dangers and picking up the scraps from the kill.

Prompted by this early wakeup call, I went out with a group to search the surrounding area. Sure enough, on a patch of soft sand near the creek, along with signs of small animal activity, we found tracks from a much larger animal, presumably the tiger. I guessed that it had come down to get a drink during the night, but after seeing our campfire, vanished again into the forest.

Most people say it would be rare and exceptional to see a tiger in this part of the forest. Perhaps, a ranger told me, the tracks we saw were just made by a leopard instead. But whatever it was that approached our camp that night, it certainly gave our group an exciting story, one that we could retell around the campfire every time we ventured into a darkened forest.

Getting to Alaungdaw Kathapa National Park

From Mandalay, the park can be reached by hiring a vehicle (preferably a 4WD) to the town of Yinmabin (about four hours, excluding the ferry crossing), where the Park Administrator's Office is located. The road from Mandalay is an all-weather paved road, but from Yinmabin onward to the park (five to six hours) it turns to dirt and vehicles must drive along a creek bed for some distance. Due to weather and road conditions, the park is usually accessible only from December to April. A trip to the park must be arranged through a licensed tour company (see page 267), as permission to enter is necessary from the relevant government departments.

About Alaungdaw Kathapa National Park

Established in 1941 as a wildlife reserve and upgraded to a national park in 1984, this park covers more than sixteen hundred square kilometers. Along with being home to wild elephants, tigers, leopards, guars, bentengs, sambars, barking deer, mountain goats, bears, wild boars, and many species of jungle cats, it also hosts sixty species of resident birds and two hundred species of butterflies. It is one of fifteen sites opened by the Myanmar Ministry of Forestry for ecotourism activities, such as elephant riding, bird-watching, and trekking.

MANDALAY & CENTRAL MYANMAR

165

Where to stay

The Forest Department provides lodging inside the park at Log Cabin Camp, seventy kilometers from the Park Administrator's Office and just a few kilometers from Alaungdaw Kathapa Shrine. Visitors are also allowed to spend the night at monasteries near the shrine. Accommodation and meals at Log Cabin Camp must be arranged ahead at the administrator's office. A village of *mahouts* (elephant handlers) is located about three kilometers from the the camp along the banks of Patolon Creek.

Spirit quest

According to Buddhist belief, Ashin Kathapa, a disciple of Lord Buddha, died inside this forest and his sarcophagus is said to be buried inside a limestone cave. On that spot, a big reclining Buddha image was constructed. Many pilgrims visit the Alaungdaw Kathapa Shrine, especially during the full moon festival in February.

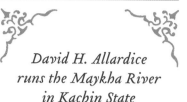

KACHIN STATE

David H. Allardice runs the Maykha River in Kachin State

Searching for potential commercial raft trip opportunities, I come to Myanmar as leader of a team to explore the rivers of Kachin State, in the far north of the country. My group, the first paddlers to explore this area with kayaks and a raft, hopes to complete the first descent of the Maykha River, a headwater of the Ayeyarwady River, literally the lifeblood of Myanmar itself, and one of the world's great river systems.

We take a flight to Putao, the northernmost airstrip in Kachin State, from which point we consider our options to reach the river. We agree on an approach that will require a day on a truck and two bone-jolting days on tractors to get to the village of Ratbaw, where the road ends. From Ratbaw, the trail is about 120 kilometers to Dazungdam, where two tributaries join forces to become the Nam Tamai, the main artery of the Maykha. This trail is normally trekked in nine days with loads; we are pushing hard and with the help of porters plan to reach it in six.

An hour out of Ratbaw, all the porters drop their packs and rush off into the jungle. This is not good. But it turns out they aren't deserting us, just off chasing a small deer they've seen on the other side of a tributary. With determination, and some dumb directional decisions on the part of the deer, they run it to the ground and are happy with the prospect of fresh meat in the pot. Even though this has wasted an hour, it is agreed to be an auspicious start to the trek.

The trail winds through dense subtropical forest, with lush vines and creepers entwined in huge, sculptured trees. We climb all day to the pass that separates us from the Maykha River Valley. It's a long day made even longer by constant rain. By late afternoon we have five hours of trekking left and only three hours of light. We descend a steep mudslide into the darkness, and the last two hours are negotiated with candles. We arrive at the village exhausted, wet, and muddy.

The next morning dawns clear, and we get our first views of the Maykha River, running blue-green through verdant forest. For the next four days we climb its shores farther into the isolated mountains. Trekking in this remote part of Myanmar, crossing dodgy-looking bridges made entirely of bamboo and rattan, is not for the faint-hearted.

Fifteen bamboo huts in a clearing mark Gawai Village, the entry point to the national park that surrounds Mount Hkakaborazi. It is pristine wilderness rich in flora and fauna. The night we arrive, the local Rawang and Lisu people we meet talk about what the park means to them. They have lived here all their lives and are concerned that their traditional hunting and slash-and-burn methods of agriculture might be threatened if restrictions force them to alter or discontinue their practices.

We continue on the trail to Dazungdam, where the whole village is waiting to meet us: a handshaking line snaking around a bend in the road. Obviously, the bush telegraph has been hard at work, and news of strange white men carrying an unusual cargo—our kayaks and a raft—has traveled fast. Sitting on animal skins around a smoky fire, we share a huge meal of deer meat in the village chief's house, then lie down to sleep. Tomorrow is the big day.

That following morning, curious villagers perch on smooth boulders in anticipation of seeing the river runners in action. As no one in his right mind would go near the cascading waves and chutes of foam, it is obvious to them that this will all end in tears. The first rapids are a maze of boulders finishing in steep chutes. The villagers are surprised at our kayaking skills and run down the river trying to watch every move. Their enthusiasm lasts about two hours and then they go back to whatever they were doing before we arrived.

In the shallows above each rapid we see phenomenal numbers of huge fish as we drift through a living green corridor. The rest of the day is liquid bliss—kilometer after kilometer of cataracts with lush jungle clinging precariously to canyon walls and surreal mountains suspended high above the forested ridges.

There is no feeling quite like being in the middle of wilderness where every rapid is a new game. Running an unknown river focuses your concentration. From the moment you put on your gear in the morning until you drag yourself onto a beach at night, the rest of your life ceases to exist. Teamwork and communication are intense as we work our way downstream. This is the hardest water any of us have run in a raft.

As we drift into the village of Ridam, drummers and dancers in brightly colored ceremonial clothing greet us. While the women sing, men wearing hats decorated with wild boar tusks swirl swords in a traditional welcome dance. It is the last thing we expect, here in the middle of nowhere, and we are all touched by the hospitality. Our interpreter explains that the villagers had heard we were coming and have been waiting two days for our arrival, many bringing their children to see their first white foreigner. They are surprised that we are planning to continue our descent of the Maykha and warn us of dangerous rapids below. The men try their hands at paddling on the raft; then we head off downstream with a gift of a dozen eggs.

The canyon beyond is breathtaking. Vertical walls of black bedrock are covered with vines and creepers. From dozens of side streams, waterfalls cascade down into the river. Indicating the height of monsoon flows, sheer granite walls

are polished twenty meters above the river's surface. It is intimidating to even consider being here when the river is running that high.

From our last campsite, nestled in the rock formations of the lower canyon, we drift down to Laugkhang, the first town we've seen for fifteen days. It isn't much, but even so it's hard to get re-accustomed to the sounds of civilization. Having successfully completed the first commercial raft descent of the Mayhka River, we are all ready for a celebration.

The expedition surpassed all our expectations: pristine jungle, great people, and surprisingly difficult whitewater. Maykha means "Mother River," but the local people call it the "Impossible River" because the terrain is so steep and convoluted. Add to that extremely remote gorges hemmed in by thirty-five-hundred- to four-thousand-meter-high sheer granite peaks, and unrelenting class-5 rapids, and it certainly lived up to its nickname. But we were totally committed to going downstream.

Running the rapids

This trip can be arranged only through a licensed tour company in Myanmar, as permits are necessary from the relevant government departments to enter the region we rafted. Ultimate Descents is planning more rafting trips on the Maykha. For information on dates and prices, check out the company's website.

www.ultimatedescents.com

THAI BORDER

Peter J. Walter border hops between Thailand and Myanmar

Making a land crossing into Myanmar offers a distinctly different introduction to local life than what you get arriving by air in Yangon. Perhaps it's the absence of sterile, air-conditioned airport corridors, or maybe it's the fascinating notion that one footstep across an imperceptible boundary carries the traveler into a completely different world, where language, customs, and food can change instantaneously.

As an alternative to flying, travelers can enter Myanmar overland from various border crossing points in Thailand. Although these points are not open at all times, making a crossing is usually easy, and can be done with either an official visa, or on a day pass with no visa required.

The first time I made such a trip was from the Thai border town of Mae Sai to Tachileik. A friend and I had been traveling around Thailand's Chiang Rai Province on motorbikes and decided to visit Myanmar on a whim. After parking our bikes in Mae Sai, we approached the Thai immigration officials

to decipher the procedure for obtaining a day pass. Our hopes were temporarily dashed when we realized that my friend wasn't carrying his passport, but were quickly revived when we learned that he could still enter by using his US driver's license.

Once across the border, we walked along the dusty streets of Tachileik, soaking up our new surroundings. Open-air teashops filled with locals dotted the main road, along with a jumble of small shops and roadside stalls selling a variety of border goods such as basic foodstuffs, clothing, and household items. We visited a teashop for a cup of sinfully sweet tea and stopped at the local market before hiring motorcycle taxis to take us to see some of the pagodas scattered across the hills north of the town. After a bit more exploring, we headed back to Mae Sai before the border closed at six.

My next border crossing was from Mae Sot, in Thailand's Tak Province, to Myawady. I approached the border with the resurging exhilaration of having another chance to see the beauty of Myanmar. Once my simple day pass application was complete, I hired a moto driver to take me around the surrounding countryside for the few remaining hours before the border closed. The brilliant green hills were dotted with golden Buddha statues and pagodas, poking out of the tree line like the giant blossoms of some spiritual flower.

About a year later, I had yet another opportunity to visit Myanmar, this time by crossing the border at the historic Three Pagodas Pass. This was the area where the Japanese "Death Railway" was constructed during WWII. From the Thai town of Sangkhlaburi, I crossed over to Payathonzu. After settling down at a teashop for a few cups of my beloved sweet tea, I found a motorbike driver to take me around town and into the nearby hills. The most surprising find was a long line of Buddha statues, what seemed like hundreds, all spaced evenly apart and stretching up to a hilltop pagoda. The gracefully undulating string of golden and white statues was mesmerizing as it followed the contours of the land.

On the way back to Bangkok the following day, I stopped at Ban Pilok. It wasn't listed as an official border crossing, and I knew traveling into Myanmar might not be possible. But on my map I had noticed a road leading to the border, and decided to give it a go to see how different it would be. As the drive wound through scenic forest roads, the mountains seemed to grow taller with each passing curve. The clouds dipped lower and lower until the air was filled with an eerie mist, befitting this mysterious junction between two nations.

When I arrived at the Thai border outpost, the road seemed to end, and I needed help from the soldiers on duty to find a narrow dirt track which led to the Myanmar border checkpoint another five hundred meters away. The post seemed deserted at first, but as some passing fog cleared, I made out a lone soldier ensconced within a tiny, concrete pillbox. Beyond him was a gate covered with barbed wire, leading down the other side of the

mountain into Myanmar. On the far side, the clouds covered the valley below, revealing little about what lay beyond, as if to remind me that this part of Myanmar was closed to travelers and voyeurs alike.

The guard emerged from his post and greeted me. I sensed that he was pleased to have a visitor to break up the solitude of this remote place. While my sheepish attempts to gain permission to cross the border were denied with a shake of the head, he motioned me over to a stone table where we sat and struggled to chat in awkward sign language. Nodding to two bottles of whiskey on the table, he offered me a drink. Unfortunately, I needed to stay sober for the long and treacherous drive home. Through a confusing array of hand gestures, I sought to politely explain why I couldn't join him.

I'm not sure he ever fully understood my explanation, but it didn't seem to matter. Instead of drinking, we sat together for a few minutes and absorbed the beauty around us, smiling occasionally to make up for the absence of words, while acknowledging our mutual appreciation for company in that uninhabited corner of the world.

Border crossing

Crossing the land borders between Thailand and Myanmar can be a bit more daunting than arriving by air, but for travelers who don't have much time and find themselves within reach of an overland border, it can be a great way to get a taste of the country even if for only one day. Crossing is actually quite easy provided you have the right documents (normally, a valid passport) and don't mind paying the fee (about $15) charged by Myanmar's border officials (no charge is levied by Thailand).

If you are planning to travel extensively throughout Myanmar, keep in mind that any onward touring plans may be curtailed if you are entering the country

from one of these land border crossings. In most cases, only travelers arriving by air at immigration points in either Yangon or Mandalay are allowed to continue to other destinations around the country. For details, check with one of the travel agencies on page 267.

Border crossing times are generally from 8 a.m. to 6 p.m. Crossings between the two countries are sometimes closed temporarily.

Spirit images at a pagoda on Mandalay Hill

ON THE ROAD

Reflections on how the journey becomes the destination

It is said that "getting there is half the fun" and this certainly holds true for travel in Myanmar. The experience of being on the road (or on the water or on the train tracks) with fellow travelers and locals makes a journey that much more memorable. Of course some of these trips may not necessarily be comfortable ones, particularly if you are a long-legged or big-bodied foreigner who gets stuck in a tiny seat between—or on—lumpy sacks of rice.

For short excursions, hiring a bicycle is an option I prefer. It's a great way to absorb the sights at your own pace and a fine way to meet people. Braving the chaotic streets of Mandalay, Leif Pettersen takes us on a pulse-pounding ride, as he dodges potholes and allows himself to be towed by a passing truck. And cycling with Viola Woodward through the back streets of Yangon reveals more than a few unconventional sights—among them, Viola herself, with her purple helmet and a bright blue handkerchief streaming from her handlebars.

If you pedal around any town, be fully prepared to be greeted by friendly choruses of "hello" and "ta-ta." You may even find yourself joined by one or two locals, as is Jeff Gracia when he takes a break from touring pagodas in Bagan. Climbing on a bike, he follows a couple kids into the countryside, where he discovers a bat colony, refreshing rural scenery ... and lots of peanuts. As for serious cyclists, Graydon Hazenberg gives tips on the best touring routes in Myanmar, a country he calls one of his top ten favorite biking destinations. One of his highlights is cycling across the historic Gokteik Viaduct, a famous attraction that Serena Bowles looks forward to photographing from a train. Unfortunately, things don't turn out quite the way she planned.

Myanmar also has less conventional means of transport such as trishaws and horse carts. When Craig Hewer attempts a trishaw ride in Mandalay, his large frame doesn't fit very well into the passenger seat, so he comes up with a solution: he pedals the

Pony cart in Pyin U Lwin

rig himself! Jan Polatschek completes the Asian equivalent of "hitting for the cycle" by taking every available type of vehicle during his trip, including a pony carriage around the old hill station town of Pyin U Lwin.

Though bikes, pony carts, and trishaws are fun alternatives, Myanmar's buses and boats are still great ways to soak up local flavor. You may find yourself zigzagging by bus to save money to reach Namshan, as Sandra Gerrits does, or marveling at the scenery along the Ayeyarwady River, like Guillaume Rebiere and Miranda Bruce-Mitford. You may also find yourself having a life-changing experience. During the excruciating long bus ride from Mandalay to Bagan, Michael Meadows is invited by some friendly locals to share their table at a roadside café during a stopover. Little does he know that tea and tattoos will help seal a bond between people from such different cultures. As the bus prepares to depart for the remainder of the journey, Michael decides that the length of the trip no longer matters. These are the moments when you realize that the best part of travel is opening yourself up to new experiences—even a ten-hour bus ride.

Yangon Division

Viola Woodward cycles and twirls around Yangon

As I set off on my first bike ride around Thingangyun, a neighborhood near my apartment in Yangon, I reminded myself to watch for certain obstacles specific to the locale: soccer playing monks, potholes, kids darting into the road, trishaws, men playing *chinlon*, mangy dogs, goats, and chickens. I was venturing off the main roads, and as I pedaled I found an endless series of alleyways and side streets that meandered past crowded markets, betel nut stalls, and snack shops.

I quickly got hooked on these rides. They were like being in an exhilarating computer game, saturated with color and loaded with constant action. Riding around the back roads of town, ringing my bell in warning—"Foreigner coming through!"—I was greeted by constant screams of "Hey, you!" or "Okay, okay." Sometimes there was speechless pointing or hysterical shrieks of laughter as I flew past. To the locals I must have looked an odd sight as I pedaled my four-speed blue Peugeot with silver fenders, wearing a purple helmet, with a bright blue handkerchief streaming from the handlebars.

At first, I would head out in one direction and just ramble around for an hour or two. When I was ready to return home, I usually stopped at a watermelon stand to have a snack and check my map. A curious crowd always gathered, ready to offer assistance: "Where you going? ... Where you from? ... How old are you?" Each time they would point me in the right direction, impressed that I had ridden all the way from Thingangyun.

After a year, I knew my way around town, and my map was tattered from each ride I had marked on it. I had a growing list of theme rides: the Neighborhood, the Rice Paddies, the Railroad Tracks, Kandawgyi Lake, Inya Lake, Taketa Township. It became a game that I played with myself to stay completely off the main roads and find the best, but never the shortest, routes for my rides. Taxi drivers gave me the thumbs-up, and trishaw drivers rang their bells in greeting.

I took the opportunity to contemplate deep questions such as, "How does that lady manage to balance a big basket full of live chickens on her head?" I took photos of people I saw and returned later with prints for those I recognized—the lady pickling greens in vats of vinegar; the shyly smiling woman frying *samosas*; the scruffy beaming children running toward me through rows of cauliflower and lettuce.

When my school term came to end, I spent my last day in Yangon cycling around town and saying goodbyes to people I'd met during the year—the crew at Angelina's, my shampoo and massage place on Thumingalar Street; Khin Khin Myint, who sold me watermelon in season, and now gave me a bag of farewell mangoes; the crew at Moon Bakery, where I had one last coffee. During that final ride, I was coming out of a side street when suddenly I heard loud music. I veered toward the sound and found a bunch of costumed dancers entering a house. Parking my bike, I walked toward it, curious to find out what was going on. Seeing my approach, a man motioned me over and invited me inside.

The living room was full of people: spectators sitting in chairs on one side, dancers in the middle. There was an overflow of more neighbors spilling out onto the narrow street. I saw that the dancers were all men dressed as women, complete with makeup and crowns! What was going on? I grinned to myself. People were pinning kyat notes onto the dancers' costumes and putting snacks, bananas, and sticks of incense on the living room mantle as offerings.

After I had been watching for about ten minutes, nearly deafened by one performer screeching songs in a loud falsetto, a man sitting nearby asked if I would like to join the dancers. "Sure," I replied, mainly wanting to be agreeable, but also confident that I could do it. Just because I was all sweaty and tired from biking, and did not know one single traditional dance step ... why should that stand in my way?

The man took me to a back room and let me select a costume from a large trunk packed with outfits. He and his assistant wrapped me up in an elegant *longyi* that had an extra long train trailing from the back. They added a gaudy gold blouse, and a crown to top it off. Did I look beautiful? Ridiculous is more like it.

I made my entrance by popping out of the side door of the living room, joining the other dancers "on stage." I twirled and pointed my fingers and hands in what I hoped was the proper style, kicking out the train of the *longyi* behind me every so often. I soon needed my own assistant to follow behind and untangle the train as I continued to twirl and kick. The audience laughed and cheered me on as I carefully copied the dancers to the best of my ability. At one point someone even pinned a kyat note on my blouse!

Only when I was ready to leave did I learn that the family had hired these dancers as part of a birthday celebration. I was invited to stay for dinner, but I bowed out gracefully, as I had a plane to catch. I posed for photos and left amidst a sea of smiles and appreciative cheers.

Needless to say, my biking trips around Yangon were never boring. I would encourage anyone who wants to see more of the city to consider the cycling option. It's always an adventure, and who knows, you may even spend an afternoon dancing with the local transvestites.

Renting a bike

Unlike in other cities and towns around Myanmar, you won't find bicycle rental shops in Yangon. If you want to use a bike just for a day, you should ask at your guesthouse or hotel. Otherwise, there are some small shops that sell Chinese one-speed bikes. Bike Market has the best selection of new and used bikes in the city.

5 Tharaphi Rd.
Insein Township
Yangon
(+95) 510-448

Cycling tips

You will find small corner repair stands all over the city. Look for an inner tube hanging on a tree. Also, you can bike around scenic Kandawgyi Lake Park, but only after paying the 1,000 kyat entrance fee required of foreigners.

Chinlon

Chinlon is similar to the sport of takraw (popular in Thailand, Malaysia, and other Southeast Asian countries). It's like volleyball, in that it's usually played between teams on opposite sides of a net. But in chinlon players kick a wicker ball with their feet, or use their heads to propel it across the net. Street versions of the game, in which players stand in a circle and kick the ball around, are also popular.

MANDALAY DIVISION

Leif Pettersen takes to two wheels on the roads of Mandalay

I arrived in Mandalay at four in the morning after a sleepless, ass-smashing, nine-hour ride from Bagan on a bus seemingly designed by torture specialists. Not even Eden would be all that appealing after such a journey, and my spirits were appropriately low upon arrival. But a five-hour nap straightened me out, and after a large meal and several coffees, I was primed to see the city.

My impulse to rent a bike turned out to be a rare flash of genius. Not only is biking by far the quickest way to cover the great distances between sights, but at less than $1 for a full-day rental, it was also easy on the budget. Moreover, cycling in Mandalay provided the most intense adrenaline rush I'd had since I'd jumped out of a plane in New Zealand, screaming all the way down.

The traffic in Mandalay is exceptionally lawless, as Myanmar is a country where most driving conventions are improvised. Certain disaster is faced and somehow magically avoided every few seconds while

MANDALAY & CENTRAL MYANMAR

MANDALAY & CENTRAL MYANMAR

plunging through traffic that would make a New York cabbie weep. At the end of the day, the clouds of dust and debris that coat your body make it look as if you really did something.

Although I have to assume that tourists on bikes must be seen on a regular basis in Mandalay, each local nevertheless stared at me as if I were riding a winged yellow hippo, executing cartoonish double-takes as I whizzed past. A slow-moving pickup-truck-cum-bus full of rambunctious guys encouraged me to speed up and catch them, and I did, at which point one guy daringly hung out the back to take my hand, towing me for about two blocks before the truck took a turn and I had to let go.

My first stop was a neighborhood in central Mandalay. Tooling down the bumpy dirt street, I stopped at Gold Rose, a shop that makes gold leaf. I was greeted the instant I dismounted the bike by a young woman named Moh Moh, who served me cold water as I recovered from the kamikaze biking.

After an hour learning about the torturous manual process for making delicate gold leaf, I departed and pedaled furiously around the perimeter of my next objective, the gigantic Mandalay Palace and Fort. The compound is surrounded by an imposing wall and colossal moat filled with water from the city's irrigation canal. The fort has been around since the 1800s, but during WWII the palace burned down. It was eventually rebuilt in concrete and aluminum.

My hastily conceived plan to avoid the government-levied entry fee to the fort by seeming naive while I resolutely pumped my bike through the entrance gate without slowing down was foiled by several alert guards, standing at the ready for people like me. My plans derailed, I had to be satisfied with what little I could glimpse through the imposing gate. From this brief peek, it appeared that the fort was far more impressive outside than inside.

Saluting the guards, I headed for my final goal, Mandalay Hill and the pagodas clustered around its base. It was difficult not to notice by this point that I was by far the fastest biker in Mandalay. I don't know if it was in deference to the fantastic heat or due to the fact that most people were riding half-busted bikes, but the locals were pedaling along only slightly faster than typical Manhattan walking speed.

I kept up my pace until after dark, which was probably not the best time to be weaving through dense traffic on unlit, crumbling streets with the occasional open, concrete ditch. Still, I raced on, defying death at every turn, dramatically careening to a stop in a cloud of dust at the bike shop, five minutes before closing.

I pitied the rube tourists, cruising around Mandalay in their vans with tinted windows, stereos, air conditioning, cold beverages, and genuine seats *with* seatbelts. If only those suckers knew what they were missing!

Renting a Bike

In Mandalay there are many places that rent bikes to tourists. You will find one no-name bike shop directly across the street from the Royal Guest House (41 25th St.). Rates for bicycle rental in Mandalay normally range from 1,000 to 1,500 kyat per day. If you plan on touring the Mandalay Palace and Fort, you must pay the $10 Mandalay Archaeological Zone fee, which gets you into Mandalay Hill and other sites.

Gold Rose

108 36th St. (77/78)
Mandalay

Craig Hewer takes control in Mandalay

The burly trishaw driver smiled just a little as he and his passenger cruised past the University of Mandalay. The scene was common enough for this part of town. Children ran to and fro, food vendors plied their trade, and the occasional vehicle chugged lazily by. On the fringes, elderly folk sat serenely under the shade of the many pine trees which haphazardly lined the street.

It was another tranquil, dusty mid-morning in Mandalay, although something was not quite right about that trishaw driver. He attracted a few second glances and stares from passing cyclists and pedestrians, but mostly just hushed giggles.

The driver was getting used to it. He appeared only nominally comfortable with the vehicle he pedaled, and with the heat even less so. One could easily imagine the beads of sweat sliding down his temples as he pushed north along 66th Street.

His passenger, in contrast, appeared disinterested with his surroundings and took no note of the cultural curiosities around him. He wore nondescript clothes and idly puffed at a self-rolled cigarette which, like the hand that held it, had a brown parched quality.

The large Sedona Hotel appeared on the left-hand side of the road, much to the secret relief of the man at the helm. Out front there was the usual chatter from the taxi drivers as the trishaw made ungainly progress up the gentle incline of the hotel driveway. Some of the younger porters looked on in disbelief, but the regular concierge crew just smiled as the Sedona's most eccentric guest came to a neat halt beside the red "Welcome" carpet.

Laboriously the driver dismounted, and in one sleek motion, his wiry passenger sprang beside him and accepted 300 kyat. Driver no more, the hotel guest trudged through reception and up to his room. By that time his former passenger was already back on 66th Street, scouting out another fare.

MANDALAY & CENTRAL MYANMAR

Riding in a trishaw

Trishaws are available on almost every street in Mandalay—you'll normally find one parked under the shade of a tree—and are a great way to get around if you have time on your hands. A short journey can be as little as 100 kyat, but longer trips around town can cost 2,000 kyat or more. Fares are always negotiable. While it is possible to rent one for the day, I pity the poor driver in this case. Trishaws are typically quite small and I never actually found one that I fit in (I'm 190 cm tall and weigh about 95 kg). Most drivers will gladly let you pedal yourself if you are so inclined. It adds a new dimension to your morning exercise routine, in any event!

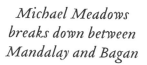

Michael Meadows breaks down between Mandalay and Bagan

Morning mist cloaks the sleeping city of Mandalay, its quiet streets a swirling sea of dawn-lit gray. After walking through the silence of these peaceful paths, it's painfully jarring to arrive at the highway bus station. Despite the early hour, it's already swarming with activity and noisy chatter. Old buses growl irritably, spewing thick smoke as they cough and sputter to life.

Blinking against the fumes, I wander through the milling crowds, nursing a bad headache and hoping I haven't already missed the bus to Bagan. A young boy selling what are surely the most popular bus station snacks, whole sparrows roasted on a stick, kindly points out my bus and I climb wearily on board.

The seven-hour journey hasn't even begun, and already I can't wait for it to be over. The aisle on my bus is best described as an obstacle course, with its flimsy plastic stools, sold at a reduced fare as "middle seats," along with coarse sacks of grain, battered tin boxes, and the occasional trussed chicken.

Squeezing through this jumble, I clamber over a box, edge carefully around an indignant rooster, and finally arrive at my suspiciously small-looking seat. Indeed, there's so little space that I have to perform a complicated contortionist act just to sit down. With my feet up on the hard seat and my knees drawn up almost to my chest, I stare blearily out of the window and let my mind wander. I've heard so much about Bagan, with thousands of pagodas strewn across a plain, and am eager to see it. I just wish I were there already.

Passing through the townships, we make frequent stops to let passengers off. Vacant seats don't stay vacant for long; there always seems to be someone waiting for a ride just a little farther down the road. I watch a radiantly beautiful girl, with elegant spirals of *thanaka* on her cheeks and tiny flower buds woven into her hair, as she emerges from a decrepit hut and hails the bus with a regal wave. A little later, we slow for a young monk in red robes, waiting serenely with his hands clasped in front of him.

There are only middle seats left when he boards, and he settles into one without complaint. Immediately, an older man calls out respectfully and offers his seat. After they change places, I notice the monk slip on a pair of earphones and reach into his robes to program an iPod. An old woman across the aisle from me is watching too, and chuckles quietly at my surprise. She reaches over and offers me a segment of the orange she's just peeled. My faltering attempt to thank her in Burmese elicits a beaming smile and offers of more orange. Maybe I'm just getting used to it, but my seat doesn't seem quite so uncomfortable anymore.

I doubt I will ever become completely at ease with Myanmar's road rules, though. Strangely, while the vast majority of vehicles in the country are right-hand drive, they are also driven on the right-hand side of the road. Needless to say, this makes it very difficult for drivers to safely judge their position relative to oncoming traffic. So it seems to be standard practice for bus companies to employ a young boy to advise the driver. Hanging out of the left-hand door, the boy calls out a constant stream of instructions, shouting warnings to avoid collisions and soothing reassurances if there's plenty of space on the road.

This boy is also armed with a long stick, and every time we stop, he vigorously thumps the tires, checking air pressure. After one such session of energetic whacking, he exchanges words with the driver, and it becomes obvious that one of the tires is flat. But apparently not completely flat. The driver pushes stubbornly on until we finally roll to a stop outside a teashop. Everyone pours happily off the bus, most thanking him for his consideration in picking a pleasant place to fix the tire. Not a single one seems to consider this an inconvenience, accepting it instead as a welcome chance to stretch tired legs and enjoy a hot cup of tea.

The tire is changed fairly quickly, but then the driver disappears under the bus with an ice-cream container full of greasy parts and rubber strips. It appears there are other repairs needed and that we may be here for a while. I wander across to the teashop, a mismatched assortment of low benches and plastic tables spread out under a shady tree, but there are no free seats. I've only been standing for a moment when some young men wave and invite me to join their table. They shuffle up the bench to make space for me, and I settle down with a grateful sigh and a smile.

The man sitting immediately next to me has an amazing collection of tattoos crawling across his chest and back, an inky menagerie of strange-looking creatures poetically caged by swirling Pali script. I've heard a little about these. Each tattoo has a purpose, endowing the wearer with a specific quality. When I ask the man about them, he hesitantly begins to explain the significance of each, gaining confidence as he goes on.

With a smile, I complain that these kinds of tattoos aren't available where I come from, and ask if he'll tell me where I can get some done. The men all laugh at this, in relief as much as amusement, and our shared laughter dispels some of their initial shyness. They begin to talk more freely. It turns out that they speak English quite well, and we manage to carry on a meaningful conversation, increasingly oblivious to both the time and the progress of the bus repairs being carried out.

They ask me questions about my home country, and when I answer, I see such wonder in their eyes. We might as well be discussing an alien world. I ask them questions about Myanmar, taking care not to stray too close to anything controversial. We discuss the everyday instead—what do they plan to do in Bagan, are they married yet, where did they grow up, have they traveled through much of Myanmar? Despite the language barrier, and the circumspect nature our conversation has to take, their quiet, assured pride in their country becomes powerfully evident.

We are startled by the sudden sound of our bus rumbling asthmatically back to life. An hour has passed quickly. Too quickly. Reluctantly, I get to my feet, and we wander back to the bus together, stretching tired limbs and sharing weary grins. As we board and move along the cluttered aisle, one of the men pats me lightly on the shoulder as he passes, and assures me that we're only one hour from Bagan now. Wedging myself back into my cramped seat with a smile, I gaze out the window at Myanmar passing by, and realize I no longer mind how long the journey takes.

Catching a bus in Mandalay

Most buses, except those heading farther north, leave from the highway bus station, which is about seven kilometers south of Mandalay. There are many different bus companies operating at this station. You can buy tickets there, through your guesthouse, or from ticket stands around the city. A single ticket for the bus from Bagan to Mandalay (about seven hours) is around $8. During most times of the year there are usually three departures daily. During peak holiday times, such as the *Thingyan* water festival in mid-April (see page 68), there are more departures, but ticket prices are usually higher.

Miranda Bruce-Mitford takes the slow boat to Bagan

The Ayeyarwady River steamer seemed to be sitting much too low in the water, as crowds of people milled around the landing stage, laden down with tiffin carriers and reed mats tied into bundles. Politely waiting my turn, unlike everyone else, I eventually made my way up the wobbling gangplank and onto the deck, which was by now a carpet of color. Every inch was taken up by passengers, who had untied their mats, extracted their belongings, and arranged themselves on the reed surfaces in their brightly patterned *longyi*, like so many butterflies.

It was late in the afternoon, and by the time the voyage from Mandalay to Bagan began, people were chattering and laughing, passing tea around from thermoses, and making cheerfully lewd jokes about the soldiers who were also aboard. The soldiers sat uncomfortably in groups on the deck, rifles upright between their legs, muttering to each other.

I was traveling first class, at the insistence of my local hosts, and had been allocated the only cabin. Feeling rather ashamed of this, I followed a sturdy crew member as he beat a path through the sea of bodies. Smiling apologetically, I was led to the stern, where I was ushered through an open door. The cabin was quite spacious and had windows on three sides; however, I was surprised to find twenty other people occupying it. My appearance excited much jovial comment, and a young man was pushed off the lower berth to allow me to sit down.

I was at once surrounded and subjected to a lengthy interrogation in Burmese—where did I come from, how old was I, what did my parents do, was I married, where was I going, where did I get my *longyi*, had I eaten yet? As the boat started to clunk and creak, and we moved out into the center of the river, my fellow passengers gradually fell silent and settled down to doze.

Suddenly the door opened and a monk walked in. Immediately, the occupants of the upper bunk jumped to the floor and the monk was ushered up to replace them. Uncomplaining, the three who had given up the bed rearranged themselves on the floor. But after a while I overheard people whispering. The monk wasn't to be respected, apparently. He had a portable radio. Naturally, by virtue of his robes, he kept his superior position, but otherwise he was ignored.

By now it was nearly dusk. I stepped out onto the deck and picked my way to the rail. Here I watched life played out on the Ayeyarwady. Beneath the salmon sun, small boys leaped into the water in great splashes of liquid gold. High up, oil lamps flickered as women prepared the evening meal in their little houses perched on stilts over the water. Lights bobbed as fishermen laid their nets, calling to each other across the water for reassurance. More lamps glowed from villages along the shore, and the pagodas, illuminated by fairy lights, were visible for kilometers.

Finally, I turned away. It was now dark, and I was hungry. The kitchen was an open fire on the deck over which a cook shook huge pans which hissed and sizzled. As I approached, I felt a sudden sense of unease. The floor seemed to be moving, as though it were living. My step faltering, I saw that it was indeed alive: there were hundreds of cockroaches running all over the deck. It would be impossible to approach the blazing fire without squashing them underfoot. Queasily, I decided that perhaps I could do without food for one night.

I made my escape and returned to the cabin where the inhabitants of my bed graciously made way for me. I curled up awkwardly beneath a grubby sheet, but it was hard to sleep in a room with twenty other people in it. I must have lain awake for two hours or more, listening to the gentle chugging of the boat and the occasional snores within the cabin.

I was woken at dawn. In this part of the world, getting up is generally a noisy affair, with much hawking and spitting, raised voices, and no thought for those still asleep. Two women had already been to fill their thermoses and were now shouting to their husbands to get up. Wearily, I repacked my bundle and went out on deck. Here, everyone was awake, laughing, arguing, drinking tea, and waiting for breakfast. As the boat approached the shore, food vendors waited eagerly to sell their wares, rice cakes, and *monhinga*, the fishy noodle soup that they'd probably been cooking since 3 a.m.

With much clanking we docked. Before the vendors were able to board, I made my exit, the only other person disembarking being a woman with a cage of hens. There were friendly shouts from the crowded deck, and I turned to see many of the passengers waving goodbye. I waved back, and lifting my reed bundle, I headed for a waiting bullock cart.

I climbed up beside the driver, and as we jerked and swayed along the dirt track into Bagan, I looked back. The vendors were walking away from the riverbank, and the boat was maneuvering back into midstream. No one was waving now. The foreign passenger was forgotten as the business of breakfast took over, and the day got underway.

Inland Water Transport

My trip was made more than twenty years ago (which explains the response to the monk with his radio), and boat transport along the Ayeyarwady River has changed considerably since that time, since there were no boats specifically designated for tourists back then. The so-called slow boat is operated by the government-owned Inland Water Transport (IWT). On it you will travel with locals as the boat makes several stops at riverside villages and towns along the way. To take the slow boat, show up at the Gaw Wein Jetty in Mandalay at 5 a.m. and buy a ticket ($10) for a plastic seat on the upper deck; you can also purchase a ticket from the company's office (below). The boat leaves at 6 a.m. and, depending upon the water level, arrives at Nyaung U around 7 p.m. This boat operates on Wednesdays and Sundays.

Yangyiaung Road (AKA 35th Street), Western End
Mandalay
(+95-2) 36035

Faster, faster

The popular option for most tourists is the express boat. It's faster and more comfortable than the slow boat, but less interesting as it makes about only two or three stops. It leaves Mandalay each day at 7 a.m. and usually takes ten to eleven hours (depending on water levels). The price per passenger is now $30. Boats are often full during high season, so it's best to book your ticket a day or two in advance. Tickets can be arranged through your hotel or guesthouse, or through the companies listed below.

Malikha Travels

57 Shan Rd. (head office)
Sanchaung Township
Yangon
(+95-1) 531-816, 537-904

OR

110, 26B Rd. (82/83)
Mandalay
(+95-2) 72279
www.malikhatravels.com

Shwe Keinnery Vessels

126 38th St. (head office)
Kyauktada Township
Yangon
(+95-1) 380-888

OR

H-SY Building, 30th St. (77/78)
Mandalay
(+95-2) 72743, 73683
www.shwekeinnery.com

Jeff Gracia gets batty on a Bagan cycling trip

My first trip to Bagan was progressing wonderfully. I'd been exploring the awesome ancient pagodas that seemed to be everywhere I turned, taking horse cart rides down narrow dirt paths, and marveling at the dusty tapestry of rural sights. In this area hardly touched by the hands of modern man, weathered farmers and sturdy water buffalo are more the norm than cell-phone-toting tourists and gas-guzzling SUVs.

But after two days of nearly non-stop sightseeing, I was starting to feel a twinge of pagoda paralysis, that uniquely Asian malady brought on by touring too many religious structures in too short a period of time. Recognizing my need for a break, my young friends Min Min and Tun Tun, teenagers who live in New Bagan and sell postcards to tourists like me, suggested a bike ride to a nearby village. Knowing that nearby— or "nearly" as these kids are always saying: "My house is nearly"—can be construed to mean treks of widely varying distances, I was prepared for more than a short ride.

The morning of our excursion, I met the kids at Silver House Restaurant in New Bagan. After a quick and satisfying breakfast of fresh fruit and pancakes, we were on the road by eight. Unsure of our exact destination, I pedaled in the boys' wake, trying to

MANDALAY & CENTRAL MYANMAR

adjust to my bike's tiny, hard seat. Then again, maybe my big, flabby posterior was the problem. About a kilometer south of town, we approached a large, bell-shaped pagoda called Sittana Paya. Tun Tun asked if I wanted to stop and see it. Though I had been hoping for a pagoda-free day, this place was one of the few I had yet to visit. Happily noting that there were no tour buses in sight, I decided to break my no-pagoda vow and check it out.

Since Sittana Paya is not on the typical "Greatest Hits of Bagan" itinerary, it wasn't strange that there weren't any other tourists around. But neither was there the usual crew of locals to be found—no key keepers, monks, students, or artists selling their paintings. A rare instance of Bagan pagoda solitude. We climbed a series of wobbly bamboo ladders until reaching an elevated platform near the *stupa*. From that vantage point, I gazed out on the plains that surrounded us: hazy outlines of other pagodas in the distance, along with fields of rice, peanuts, and corn. Not a skyscraper or billboard in sight.

After poking around a bit, we resumed our journey, only to stop a few minutes later when the chain came off Tun Tun's bike. Half an hour after that, starting to feel winded, I asked Min Min how much farther it was to the village. "Nearly" was his predictable answer. But in this case he wasn't too far off the mark. A few minutes after my query, we veered off the main road and rolled down a shady dirt lane, surrounded on both sides by small, thatched-roof houses.

One of the reasons the boys chose this particular village was because some of Min Min's relatives lived in it: a grandmother, along with assorted aunts, uncles, and cousins. We parked our bikes outside Grandma's house and were promptly ushered to a nearby porch, where we sat in very nice wooden chairs, all handmade by one of the uncles. Min Min chatted with his relatives in Burmese for a minute before switching to English and introducing me to everyone.

After making polite conversation and indulging in several cups of hot tea, along with a big bowl of peanuts, the boys suggested a walk to the Ayeyarwady River, which lay only a few hundred meters away. As we strolled down the village's main road, groups of children played games in dirt yards. Some of the kids stared in fascination at the sight of a foreigner marching through their village, while others gleefully shouted "hello" and "bye-bye."

As we got closer to the river, I caught sight of several large black birds circling a cluster of tall trees. On closer inspection, I realized that the flying creatures were bats. There seemed to be hundreds of the darn things, either hanging from tree limbs or darting about in the air. It appeared that I had stumbled upon big-time bat territory. Near the base of one tree, someone had posted a hand-written sign, confirming my theory: "Ph.D. research in progress. Please do not disturb the bat colony. Can shoot through lens."

I took a few photos, shooting through the lens as instructed. What else was I going to do, try to shoot one with my umbrella? I followed the boys down to the river's edge and surveyed the vista: small bamboo shacks hugged the opposite shore, craggy mountains rose in the distance, and a sole villager paddled a wooden canoe.

Back at the house, more cups of tea were offered, along with another avalanche of peanuts. I didn't want to be rude to my hosts, but I suggested to the boys that it might be a good idea for us to get going soon. I wanted to resume our ride and get back to Bagan before the day got much hotter. Besides, I was in danger of exploding if I consumed any more peanuts and tea.

Returning to Bagan, we stopped three more times, as the chain kept coming off Tun Tun's bike. Poor kid. His bicycle was cursed, but he cheerfully fixed it each time without complaint. Besides those interruptions, the ride went smoothly. My legs and backside were starting to feel the effects of the workout, but my stamina remained strong. The occasional truck or mini-bus, packed unmercifully with passengers—some balanced on the tailgate or sitting on the roof—would pass us and we'd exchange waves and big smiles.

The country road unfolded before me, kilometer after kilometer of rural majesty. I felt completely relaxed. What a marvelous side trip this turned out to be. I'd do it again in a heartbeat, but only after giving my legs a well needed rest.

Nyaung Hla

The village is approximately thirteen kilometers south of New Bagan. Follow Bagan-Chauk Road until you see a monastery called Nyaung Bin Kyaung on the left side. The dirt road leading to the village (and the river and bat colony) is on the right side. If you come to the Pato Gyi Pagoda, on the left, you've gone a little bit too far and need to turn around.

Hiring a bike

Bike rental was 2,500 kyat for a full day from Silver House Restaurant (see page 27). Half-day rates were 1,500 kyat.

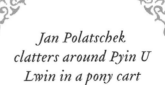

Jan Polatschek clatters around Pyin U Lwin in a pony cart

My transport to Pyin U Lwin, an old British hill station east of Mandalay, is a share-taxi, an old, very small, four-door vehicle that looks like a refugee from the used car scrap heap. This long-legged foreigner pays extra for the front seat. Four local passengers cram into the back. The drive takes about two hours, including a brief stop at a service area that doubles as a teashop, where young boys fill up the radiator. Afterward, they let the hose continue to pour water over the motor, cooling it down in preparation for the continuing climb up into the mountains.

During my travels in Southeast Asia, I have seen some unconventional means of transportation, including trishaws, tuk-tuks, canoes, motorbike taxis, and beat-up old cars like this one. For my first ride in Pyin U Lwin, I discover yet another unusual mode of transport: the pony cart. Think of your favorite Western movie from the 1950s. Can you hear the clatter of the Wells Fargo stagecoach racing across the dusty plains with the payroll on board, bad guys in hot pursuit? In your mind's eye, miniaturize the coach, decorate it colorfully, and hitch up a single pony. Now you have a Pyin U Lwin "taxi." I hire one and ride shotgun.

The driver drops me at the base of a tall hill in the countryside. I make the climb to the pagoda at the top, huffing and puffing, but pleased with the reward: a grand view of the valley and town below. Inside the pagoda are eight small niches for the days of the Burmese week; the extra niche is for Wednesday, which is divided into two parts, morning and afternoon. I locate Wednesday morning, my birth day, and sit in front of my Buddha. On the sides of each niche are the symbols for that day. Mine is an elephant with tusks. I think how lucky I am to have been born on Wednesday morning. How lucky to have been born at all. How lucky I am to be riding around in a pony cart.

Back in town I mosey on over to Pyin U Lwin's answer to Starbucks, the Golden Triangle Café and Bakery. My lucky day ends with a blueberry muffin and a large mug of hot, frothy real coffee. What a treat it is. Most of the coffee I have been served in Myanmar comes from a packet of instant with sugar and powdered creamer. Just add hot water. Thankfully, in this area, the real thing is grown in the nearby hills, and I have found a place that serves it.

By the way, the only "bad guys" chasing my coach on this day are a couple dogs, barking at the pony. I haven't met any bad guys at all, in fact, not here or anywhere else in Myanmar. Only happy folks: happy to meet me and happy to chat, happy to be of service and happy to welcome me into their shops, restaurants, and places of worship. As for me, I'm happy to be here ... and oh, that lovely coffee.

Getting to Pyin U Lwin

See fact file on page 100.

Pony cart rides

Pony cart rides around Pyin U Lwin average around 2,000 kyat, depending upon the distance. You should agree on the fare prior to departure.

Golden Triangle Café and Bakery

Mandalay-Lashio Road
(+95-85) 24288

SHAN STATE

XXXXXXXXXXXXXXXXXXXXXXXXXXXXXXXX
oooooooooooooooooooooooooooooooo

Graydon Hazenberg cycles from Lashio to Mandalay

During my first year of living in Yangon, I found the time to get out of town for a few bike trips. These long weekend escapes were a major highlight of my experience in Myanmar, vaulting the country into my Top Ten list of favorite countries for bike touring. Though it is one of the least visited destinations for cyclists in Southeast Asia, it deserves to be much better known, with friendly people and scant, slow-moving traffic, along with a colorful panoply of local culture unfolding along the roads.

In terms of quality, these roads often leave a bit to be desired. Asphalt sometimes seems to date from the days of the British Raj, with a surface like Swiss cheese. More dangerously, road builders often economize by only providing one lane's worth of pavement, so you will have to veer off to the side on occasion to let motorized vehicles pass. On the positive side, poor road quality keeps driving speeds down, which means you are far less likely to get flattened by speeding buses and trucks than you are in Thailand, Malaysia, or Vietnam. As well, the volume of traffic is low by Southeast Asian standards, making for a more pleasant experience.

My favorite cycling trip was a four-day ride from Lashio to Mandalay. The route was much less hilly than I had anticipated from looking at the map, and had some of the best road surfaces in Myanmar, no doubt due to it being a major trade route with China. In addition, the air in this region is cool and fresh, and the scenery superb.

The first day from Lashio to Hsipaw (or Kyaukme, if you're feeling energetic) is relatively level, through a landscape of prosperous-looking Shan villages dotting the plateau. Hsipaw's setting, nestled in a broad valley, is quite pretty indeed. From Hsipaw and Kyaukme, there are ample opportunities to explore off the main road, either on your bike or by taking to your heels and hiking into the surrounding hills. I had a marvelous first day on my bike, undulating across the countryside, stopping to take dozens of photos of the smiling villagers I passed along the way, and sipping tea in roadside teahouses while practicing my lamentable Burmese language skills.

From Hsipaw to Pyin U Lwin, the gently rolling pattern continues, with one glorious exception: the precipitous plummet into Gokteik Gorge and the equally steep climb back out. This was my favorite stretch of the entire trip, hurtling through bird-rich forests down to a tumbling river, perfect for a mid-day dip.

MANDALAY & CENTRAL MYANMAR

MANDALAY & CENTRAL MYANMAR

There's no such thing as a free lunch though, and the grind up the other side was one of the sweatiest hours I've ever spent in the saddle. To distract me from my exertions were perfect views of the famous, century-old Gokteik Viaduct, a railway bridge spanning the full width of the chasm. If you want pictures of this engineering marvel, you should cycle the route, rather than ride the rails, as the spoilsport security folks on the trains will try to prevent any photography.

Pyin U Lwin offers a touch of faded colonial elegance and weird Wild West pony-drawn stagecoaches (the local taxi fleet) in the cool of a leafy, British-era hill station. It also has a large botanical garden, although I had the misfortune of running into its seventy-fifth anniversary festival, an event that attracted tens of thousands of celebrants, making it impossible for me to contemplate the beautiful flowers and plants.

Instead, I spent an enjoyable morning cycling around the old cottages and hotels on the southern outskirts of town, stopping often to watch the impressive variety of birds adorning the trees. When I finally hit the road, I reveled in the final screaming descent into the heat and dust of the Ayeyarwady Valley. I covered the sixty-five kilometers into Mandalay in well under three hours, losing eight hundred meters of elevation along the way.

The next morning, I pedaled through the streets of Mandalay, around the immense, placid palace moat, to the foot of Mandalay Hill. I made the sweaty climb to the top and sat in the cool breeze looking out over the city, reflecting on the sights and people who had filled my four days. The indulgent smiles on people's faces as I passed, the friendly races with locals on bikes, the rolling green scenery glimpsed from the saddle—all made me determined to see more of this enchanting land from atop a bicycle. The Inle Lake to Kalaw route is high on my to-ride list, as is the Ayeyarwady Valley. I can't wait!

Cycling routes

The most popular routes in Myanmar are from Lashio to Mandalay and on to Bagan, and around the Inle Lake area. You can continue south from Bagan along the Ayeyarwady River through Pyay and on to Yangon, and then as far southeast as Mawlamyine and the Allied War Cemetery at Thanbyuzayat. Some bike tourists string all of these routes together, along with some more off-the-beaten-track exploration in Sagaing Division (near Mandalay), for a satisfying tour of a month or two. For practical information on biking in Myanmar, check the following website. Though the Myanmar trip described was taken in 1998, it contains good practical information on distances, altitudes, etc.

www.cyclingaroundtheworld.nl

Roadblocks

The biggest impediment to would-be cyclists in Myanmar is the changing fiats that dictate which roads are open to foreigners for travel, and which towns are approved for overnight accommodation. The road south from Thanbyuzayat to Kawthaung is normally closed to foreigners, unless you opt to pay for an expensive permit. Much of Kayin and Kayah States, along with eastern Shan State, are also off-limits. The road to Mandalay through the new capital of Naypyidaw is open to bus travelers, but bike tourists may not be allowed to sleep in Naypyidaw and will be strongly discouraged from riding along the central stretch of the Bago-Mandalay road. Many rural towns do not have officially licensed accommodation to take foreigners, and the distances between permitted stops are often unrealistically long for cyclists. This is rarely a serious problem, however, as the police can usually be prevailed upon to let you bed down in a local guesthouse if you politely explain the need.

Serena Bowles sets her camera aside at Gokteik Viaduct

I like bridges. In fact, I'd even go so far as to say that I have a bridge fetish. So when I read about Myanmar's old Gokteik Viaduct, which allows trains to traverse Gokteik Gorge, I knew I had to see it. Built by the Pennsylvania Steel Company at the turn of the twentieth century, it was at that time the second highest railway bridge in the world: almost one hundred meters high and nearly seven hundred meters long.

To see this wonder, I needed to take the train from Pyin U Lwin to Hsipaw. Traveling by rail takes twice as long as going by bus, and is relatively expensive, but it seemed to be the only way to see the viaduct up close. At the station, a guard beckoned me into the ticket office, asking whether I wanted a first-class or ordinary ticket. I opted for first class, then popped over to a teashop on the platform.

While I waited for the train to arrive, I nibbled on a tasty strip of fried dough. When the hawkers burst into a flurry of activity, hoisting plates of assorted goodies onto their heads and securing prime sales positions along the platform, I knew the train was coming. I boarded, found the first-class compartment, double-checked that the basic carriage really was first class, and took my seat.

The man sitting opposite me, a teacher from Yangon, told me he was getting off at the next stop to visit a waterfall. That "next stop" didn't appear to be a stop at all; it was in the middle of nowhere, not a building in sight. The only thing to mark it was the twenty or so women standing alongside the track, each carrying plastic bags full of carrots, which they sold to passengers through the open train window. From here, the journey continued past ploughed fields, men washing tractors in a river, glinting pagodas, and distant hills. After a couple hours, I glimpsed an approaching gorge and figured this was it, the highlight of my trip: Gokteik Viaduct.

Leaping over a lady asleep in the aisle, surrounded by her bags—ah, the joys of "first class" travel—I moved to the front of the carriage, so I could get an unobstructed view of the viaduct from the open doors. The bridge was still far away, but I decided to take a couple of warm-up shots. It was then that a man in uniform approached me, waving his hands. I recalled a note in my guidebook: "The military supposedly forbids photography from the bridge, but everybody seems to do it." Believing what I had read, I didn't think it would be a problem. Apparently it was.

Muttering irritably to myself, I returned to my seat and tried to take a surreptitious shot through the window. This prompted a different uniformed man to tick me off. I was gutted. Spectacular scenery, a fantastic bridge, a train moving slowly enough to take well-framed shots, and I wasn't allowed. It was painful, but what could I do? I had pushed my luck far enough. I would have to make do with committing the scene to memory.

As we crossed the precarious viaduct, I looked down the length of the steel struts, which disappeared far below into the green trees, and was struck by the juxtaposition of shiny, man-made metal and rugged, organic jungle terrain. The train creaked and shuddered, deliberately inching along to avoid undue stress to the aging structure. After a few minutes, we reached the other side of the gorge, leaving the old bridge behind. It was a memorable train journey, even without the pictures to prove it.

Taking the train

The trains in Myanmar are government run, and foreigners must pay in US dollars. It is advisable to book trains at least the day before you wish to travel, although you will sometimes be told to come back and pay on the day of departure. Larger stations have special windows for foreigners to book their tickets. At smaller stations you will be ushered inside the ticket office. Bring your passport and the exact fare, if possible. Many stations will not have change in dollars.

There are three different classes (Upper Class, First Class, and Ordinary Class), although these are not all available on every route.

The exact standard of seating varies, depending largely on the age of the train. Upper Class should give you a padded, reclining seat. First Class has wooden seats with a thinly padded, vinyl cushion to sit on. Ordinary Class provides plain wooden, slatted seats. I paid $4 for my first class seat.

Certain trains have sleeper carriages, where a sheet, pillow, and blanket are provided. Women should note that they may not be allowed to ride in an upper bunk, as it is considered a great cultural insult for a woman to be above a man.

Jan Polatschek pedals the rocky road beyond Nyaungshwe

The manager at my hotel in Nyaungshwe persuades me that a cycling trip to a place called "the hot springs" will be a pleasant activity for the day. Given my past, I approach this with reluctance and apprehension. I have been on a bicycle exactly three times in the past four years. And the time before that? Twenty years ago? Thirty? Maybe longer?

The manager informs me he makes the trip to the springs in thirty minutes. He adds that most foreigners take forty-five. I estimate it will take me at least two hours.

"The road will be a little bumpy in places," he says. That's the understatement of the millennium. About fifteen minutes out of town, the asphalt turns to dirt, filled with rocks. After a few minutes of this roughshod road, I park the bike at the side and stand under a huge tree surrounded by a forest of thin green bamboo. All around me are houses on stilts, farms, wild plants, and lots of birds.

The road ahead is uphill. No way can I pedal it, rutted or smooth. I remember that today is Saturday. Shabbat. A day to rest. Why not head back and have a nice rest at the hotel? Then I think, on Shabbat it is a tradition to take a nice walk. I motivate myself to walk my bike up that hill on that rough dirt road to see where it will take me. I am rewarded. At the crest is the turnoff that leads to the hot springs. And it's downhill!

Though the road is "paved," it is uneven and patched. As I maneuver along, I encounter all the local means of transportation: small trucks, tractors, horse wagons, and pairs of bullocks grudgingly pulling carts. I spot a stone stairway. Down comes the kickstand and out comes my bag with water and camera.

The climb is easy and at the pagoda at the top, I gaze upon the valley below, the best vista I have seen so far in Myanmar: a vast expanse of watery farms crisscrossed with canals, Inle Lake to the south, mountains on the horizon, farmers in the fields, men paddling small wooden canoes, women caring for their children, and small boys riding on the backs of huge bullocks.

I descend, get back on the bike, and pedal onwards. Located next to a hotel that is landscaped with lovely gardens and small ornamental trees, the hot springs are nothing more than an ordinary outdoor concrete compound with changing rooms and showers. There are two pools, one small round pool with very hot water and one oval pool with not-so-hot water. Between dunkings, I rest under an umbrella on a chaise lounge and try to relax my old muscles. I chat with a young Italian couple who are also enjoying the hot sun and hot baths. I take a break and wander over to the gardens. At one end is a stand, and I buy a cold drink. A few kids stare at me from across the road.

Faced with the tiring prospect of another long ride, I decide not to make the return trip by bike. I figure that with all the traffic, I should be able to hitch my way back. After several failed attempts, I finally wave down a pickup truck. I sit on a steel shelf near the side of the bed. I regret this after about three seconds.

The truck has absolutely no springs or shock absorbers. Every bump, rut, or patch in the road goes straight to my backside. I think my behind will break into about fifty pieces. The six women sitting with me are stoic and utterly unaffected. I can't understand how they endure this bone-jarring, teeth-shattering ride. Can it be that they possess more fully equipped posteriors?

As we return to town, the sun is setting, the golden rays painting the sides of wooden houses. Flocks of birds paddle around in canals, and kids play games, yelling "hello" when they notice me in the truck. All my weariness and pain aside, it is a splendid way to end the day.

Getting to the hot springs

The hot springs are located near the village of Kaung Daing on the northwest shore of Inle Lake. They are open daily from 7 a.m. till 5 p.m. I paid $2 to use the facility. If you want to cycle there, bikes are rented at many travel agencies, restaurants, and small rental businesses along the main road in Nyaungshwe. The average price is 1,000 to 1,500 kyat for a full day. Make sure you get one with good brakes!

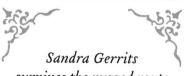

Sandra Gerrits survives the rugged route to Namhsan

After spending a few days trekking in the area around Hsipaw, I found myself faced with the decision of what to do next. I still had ten days before I needed to be in Mandalay, so I agreed to accompany my Burmese friend, Kyaw Kyaw, on a visit to Namhsan, a picturesque tea-growing town surrounded by mountains, about eighty kilometers west of Hsipaw.

In Hsipaw we hired a guide named Tun Tun, whose family lived in Namhsan. Rather than traveling directly to Namhsan from Hsipaw, he suggested that we take a bus to Kyaukme, spend the night there, and then double back through Hsipaw before continuing on to Namhsan. That didn't make much sense to us, but he claimed doing it this way would help us secure seats on the bus. If we started the journey in Hsipaw, he warned, the bus would most likely already be full, and we would end up standing in the aisle the whole journey.

The following afternoon we left for Kyaukme. Our seats for this trip were in the back of the bus on some big bags of rice. This turned out to be good practice for the next day—we just didn't know it at the time. In Kyaukme everybody tried to convince us to hire a jeep, but we were not inclined to spend so much. The cheapest price quoted was $75, a big difference from the $5 it would cost for a bus ticket.

We showed up at three thirty the next morning, not at the bus station, but at a street corner where the bus was being loaded with various goods. After waiting more than an hour, we climbed into the vehicle, which was more like a hybrid bus-truck. It turned out that even at this juncture we were too late for real seats.

We found some sacks in the back, next to the last row of seats, and made ourselves comfortable, thinking we would have the luxury of all this space for the rest of the trip. Wrong. At the station, the bus was loaded to capacity with passengers. I'm talking about Myanmar's version of full capacity, not some wimpy Western standard. I found myself crammed on top of the lumpy sacks along with Kyaw Kyaw, Tun Tun, and seven other people—all in a space less than two square meters.

When we reached Hsipaw, even more people and goods were added. Tun Tun decided to flee our cramped quarters and took up residence on the roof with some other men; women aren't allowed to sit on top of vehicles in Buddhist Myanmar. Then the whole overloaded vehicle got on its way. The journey was supposed to take around eight hours, but it ended up lasting more than thirteen. It wasn't even the rainy season yet, but the road conditions were that bad. There were no broken trucks full of tea blocking the road, as I had seen in another town, but when we came to a damaged bridge, everyone had to get out and wait for over an hour before the journey resumed.

After finally arriving in Namhsan, we were ready for the final leg, the walk to Tun Tun's village. He said it was only ninety minutes, but he forgot to mention that this hike would take us up a mountain, and then down another one, before crossing a small stream with no bridge.

When we reached the village, the warm reception by Tun Tun's friendly family made the whole tiring journey worthwhile. After we were "shown around" at all the houses, the family announced that they wanted to throw a party in our honor. Unfortunately, our trip had seriously worn Kyaw Kyaw and me out, so we politely declined, and like the rest of the village, turned in early.

The next day we took a pleasant walk, taking in the gorgeous mountain scenery, and visiting a few of the many tea plantations in the area. Some of those plantations are set up on hillsides, where it seems not even a mountain goat would feel comfortable. But the Shwe Palaung people get up and down these incredibly steep slopes with ease, carrying huge baskets packed with tea.

Before I left, I bought a big bag of tea from Tun Tun's village. Honestly, it is the best tea I've ever tasted. I still think of it a year later. Namhsan and the scenic area around it are high on my list of places I want to visit again.

We stayed two days in Namhsan before taking a bus back to Kyaukme. This time the experience was a bit more comfortable—we had actual seats. And the bus didn't have an extra layer of bags covering the floor, so we could actually put our feet down. Oh, such luxury!

Getting to Namhsan

From Hsipaw the trip to Namhsan by truck or bus normally takes about six or seven hours. If you want to secure seats, however, Kyaukme (about fifty kilometers south of Hsipaw, on the route to Pyin U Lwin and Mandalay) might be an easier point of departure. Surrounded by mountains, Kyaukme is also a beautiful little

town that sees few tourists. It's important to note that there are currently no "official" guesthouses in Namhsan, although it's common for local families to rent rooms to tourists. Inquire about accommodation at one of the restaurants in town.

KACHIN STATE TO MANDALAY DIVISION

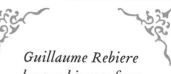

Guillaume Rebiere dreams his way from Bhamo to Mandalay

After a night in Myitkyina, the capital of Kachin State, a group of friends and I board an early morning shuttle boat that will take us to Bhamo, a town about six hours down the Ayeyarwady River. The small ferry is full of people from the countryside, joyful students, and sleepy merchants. As it travels fast between rocks, I feel more than a little anxious. We are near the river's source, and when the flow is this strong, especially now just after monsoon season, crashes—and drownings—are quite common.

After we reach Bhamo, we transfer to a large charter boat, an old but charming vessel that will take us farther south to Mandalay. Comfort is minimal but sufficient. We leave our bags in a room on the main deck, which will also serve as our dormitory, and go to the upper deck where chairs and fruit juice await us. As the boat starts down the river, we look back one last time at the highlands, burned by the sunset, disappearing behind the cliffs that surround us.

We travel between hills and cliffs that few Western tourists have ever gazed upon. Each day we visit new villages and discover different landscapes. Some scenes look as if they have not changed in centuries: bamboo houses on stilts, buffalo grazing in sugar cane fields, craggy mountains in the distance. The closer we get to Mandalay, the bigger the villages become. River dolphins come to the surface and play in the waves. Knowing that there are very few of these magnificent creatures left in the river makes me sad.

One night we stop in Kyauk Myaung, a village famous for its clay pots. Merchants transport these pots on large bamboo rafts and then sell them to dealers, who in turn distribute them throughout the country. When we enter the village, children flee, apparently frightened by the sight of our foreign faces. Our guide tells us that they have never seen white people before. Moreover, he explains, foreigners are quite often the bogeymen in stories the children are told when they misbehave. Despite our evil reputation, after a few minutes some of the children dare to come out of hiding and greet us with shy smiles. Determining that we're harmless, they take us to meet

their parents, whose local hospitality includes offers of tea and cheroots.

Later, as we sit around a fire on the sand bank, dining on grilled fish, I watch elephants bathing in the river. They have ended their long working day, and the teakwood they hauled is being gathered to be floated on rafts to Mandalay. In this village, time seems to flow at the same rhythm as the river here: slowly and quietly. There is no other light but that of the stars, and no other music than the hum of the water. As I soak up the tranquility, I reflect on all that we've seen today, and I realize I would like to be nowhere else but here right now.

The next morning, we find our boat surrounded by fog. We travel slowly, waiting for the sun to part the thick white curtain. When it finally does, we can see the shadows of the pagodas in Shwebawkyun village, one of which has sheltered relics of the Buddha for two thousand years. The river now grows wider, which means that we are getting closer to central Myanmar.

Finally, on the fifth day, the royal city comes into sight. While I watch the busy docks approach, I feel as if I have just woken from a beautiful dream

Bhamo to Mandalay

The cruise between Bhamo and Mandalay takes around five days on a charter boat. The river along this stretch is open for travel between October and February. During the rest of the year it is either too rough because of monsoon rains or the water level is too low.

Getting to Bhamo

To reach Bhamo, you must fly from Yangon to Myitkyina. Then, depending on weather conditions, you can travel to Bhamo by shuttle boat (five to seven hours) or by car (eight to ten hours). Shuttle boats are only available when weather conditions are safe (usually October and November), since accidents are common on this part of the river.

Booking a cruise

Prices depend on the kind of boat you book and the number of passengers involved. Our group paid $1,000 per person for the five-day trip, including all meals and beverages (except beer and alcohol). Though our eight-to-ten person boat was comfortable, it was not top of the range; accommodations were dormitory style. A similar trip is offered with luxury companies such as Pandaw River Cruises, which is much more expensive. Regardless of the boat, you have to arrange your cruise using a local travel agency (see page 267), which will help you hire a local guide and get a permit, since traveling in Kachin State requires authorization. You can also book cruises directly through some boat companies (see page 184).

Boy rowing on a canal near Inle Lake

WHEN IN ROME

Lessons on living local and making yourself at home

As soon as you enter Myanmar for the first time, it's obvious that you have stepped into a very different corner of the world. Western visitors are often curious about the wide range of new images they see. Why do the men wear skirts? What's that pale yellow paste on the faces of all the women and children? Why are there bright red stains all over the sidewalk? Where are the Starbucks?

Happily, there are no Western food and beverage franchises blotting the local landscape. But there are plenty of distinctive local practices such as wearing a *longyi*, applying *thanaka* to the face, and chewing—and spitting—betel nut. The people of Myanmar are justifiably proud of their culture and the centuries-old traditions they still practice, and are more than happy to share it all with visitors.

Tourists remark that visiting Myanmar is like traveling back in time, and there's no doubt that Modern Man has been very slow to leave his imprint. As a result of several factors, not least of which has been isolation from the world stage over the past several decades, Myanmar has arguably retained more of its traditional customs and culture than any country in Southeast Asia. Certainly, that lack of "progress" is part of the appeal for travelers. As Jan Polatschek writes in one essay, "Where else in the world can I take a horse cart to the airport?"

But the times they are a-changin', even in Myanmar. Just a few minutes of watching a Burmese hip-hop video, or seeing a Yangon teenager sporting dyed red hair, a nose ring, and a Linkin Park T-shirt, is proof enough that Western culture is already leaving its indelible mark on a new generation. Yet even with such changes, traditional practices continue to play an important part in society, as Isabelle Abreu learns when she has her future told by an astrologer on the outskirts of Yangon.

Teashops are the public houses of Myanmar. More than just a place to sip a cup of tea, they are where locals catch up on

Woman smoking a cheroot

the latest news and gossip. While Yangon native Aye Aye Maw reminisces about going to teashops with friends when she was a student back in the early 1990s, these cafés aren't just for locals. Don Gilliland also enjoys the social aspect of teashops, which he considers sources of cultural enlightenment, and in Mandalay, the best places to sample local noodle specialties like *mondhi*.

Some cultural aspects of daily life may be off-putting to a visitor at first, but when it comes to all those crimson blotches staining the sidewalk, Michael Pugh proves that if you can't beat 'em, join 'em, giving insight into the habit of betel nut chewing when he bravely accepts an offering of the local chew. Want a new look? John Buckley tells you how to get the hang of walking—and swimming—wearing a *longyi*. And have you ever eaten, or even heard of, tamarind flakes? If you are anything like Manjit Kaur, be prepared to become addicted to these delightful sweets, along with so many other traditions unique to Myanmar.

YANGON DIVISION

John Buckley drops his pants in Yangon

To be honest, I've never quite been sold on the concept of pants. I was raised in a cold weather environment in the United States, which made them an elemental, not to mention cultural, necessity, but secretly I've always yearned to be freed from their form-fitting restraint.

When I began reading about Myanmar in preparation for my first visit, I was introduced to certain interesting facts. Upon arrival, I would quickly come into contact with women who wore a powdery, yellow substance called *thanaka* on their faces and—of particular interest to me, due to the aforementioned reason—men who would be dressed in a skirt-like garment known as a *longyi*.

Sure enough, when I arrived at the Yangon International Airport on a hot October day, I was greeted by smiling women with *thanaka* smeared across their cheeks, along with taxi drivers seeking my business, all of them wearing ankle-length pieces of cloth tied neatly around their waists. I was instantly intrigued.

After wandering the chaotic Yangon streets, it soon became apparent that the *longyi* was not a costume worn by the locals for the benefit of arriving tourists. Both the use of *thanaka,* which serves as sunscreen and make-up, and the wearing of *longyi* are traditional practices preserved in a country that has essentially been cut off from the "modern" world for the better part of the last half century. While visiting a *longyi*-wearing travel agent in Yangon, I curiously asked about the garment. After a brief explanation of its practicality, the agent then produced a small plastic-wrapped package containing a neatly folded *longyi*. With a smile, he offered it to me as a gift.

Later that day, I visited the Shwedagon Pagoda, Myanmar's most sacred Buddhist site. As I was paying the entry fee, one of the ticket takers noticed that I was wearing shorts and shyly asked if I had a pair of trousers to cover my knees. I remembered the *longyi* in my backpack and asked if that would suffice. The young man looked relieved and told me it would be much appreciated if I would be so kind as to put it on.

It then occurred to me that there was one small problem. I had no idea how to go about fastening the large piece of cloth around my waist. Attracting a small crowd of giggling locals, I received my first lesson on properly tying a *longyi*. You must first "step into" the cylindrical garment,

and then pull up the top end until it reaches your lower chest. The next key step is to secure two separate ends of fabric in each hand at both sides of the waist and then to pull each end in opposite directions. The right hand then drops down to hold the loose middle section firmly in place before bringing the left hand down to meet the right hand in the middle. Are you with me so far?

Maintaining a tight a grip on each portion, you then encircle the two pieces of fabric in each hand into a tight cross section at the waist, while still holding the middle. This leaves the two ends free for a final motion where one end gets tucked into the waistline. The other end sticks out like a clump that resembles a knot. Though more intricate, the *longyi*-tying process is essentially akin to wrapping a towel around your waist.

I felt slightly awkward at first, but as I walked the grounds of Shwedagon, I began to take to the concept of *longyi* wearing. Free-flowing, yet conservative. Casual, yet stylish. I felt the need for pants in my life diminish.

Several days later, on a visit to the riverside town of Mingun, I received another lesson in the practicality of the *longyi*. Having engaged in a rather lengthy tour of the Mingun Paya—that large, unfinished pagoda on the Ayeyarwady River—I was soaked through with sweat. Noticing that the sun was taking its toll on me, my guide asked if I would like a shower. In local parlance this meant bathing in the river. Though tempted, I did not want wet clothes for the

YANGON & SOUTHERN MYANMAR

remainder of the day and politely declined. Undeterred, my guide told me that I could borrow a *longyi*.

The beating sun soon weakened my resistance, and I followed my guide to his modest house, where I re-enacted the motions of my earlier *longyi* experience. I then walked down to the river, doing my best to keep the *longyi* firmly in place so I wouldn't expose myself to the other tourists who were already shooting surprised looks in my direction. Joining a group of elderly local women and my guide in the water, I spent the afternoon swimming along the banks of the river and washing myself with borrowed soap. Though the Mingun Paya was indeed a grand sight to see, it was that moment in the river that I will remember best—and I owe it all to the *longyi*.

Throughout the remainder of my trip, I would wear my *longyi* in private, secretly longing for this to become an accepted look for an American. On my way out of Yangon, I purchased two more in various patterns. Though I know it will take some convincing, I have vowed to friends that I will make the *longyi* the latest craze in a society that could benefit from loosening up a bit and dropping its pants.

Longyi lessons

For a regular men's *longyi*, which locals also call *paso,* prices usually range from 2,000 to 6,000 kyat (about $2 to $5), depending on the quality. Pure silk versions can cost around 20,000 kyat, and women's *longyi*, also called *tamein*, are normally more expensive, ranging from 3,000 to 30,000 kyat. The finer ones might cost up to 120,000 kyat (around $100). Besides price, there is another difference between men's and women's *longyi*. Women tie their *longyi* on the side. Most locals buy their *longyi* at markets or department stores.

Isabelle Abreu consults a Yangon astrologer

People in Myanmar have a strong belief in astrology. It is so pervasive that astrologers are an important part of the social fabric. It's common for locals to seek the advice of an astrologer or palmist when they are thinking about moving to a new house, seeking a job, taking an exam, opening a business, or getting married.

I have always been skeptical when it comes to things like predicting the future, but the ways of the Orient intrigue me. After talking about astrology to a local friend of mine, who is definitely a believer, my curiosity finally got the best of me. During my last visit to Yangon, I decided to have my fortune read.

We drove to the Yangon suburb of North Okkalapa for my consultation. The astrologer my friend uses is based at Mei La Mu Pagoda, nestled among mangroves on the banks of the Ngamoeyeik Creek. Legend tells of a beautiful princess, Mei La Mu, who was born out of a *la mu* tree at this spot. After she married, she gave birth to King Okkalapa, the original builder of Shwedagon Pagoda. Later, she commissioned a pagoda of her own built on the site where she was born. Ancient relics were found there in 1959, and pilgrims now come to worship, meditate, and seek the advice of astrologers.

I had expected to find something resembling an outdoor fair, with scraggly gypsy hags in tents, gazing into crystal balls and cackling at their predictions, but it wasn't like that at all. There were more than a dozen stalls scattered around the pagoda compound, each one housing an astrologer. Despite the number of stalls, the atmosphere was serene. A few people walked in and out of the stalls, and others made their way inside the pagoda to pray.

My friend recommended his regular astrologer, a stout, middle-aged woman whom he claimed gave very accurate readings. On the left side of her stall was a basket with three bunches of bananas and a single green coconut adorned with Eugenia leaves. This was an offering to the various guardian spirits who look after the world. There were also small shrines with pictures of "many exalted personages." I asked what made those people so "exalted" and my friend said that it was because they had devoted themselves to

religion. After such pure and saintly lives, they "transitioned to a higher plane of existence."

The astrologer spoke only Burmese, but my friend translated everything she said. I was told to sit in front of her and hold out my hands. She then took a ballpoint pen and traced the lines on both of my palms. After doing that she asked for the day of the week when I was born. I knew the date, of course, but I sheepishly had to admit that I didn't know the day. Coming to my rescue, she brought out a hundred-year calendar that showed I was born on Wednesday. She drew some complicated diagrams on a black slate and after making more calculations she gave me the results.

She predicted that I would be successful with things concerning literature, teaching, and writing; I would do a lot of traveling; I would continue to have good prospects in my work; I would make many friends, especially with people of different races. As for my health, I needed to be cautious about my stomach and heart. She also told me I would be hearing some good news within a couple of days, and there was a distinct possibility that I would inherit something mechanical.

There was, however, one bit of negative news. She said my fortunes seemed a little down at the moment due to the influences of a certain planet, but by my next birthday, when this "menacing planet" shifted to another position, things should improve. To prevent any misfortunes while under this dark planet, she advised that I should go to a pagoda, select the day of my birth at its planetary post, pour many cups of water on the post (the number of cups should be equivalent to my age!), set nine birds free, and give nine bits of candy to nine children at nine o'clock on a Wednesday morning.

I visited another pagoda in Yangon the very next day and did everything the astrologer advised. I'm happy to report that no misfortune has struck me since my visit. In fact, by the time my next birthday came around, my situation in life had definitely improved, and everything concerning my job, travel, and friendships seemed to concur with the astrologer's predictions. But I'm still waiting to inherit that mysterious mechanical item. Maybe it will be my brother's old Mercedes!

Mei La Mu Pagoda

The pagoda is in North Okkalapa Township about thirteen kilometers north of central Yangon near the airport. Most local taxi drivers know it. Don't forget to negotiate the fare before you go. Most drivers will be happy to wait for you while you have your consultation.

Negotiating the future

For an ordinary consultation from a typical astrologer, the price is around 1,500 to 3,000 kyat. Some astrologers will upgrade their services, such as giving a more detailed forecast, for an extra charge. This is what I did for 5,000 kyat. In rural areas and small towns, astrology services cost less. I was told of one highly regarded astrologer in Shwebo (near the Chindwin River in northern Myanmar) who charges only 1,000 kyat for a one-hour session. Astrologers who advertise in magazines usually charge more than 10,000 kyat. More "upmarket" astrologers command even higher fees. U San Zarni Bo, one of the most famous astrologers in Myanmar, charges around 30,000 kyat for readings that last an hour. It's also not unheard of for clients to pay 100,000 kyat for a detailed consultation that includes horoscopes.

Aye Aye Maw reminisces about teashop culture in Yangon

When I was in my late teens and living in Yangon, I started going to teashops without my parents. For a young woman from Myanmar, this was a big step. In those days, back in the early 1990s, people in Myanmar frowned on girls sitting at teashops with boys. Nowadays nobody cares who sits with whom, but back then I was usually the only girl sitting with the males, unless one of my female friends joined us.

At these teashops I would chat about exams, college choices, and future job prospects. I was quite thankful that my parents did not stop me from going. As a high school student, I studied hard and took few breaks. Teashops were my chance to relax and hang out with my friends.

The other reason I liked going was to listen to music. When I was growing up, many families did not have stereos at home. High school students did not have much pocket money, but hanging out with friends while listening to the latest music in teashops was a luxury we could afford. These days, many teashops in Myanmar also have TVs and show videos in addition to playing music.

I'm now living overseas, but when I return to Yangon, I still enjoy teashops. One new place I frequent is Zin, located north of town near the airport. It serves various types of tea, soft drinks, and coffee, as well as traditional noodle dishes such as *monhinga* and *ohn no kauk swe*. It also has good cakes, sweet sticky rice, pancakes, and *nan*. For a nice snack between lunch and dinner, I like munching on *ar pu shar pu,* a spicy Rakhaing noodle dish.

When I go to teashops like Zin nowadays, I often see some of my old friends. Sadly, we don't sit together and chat like we used to. Times change, and now that I'm living overseas we don't have as much in common to talk about.

With the opening of more modern cafés and bakeries in Yangon, the popularity of teashops among the middle class is waning. However, I highly doubt that they will disappear anytime soon. Owners will learn to keep up with the times, and there will

always be enough people who prefer tea made skillfully at a local venue as opposed to something poured from a packet. More importantly, teashops will remain a part of the social fabric: places where people can not only eat and drink, but also socialize and gossip as they have been doing all their lives.

Zin Teashop

Teashops in Myanmar open very early, usually at around 5 a.m., and offer a variety of dishes for breakfast. Some noodles dishes are only available in the morning and sell out quickly, so get there early.

92 A Pyay Rd., 10 Mile
Mingaladon Township
Yangon
(+95-1) 707-156

MON STATE

Michael Pugh spits like a local in Kyaiktiyo

Red splotches everywhere—on streets, sidewalks, storefronts, shirtfronts, and even stray dogs—signaled that I was in betel nut country. Popular across Myanmar, betel nut was pervasive throughout the town of Kyaiktiyo, with every other man on the street nursing a hefty plug between his cheek and gum.

I stepped over and around the stains, and the dogs, as my hotelier, Tun Tun, and I walked past open-air teashops and sleepy stores toward a large banyan tree at the center of town. The ground beneath the tree was stained almost completely red, like the floor of a slaughterhouse. At the center of this mess a frail old man stood behind a ramshackle wooden stall. The man smiled as we approached, exposing an impressive set of blood-red choppers. Tun Tun flashed his own crimson grin and greeted the man in Burmese.

This was Sitila, the local betel nut distributor.

A dark red seed from the betel (areca) palm, betel nut acts as a stimulant when mixed with lime powder. Chewing betel nut produces copious amounts of brick-red saliva, which explained all the splotches around town—and all the scarlet smiles.

The act of chewing betel nut in Myanmar goes back to the beginning of the country's recorded history. Long the habit of royalty, it is part of a tradition which states that dying men be given betel nut as a final earthly pleasure. I'd seen Tun Tun enjoy several such pleasures throughout the afternoon, and now he ordered two more: one for immediate use and one for bedtime.

Sitila plucked two fresh leaves out of a plastic bag, laid them flat on his counter, and smeared lime paste across them with a short knobby stick. He dropped small mounds of

crushed betel nut on top, drizzled tobacco over it all, and twisted each leaf up into a neat package the size of a bonbon.

Tun Tun shoved one in his mouth and the other into his pocket. He grinned and said, "You want try?"

Growing up in Wisconsin, I was no stranger to chewing tobacco. I figured betel nut wouldn't be much of a stretch. "Sure," I said.

Tun Tun spoke to Sitila, and the old man smiled at me.

I tried not to look at his teeth.

"Tobacco or no tobacco?" Tun Tun inquired.

"No tobacco."

The old man slathered a new leaf with lime paste and dropped a few broken hunks of nut atop it, repeating the ritual to create a package about half the size of Tun Tun's. He handed it to me and nodded with encouragement.

I popped the wad into my mouth and held it between my cheek and gum. Watching me, Tun Tun and Sitila gnawed on wads of their own.

"So, you chew it?" I asked.

Tun Tun nodded. His mouth was full of spit, and he tilted his head back to speak. "Chew, yes, but no swallow," he gurgled.

The leaf felt smooth and fresh in my mouth. The chunks of betel nut were sharp and unyielding. As I gnawed them, the leaf wrapper broke up and I could taste the gritty, alkaline paste and the peppery nut. I detected hints of baking chocolate, soil, and hand soap. I chewed and chewed and gathered saliva. Finally, I spat a gob of pinkish juice into the dust.

Tun Tun and Sitila smiled. "You like?" Tun Tun asked.

"Very good," I said. In fact, it wasn't bad. I began to feel a little buzz, like the kick of a double espresso.

I plucked a wad of kyat out of my pocket and gestured "how much?" But Sitila waved me off. This one was on the house.

Finding a betel nut vendor

With their portable stalls, betel nut sellers like Sitila conduct business on streets and sidewalks across Myanmar. If you don't spot one immediately, ask around. There's probably a stand right around the corner.

Custom ordering your betel

To order betel nut, simply specify whether you want tobacco, peppermint, or other spices added, and then watch the seller prepare your serving with betel nut and lime paste smeared on a leaf. Pop the morsel in your mouth, chew lightly, and—voilà!—you're participating in an age-old custom. A serving of betel nut can cost 40 to 100 kyat, depending upon the size of the "package" and the ingredients.

MANDALAY DIVISION

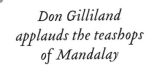

Don Gilliland applauds the teashops of Mandalay

Mandalay. The name alone conjures up cinematic visions of an exotic Burmese oasis. It's enough to convince first-time visitors they are about to embark on a fabulous road to adventure.

The reality, as I discovered during my first visit, is much different. Modern Mandalay is a loud, dusty, and fairly unattractive city that's clogged with a staggering amount of traffic—everything from motorbikes and trucks to trishaws and ox carts. Even the city's much-vaunted tourist attractions, such as Mandalay Hill and the Myanmar Palace and Fort complex, did not rank among my trip highlights.

But I found at least one must-see sight in Mandalay: the teashops. Besides offering a place to indulge in addictively sweet cups of hot tea and filling meals, teashops are where I can enjoy the company of affable and curious locals, and experience one of Myanmar's true institutions.

Natives of Mandalay claim that their teashops are the best in the country. The subtleties that determine such a lofty ranking—type of tea that's used, staff's tea-making skills, choice of noodle dishes—may be lost on most foreigners, but to a teashop connoisseur, it's no contest. Mandalay teashops rule! Whatever the time of day, I'll find something tasty to eat, from noodle and rice dishes to snacks such as *parathas* and *samosas*, along with cups of sweet hot tea.

Besides the menu offerings, what I love most about Mandalay teashops is the lively atmosphere. Regardless of the time of day, they are packed with chattering customers and buzzing with activity. These are not the sort of places where people dine and dash. Most people lazily pass the time away by eating, sipping tea, chatting with friends, or reading newspapers. Virtually all the teashops in town are open-air affairs and comforts don't extend much beyond ceiling fans (if the electricity is working) and plastic chairs or tiny stools. It's safe to say you can forget about frosty air conditioning, non-smoking sections, comfy seats, or Wi-Fi access.

Traditionally, teashops are perceived to be all-male bastions, but during my Mandalay teashop hopping, I often see tables full of women, couples, or even entire families. Although the clientele is no longer entirely masculine, for some odd reason the serving staff remains that way, always teenage boys. The constantly moving packs of young waiters bellow out orders to the kitchen and deftly wipe tables with just a flick of the wrist.

But what are those omnipresent kissing sounds? No, this is not an indication that anything amorous is transpiring between tables. The explanation is simple. Whenever a customer wants to order another bowl of noodles, or pay the bill, a symphony of lip-smacking commences. Making kissing sounds, I've discovered, is the way that locals get the waiter's attention.

As much as I try to adopt local customs, I just can't bring myself to do this. When it comes time for me to pay, and I've managed to catch the eye of a waiter (who is probably puzzled as to why I'm waving my hand and not making the kissing sound), the youngster does an amazing thing: he surveys the carnage of empty plates and cups on my table and quickly tabulates the total in his head. No need for a calculator or a cash register here!

I've visited at least a dozen teashops around Mandalay, ranging from tiny hole-in-the-wall joints to barn-sized monstrosities. My favorite is the spacious Minthiha branch at the corner of 28th and 72nd Streets. Besides the rare bonus of having an English-language menu on each table, Minthiha is spotlessly clean, the service is attentive, and the food is beyond yummy.

Most teashops in Myanmar get so busy that you sometimes find yourself sharing a table with other customers, and during one of my Minthiha visits that's exactly what happened. I was huddled over a plate of *htamin thoke* (rice salad), spoon in one hand and my Burmese phrasebook in the other, trying to digest both my meal and some new vocabulary words. Every few minutes I would call over my waiter, point to a particularly tricky word in the book, and ask him to pronounce it for me.

A local man sitting across the table noticed that I was studying my phrasebook and struck up a conversation. As we chatted, he would take the liberty of refilling my cup with the free Chinese tea offered from a thermos on each table. After he had finished his own plate of food, he paid his bill, shook my hand, and waved goodbye. It was only a few minutes later, when I was attempting to pay my own tab, that I realized this kind gentleman had already taken care of both of us.

Morning Star is another one of my favorite teashops in Mandalay. Although the equally excellent branch in Yangon is spacious and brightly lit, the Mandalay location is much smaller and a bit worn around the edges. But that's part of the appeal. Nothing fancy here, just good grub. I'll sometimes go in the morning with Myint Shin, my trishaw driver buddy, and order a bowl—or two—of *mondhi* (thick rice noodles with chicken in savory gravy). That, along with the prerequisite cups of tea (I can never order just one), always satisfies.

Another of my regular haunts is Shwe Pyi Moe Café, just a block from the southwest corner of the palace wall. Don't be surprised if you run into Lu Maw of the renowned Moustache Brothers troupe, who also frequents this popular teashop. During one of my visits to Shwe Pyi Moe, Lu Maw was sitting alone at a table in the middle of the room. Noticing me enter, a familiar face from the audience at the previous night's performance, he waved me over with an invitation to share his table. Lu Maw loves English slang and idioms, and I discovered that his use of such language is not confined to his nightly performances. Lu Maw's verbal barrage at the teashop—which included requests such as "Don't tell my wife!" after a particularly raunchy joke—felt like an extension of his show.

You may not run into any Moustache Brothers during your teashop tour, and perhaps a kind customer won't pick up your tab, but I venture to say you'll gain a better appreciation for Mandalay and its hidden charms. Who knows? You just might find yourself brave enough to make that kissing sound.

Minthiha Teashop

Minthiha has several other branches in Mandalay, including one on 38th Street between 83rd and 84th Streets.

Corner of 28th Street and 72nd Street
Mandalay
(+95-2) 33960, 64623

Morning Star

166 32nd St. (81/82)
Mandalay
(+95-2) 38519

Shwe Pyi Moe Café

There is also a new branch next to the Royal City Hotel on 27th Street.

25th Street (80/81)
Mandalay

Moustache Brothers

See page 27.

Miranda Bruce-Mitford explains Buddhist etiquette in Bagan

The ancient city of Bagan lies embraced by the Ayeyarwady River, where it swings eastward toward the Shan Hills. Nearly a thousand years ago this was a mighty Buddhist city of pagodas, monasteries, and monks. Of course there were houses and lay people too, but all life revolved around the upkeep of the monasteries and the worship of the Buddha.

Sadly, the houses have long gone, and the people with them. Bagan stands ruined on an arid dusty plain. Of its former grandeur, thousands of religious monuments remain, in varying states of decay. Although no one lives here, it stands for the people of Myanmar as the pinnacle of their ancient Buddhist culture. A café owner once told me that he prayed to be reborn in his next life as a *nat*, or spirit. That way he would be able

to spend eternity drifting happily and watching over the pagodas of Bagan.

For me too this is a place of great spirituality. I have been here often. I feel drawn as though by an invisible thread. I feel all of it: the river, the dust, the shimmering heat, the light of the late sun on the red-bricked monuments, the thick stillness of the air. Many times I have climbed shoeless up the narrow dark stairs to the high terrace of the Sulamani Pahto and waited quietly for the sun to sink orange behind the river. A profound calm washes over me as I sit, insignificant against the weight of the past.

During one of my visits to Bagan, I was escorting a group of elderly travelers around the main tourist circuit. It was late afternoon of our second day in town and I lagged behind at Shwesandaw Paya—a distinctive, white, pyramid-shaped pagoda—while our guide, Zaw, led the group to view the gigantic reclining Buddha, which lay in a low, cramped building nearby.

I can't remember what I was doing, maybe photographing some reliefs, but as I walked toward the reclining Buddha I heard shouting. I rounded a corner to see my group gesticulating angrily at five young Italians. The Italians, in turn, were shouting back. This behavior was quite out of character for these elderly, educated travelers. When they saw me, they shouted even louder.

"Quick," said Zaw, "Sort this out before you all get deported."

"What's happened?"

"Those two girls were sitting up on the image, next to the Buddha's face, having their photos taken. Luckily there aren't any other Burmese around or it would be a serious incident."

I looked from my angry group to the bewildered and defiant young Italians. How to explain to them the enormous sacrilege of a woman's "unclean" lower body coming into contact with the head of the Buddha—the seat of his Enlightenment? How could I deflate this situation, as everyone clearly expected me to do?

"It's okay, you didn't know," I said. "This place, it's sacred, like a church. Holy." I made the sign of the cross, and several ladies in my group nodded severely. "Imagine this was St Peter's in Rome. You know, St. Peter's? Well, would you sit on the altar to have your photo taken?" I patted the Buddha's podium, and with much waving of arms I put my point across.

Gradually the mood changed. The young travelers, shocked to find that they had committed such a grave offense, became embarrassed and regretful. To them, this was just a beautiful place that had once been a great city. They hadn't thought that the pagodas were still holy. They hadn't meant to upset anyone. Realizing their discomfort, Zaw and the elderly tourists were at once all reassurance and kindness.

"Never mind." ... "It was a simple mistake." ... "Anyone could have done it." ... "Enjoy your holiday." And with that, we parted.

By now it was getting late. The group was tired and wanted to go back to the hotel and change for dinner. Hot and weary, we piled into three bullock carts for the slow, jerky, but infinitely pleasing journey back to the riverside.

"Ooh, isn't this fun!"

"How nice not to see any cars!"

"Isn't it peaceful?"

Then suddenly, one woman muttered, "Silly people." At once they all murmured their assent.

"But they were so young," said another, as though that explained it all. There was a pause. "And after all, everything is so different here."

Zaw looked at me with a wry smile. It had been a long day and thank goodness we'd managed to salvage that one. With a leap he jumped from the cart and with a small bow held out his hand to me.

"Care for a walk in the dark?" he asked. I took his hand and hopped out. We stood together and watched as our charges were driven off into the Bagan night.

Buddhist etiquette

At pagodas and monasteries around Myanmar you will see signs such as "No Footwear Allowed," or grin-inducing variations such as "No Footwearing." Not only does this mean that you should not wear shoes, but you also need to take off your socks before entering. This goes for all temples, even those disused and/or in ruins. If you're on a tour of temples and pagodas, it can be a nuisance to constantly undo laces, so it's best to wear slip-ons or flip-flops. You should also do your best to dress appropriately, meaning long pants for men and skirts for women, preferably long but at least below the knee. Definitely no shorts! Shoulders should be covered; sleeveless shirts and tank tops are considered improper.

When sitting on the floor of a temple, it's best to sit cross-legged, or for women, with legs folded behind. As the feet are the lowest part of the body and considered unclean, one should never point them at a Buddha image or at another person seated in worship. Also, women are prohibited from approaching or touching Buddha figures in many pagodas. Male or female, if walking past people seated on the floor, you should lower your head as though bowing slightly. The head is the most sacred part of the body, so you are showing respect by symbolically not standing higher than another. Yes, all of this can be a hassle, but remember to be respectful of Buddhist etiquette while you are in the country.

Sunset tip

The tall Shwesandaw Paya is the most popular pagoda in the Bagan area for watching sunsets. The large terrace at the top makes a great vantage point. Another nice, less crowded spot for sunset viewing is Minyeingon Pagoda (see page 99).

Manjit Kaur flakes out on holiday in Bagan

The first time I tasted tamarind flakes was just after moving to Myanmar in 1993. That year, taking a break from my job in Yangon, I visited the famous pagoda ruins in Bagan. On the bedside table in my hotel room, in place of the usual fruit basket, was a lacquerware bowl full of what looked like candy, the tiny pieces wrapped in rice paper.

After I took the paper off, I was struck by how unusual it looked—thin circular-shaped layers of brown candy with a light coating of sugar on each one. I popped it into my mouth and an integration of sweet and sour flavors immediately flooded my taste buds. I savored the lush levels of ripe fruit, the sugar masking hints of light acidity. What were these delightful sweets?

When I was out with my guide, he told me that they were tamarind flakes. In Asia, a large percentage of tamarind, a seductively fleshy fruit, is used as a spice and to make curries. But in Myanmar, tamarind is more commonly eaten in the form of tamarind flakes, as bonbons. I discovered this custom when I went out with a group of friends to a restaurant in Bagan the next evening. At the end of our meal, the waiter brought out a bowl of tamarind flakes and left it in the middle of the table. Like the others in my party, I helped myself. As we left the restaurant, I stopped by the gift shop and bought a few bags to take with me.

During my stay in Bagan I spent six full days sightseeing, cycling around the old pagodas, and relaxing. On my fourth day in the hotel, I noticed the housekeeper staring at me and acting peculiar whenever she was in my room. I told my guide about it, thinking he would know the reason. Perhaps I was wearing my *longyi* the wrong way.

My guide asked me if I was still consuming the tamarind flakes I had bought. I told him yes. I had been eating them when I read a book before going to bed each night. He advised me that eating too many tamarind flakes was not really a good idea, and could cause severe stomach upset. But this did not explain the housekeeper's unusual behavior, so I persisted. Finally, he smiled and told me a story.

According to legend, several centuries ago there was a Bagan king who was married to a barren queen. After being informed that tamarind enhanced a women's sexuality, he ordered sweets to be made from the tamarind fruit. The result was tamarind flakes. The king fed his queen the now sweets and eventually she gave birth to twins. Even in Myanmar today, my guide said, it is believed that tamarind contains "special" properties. I began to wonder if I couldn't just make a fortune coming up with a new way to market tamarind flakes.

That night, I made arrangements to go out for dinner with my guide at Sarabha in Old Bagan. The restaurant serves wonderful local, Chinese, and European cuisine, along with fine wines. During dinner, the restaurant presented a puppet show depicting scenes from the *Jataka* (a collection of classic Buddhist fables). This was followed by a performance featuring dancers dressed as *nat*. One of the dancers, acting out the part of Ma Hnai Lay, a child spirit, began distributing some sweets to the audience. My guide urged me to go up and receive one, saying, "This is a good sign." I looked at what the *nat* dancer had given me, and I couldn't hide my amazement. There it was again, tamarind flakes!

When I returned to my seat I asked my guide what he meant by "a good sign."

"Well, if you recall the legend I told you about tamarind flakes, I never really told you the ending."

"Yes you did, you said the queen had twins."

"Well, yes and no. There is more to it. Yes, the Queen had twins, but one of the twins died and became this *nat* child spirit, the one you just saw dancing. When you received a tamarind flake from this child spirit, it means you are now blessed to receive children."

The next day I boarded my flight back to Yangon. After getting comfortable in my seat, my mind started to drift, thinking of my experiences in Bagan. Suddenly, I heard my name. A flight attendant came over and handed me a plastic bag. "Madame, I believe this is yours. Your guide insisted you take this home."

MANDALAY & CENTRAL MYANMAR

I opened the bag and was surprised to find a beautifully carved wooden box. I opened it, and there yet again were tamarind flakes. They were wrapped in white netting, along with a thank-you card that said "The Secrets of Bagan." I felt quite guilty. Did my guide suspect my risque thoughts on marketing tamarind flakes?

I reached into the box and picked out one of the candies. I unwrapped it and placed it onto my tongue. Closing my eyes, I thought, who am I to exploit these sweets? They should be left as they are, in this magical place, preserving tradition.

Sarabha Restaurant

This restaurant is divided into two parts. I recommend the front section facing the main road.

Main Road (near Sarabha Gate)
Old Bagan
(+95-62) 70125

Tamarind flake tours

Robert Carmack, of Asian Food Tours, is another tamarind flake addict. He adds, "My partner, Morrison, and I were taken by the sweet and slightly sour taste of tamarind flakes the first time we ate them in Bagan. We sleuthed the manufacturer in Chauk (about a two-hour drive from Bagan), where we saw huge piles of taffy-like tamarind pulp sitting on dusty tables along the roadside, readied for production. Inside, literally hundreds of girls were rolling the fruit "leather"

through antique cylinders, reminiscent of an old top-loading washing machine. Then, in a dust storm of confectioners' sugar, they manually cut each layer with dime-sized cookie cutters, piling them five high, and wrapping each pile in individual tissues. Quite a sight! We now take our food tour groups to the Chauk factory whenever we visit Bagan.

www.asianfoodtours.com

SHAN STATE

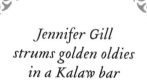

Jennifer Gill strums golden oldies in a Kalaw bar

The people of Myanmar are music lovers. In every town, on every street, there is at least one person playing guitar on his front stoop. A bookshop owner I visit in Yangon has his axe leaning against the wall among stacks of old hardcover books. We play Beatles songs for each other. In Kandawgyi Lake Park I listen to a group of rebellious teenagers take turns on the guitar after passing around a plastic bottle full of moonshine.

I take this love of music as a good sign. A sign of hope and passion and soulfulness. I've never understood people who say they aren't into music.

When I reach the Shan State town of Kalaw, I'm not at all surprised to hear other travelers talk of a bar that has guitars decorating the walls. The Hi-Bar might just be the smallest bar in the world. I arrive with two female friends, and with the help of five local men, we manage to pack the place.

When one of the local patrons excuses himself to go to the loo, I realize that there is nowhere for a woman to "go." As local women don't usually socialize in bars, the broom closet of a bathroom at the Hi-Bar contains only one urinal and, with its frosted glass door, allows the gentleman's backside to remain visible as he takes a leak. Charming. And it looks as if someone has employed the use of hyperbole in that "guitars all over the walls" statement. There is one lone guitar on the wall, and like every other guitar I have found in the country, the strings are old and it's out of tune.

We have the bartender turn off the ubiquitous Iron Cross video so I can play. And I become a super-cool guitar-playing chick once again, reprising similar performances from the beaches of Bali, ex-pat bars in Cambodia, and the banks of the Ganges River in India. Why just the night before I was rocking out John Denver covers at the request of a guesthouse owner.

I do every song I learned in my first three years of playing the guitar. Thus, my set might be qualified as somewhat "classic," and it causes the owner to ask my age. One of my friends, thinking she's saving me from some horrible embarrassment, tries to cover for me, saying that I just like old songs. All this because I happen to remember the lyrics to "Jack and Diane." I wonder what the younger generation of mediocre guitar players is strumming these days. Britney Spears? Linkin Park?

As is often the case, one smiling gentleman in the bar watches me attentively. He says he's never seen a woman play so well. I imagine he's never seen a woman play at all. My only hope is that his impression of me and what I represent—as a woman and as a Westerner—is equally as positive as my perception of these kind and gentle musical people.

Eventually the evening ends for one simple reason: three girls full of beer and no bathroom we can use. Even with that setback, I judge the evening a success. The audience was mostly attentive and always happy, a nice balance of tourists and locals brought together once again by the lube of life: beer and music.

Hi-Bar

The bar is also known as Hi Snack and Drink. It is located in central Kalaw, near the intersection of Aung Chantha Road.

Merchant Road
Kalaw

Advice for nomadic guitar players

Bring your own capo and pick. Also, a great gift to offer a guitar player in Myanmar is a new set of strings.

GENERAL MYANMAR

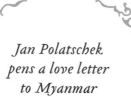

Jan Polatschek
pens a love letter
to Myanmar

I could begin my first letter about my travels in Myanmar this way:

I am relaxing at a sidewalk café at a busy intersection of downtown Yangon. Dizzy from the dust and the teeming traffic, I munch on breaded, deep-fried greens (don't ask) and wash down my oily snack with an energy-boosting glass of juice, freshly squeezed from a stick of sugar cane. I add a splash of lime.

Or I could begin this way:

I am digging in at a crowded outdoor restaurant in Mandalay. An animated assembly line of men and women first knead, then roll and grill hot *chapattis* that accompany my curry and Chinese tea.

But I will begin my letter this way, with my favorite image of Myanmar:

After a tour of a lakeside tribal market, where I nearly choke to death on my first puff of a cheroot, I am sitting in a long, wooden motorboat, cruising on sun-drenched Inle Lake. Tun Win, my patient driver, navigates past the leg-rowing fishermen into the narrow channels. We are surrounded by floating tomato farms and flower nurseries.

Suddenly from a distance I hear a gentle "hello." A young boy, tending his fields, paddles over to us in his wooden canoe, smiles, and tosses me a gift of purple and yellow "daisies."

This is Myanmar. Polite. Kind. Welcoming. Friendly. Surprising.

"You've Got to Be Carefully Taught," the controversial song from the Broadway musical *South Pacific,* comes to mind. The theme of the lyrics is that young children are naturally friendly and tolerant of everyone, so, "You've got to be taught to hate and fear ... You've got to be carefully taught."

Happily, in Myanmar the opposite is true. Parents teach their children to welcome foreigners. I observed one young woman grasp the arm of her son to demonstrate the proper method of greeting a stranger. And just like on the lake, as I take my city strolls, I am hailed by choruses of "hello" and "goodbye," and vigorous waves and bright smiles. "See you later alligator," followed quickly by "after a while crocodile," are the parting words of the cheerful young shop girls. How enchanting! I am moved by all this happy talk.

To be clear, Myanmar is not a destination for the finicky, faint-hearted, demanding, impatient, sanitation-conscious tourist. There are almost no traffic lights or streetlights in Mandalay. There are frequent power blackouts all over the country. The cities and small towns are just plain dusty. Main roads are paved, but shoulders and side streets are dirt. Dust migrates around town following the swirl of traffic, coating all the green leaves red. Everyone is sweeping, sweeping, sweeping.

Despite the dust and the din, I love it here!

I am having fun, carefully threading my way down the streets and around the markets. Sidewalks are teeming with books, brassieres, boxer shorts, shoes, pink party dresses, T-shirts (all too small for my extra-large frame), new and used tools, assorted electronics, pots, pans, toothbrushes, luggage, soccer balls, plastic toys, CDs, VCDs, batteries, and balloons.

In the midst of this mercantile madness there are abundant miniature outdoor teashops. A thermos of hot tea and several dainty teacups sit on the tiny wooden tables that are surrounded by half-size plastic chairs. Men relax and chat about whatever the men of Myanmar chat about. I sit among them. They are amused and pleased with my awkward attempts to speak Burmese.

Folks don't own much here. Their treasure lies with family and friends. On any street, on any day, young mothers nurse their infants, boys walk with their arms around their brothers, and girls walk hand in hand with their friends. Gentle, smiling men offer me rides in their taxis, trishaws, and horse carts. I ask you, where else in the world can I take a horse cart to the airport?

And so, let's hitch up the cart. There are glorious golden temples to discover, serene Buddha images to contemplate, and tall teak towers to climb.

But first, for an energy boost, another stack of hot *chapattis*, please, to scoop up my curry.

There are many memorable sights in Myanmar. My favorite? Everyone smiling and saying "hello."

I love it here!

Favorite teashops

There are outdoor teashops in cities and towns all over Myanmar. My favorites are those near Sule Paya in Yangon, and the one across the street from the Unity Hotel in Mandalay, near the corner of 27th Street and 82nd Street. On that same corner, the evening-only *chapatti* stand, Nay Café, is also wonderful.

PAYING IT FORWARD

Suggestions for giving back while you're on the road

Noticing our arrival, the young village girl squealed with glee and ran toward my travel partner and me, her hand outstretched. "Money present!" she exclaimed.

Sadly, such monetary expectations are becoming more common in tourist areas around Myanmar. It doesn't matter whether they are young children, old hill tribe women, or cheroot-smoking gents—many of the locals are now wise to the generous ways of foreign tourists.

Most often foreigners have a sincere desire to help poor people in Myanmar, especially in the wake of Cyclone Nargis. But rather than acting as a walking ATM, passing out bank notes, what can a tourist do to help those in need? Myanmar does not have the wealth of Western-based NGOs or aid organizations that are often found in other Asian nations, so the needy are still quite dependent on individual donors.

There are many schools and orphanages that need money, school supplies, and even just a little personal attention, as Ray Waddington finds out when he visits an orphanage near the shores of Inle Lake and encourages the bright children in their studies by setting personal challenges. Tour guide Kyaw Zay Latt is also a frequent visitor and donor to orphanages around the country, and he offers some thoughtful and practical ideas for helping the children.

From constructing cisterns and providing books for a local library, to aiding "orphaned" grandmothers and serving as a "godparent" for orphaned children, each essay focuses on a specific need. You will also learn what's appropriate to give, particularly from Janis Nieder, who provides a comprehensive list of suggestions. Keep in mind that a donation can include more than just money. If you have spare time, you might follow in the footsteps of Jan Polatschek, who volunteers to teach the English class of the personable receptionist at his hotel. Or gain

Buddhist nun taking morning alms in Nyaungshwe

inspiration from Viola Woodward, who helps to landscape and paint a Yangon preschool and the neighboring monastery. This is one of the chapter's most poignant stories, since the Growing Together School was severely damaged by the cyclone.

The biggest debate about helping is whether or not tourists should directly give money. Some are adamant that doing this sets a bad example, while others believe that every little bit helps. I suppose my feelings are somewhere in the middle on this issue. I certainly don't think I should be giving money to every open hand I see. But for individuals and families I've met during my travels, I often hand them an envelope with cash before I leave town. In most cases it is for a certain purpose, such as paying a child's school fees or buying new clothes. Once, I gave some money to two children I had met, wanting to ensure that they had enough for school and other expenses. One child gave it to his mother and requested that I not tell his father. "I worry he will take it and buy whiskey," the boy said. That's always the dilemma. If you do give money, will it be put to good use?

In many cases, the answer is yes. On a trip to Bagan, I noticed that the thatched roof of the house of one of the families I had befriended had several large holes in it. This made for nice stargazing at night, but when it rained the family was forced to seek shelter with the neighbors. Upon leaving, I gave them some money, and when I returned four months later, I discovered a new roof on the house. Money well spent? Definitely!

Yangon Division

XXXXXXXXXXXXXXXXXXXXXXXXXXXXXXXX
oooooooooooooooooooooooooooooooo

*Ma Thanegi
offers advice on choosing
a charity in Yangon*

While the cities of Myanmar aren't rife with beggars compared to other developing nations, the practice is becoming more common, even in the relatively prosperous city of Yangon. It is understandable to want to hand out money and other items when you encounter poor people, but please think about the consequences of these gifts before you give them.

The money that children receive from begging can encourage others to follow their lead and won't help free them from poverty. As with adults who beg, it can get them into the habit of looking for handouts and becoming dependent on such "gifts." You might also occasionally see monks or nuns asking for money. They are fakes. The Buddhist Order explicitly forbids monks from handling money.

Although the people of Myanmar are poor, they are proud, and accepting money, especially from strangers, is very much against their tradition. Thankfully, there are several well-run organizations in Yangon that cater to those in need.

Eden is a small NGO where mentally and physically handicapped children and young adults come for physical therapy, to study, and to play. Instruction is geared to the specific needs of each student. This is a warm, close-knit community center where youngsters can enjoy themselves, whether celebrating birthdays or learning to paint.

Among the young people this organization has assisted is Ko Htaik. In his early twenties and suffering from cerebral palsy, he has attended the center for over a decade and is now an informal instructor, helping to look after and teach the younger ones. He is an inspiration to other students for his humor and total lack of self pity. In spite of his handicap he is full of fun, cracks jokes, and paints lovely watercolors.

Commonly known as **Wingaba Home for Girls**, The Myanmar Women's Development Association and Home for Girls was founded in the 1940s. This NGO is home to nearly a hundred orphans and children from poor families. They attend regular school classes, and after graduating they are able to find work in Yangon thanks to a job placement program and network of local donors. The facilities also include a nursery school where the home's older students assist with the teaching. These girls grow so attached to the toddlers that it is heartbreaking when they must leave the younger ones and move on to regular schools at the end of the year.

At Wingaba the wounds run deep. One girl who was adopted at the age of two by a childless couple was re-

Yangon & Southern Myanmar

turned when she was twelve after her "parents" were able to have children of their own. They never came to see her again; she is now in her mid-twenties. Another girl was taken in by a kindly older neighbor after she was orphaned. The man re-named her Pwint, which means "Blossom," in the hopes that her future would bloom. But the man was too old to earn much money, and his grown sons and daughters insisted that the girl be given away, for they had several children of their own to feed. Unable to look after her, the man sent her to the home.

Operating under the Social Welfare Department, **Mary Chapman School for the Hearing Impaired** has been in the same location since the 1920s. The principal and teachers do what they can under the restraints of a limited budget, and it is here that the students—many of whom attend regular schools—learn crafts and sign language. They also find a nurturing environment. For example, one deaf boy in his early teens is now slowly losing his sight to an incurable genetic disease. A group of his peers looks after him tenderly, but at the same time making him feel as independent as is possible. Their time together is not one of despair or sorrow, but one of camaraderie, full of affectionate teasing and warm compassion, never pity.

The monasteries of Myanmar have a strong, traditional network that allows monks to send orphans from their villages, however remote, to monasteries and orphanages around the country. The **Parahita Kyar Mo-nastic School** is one such place. *Kyar* means "tiger," and many "tigers" from this orphanage have grown up to become educated men in good professions.

Funerals are an important way to honor deceased persons and their families. Even the poorest families would be very ashamed if they could not afford a decent funeral for their loved ones. The **Free Funeral Services Society** is an NGO that offers such services to the poor, ensuring that they are able to hold up their heads in the community. More importantly, it has also started providing free health care. Run by award-winning actor and film director U Kyaw Thu and his writer friends, this respected group has branches in many parts of Myanmar.

There are also several homes in Yangon for elderly people without families or financial support. At these homes, you can donate money or bags of rice, or even host a lunch or dinner. Caretakers will cook the meal if you give them the money to shop for the necessary groceries. Alternatively, you can ask about the number of residents and give each one a sum of money (using both hands to present it to them) that can be used for their personal needs.

If you would like to help the disadvantaged in Myanmar, consider contributing to one or more of these organizations.

What to give

At places that look after orphaned, abandoned, and poor children whose families cannot afford to feed them, donations of money or food are always welcome. You can also give clothes, books, notebooks, and pens for the children to use in school. At many primary schools in rural areas, the children especially need notebooks, pencils, and pens. The schools might also need new blackboards, desks, chairs, pencil sharpeners, or even repairs to a leaking roof. It is acceptable to distribute pocket money to the children, perhaps 500 or 1,000 kyat, which can be used to buy small personal items that the orphanage can't provide. Some institutions may not allow such cash gifts so ask first. As an afternoon treat, you can bring cakes or ice cream.

Yangon charities

Eden Centre for the Handicapped

56 4th St. (off Wa Oo Street)

Insein Township
Yangon
(+95-1) 640-399
www.edencentre.org

Free Funeral Services Society

Brahma Vihara Pariyatti Monastery
Thudathana Street
Ward 16/2
Thingangyun Township
Yangon
(+95-1) 578-183/184, 560-333
www.ffssyangon.com

Kyimyindine & Insein School for the Blind

This school operates under the Social Welfare Department where the budget is limited. The students here learn Braille and crafts, as well as computer skills.

152 Panbingyi St.
Kyimyindine Township
Yangon
(+95-1) 535-548

Mary Chapman School for the Hearing Impaired

2 Thantaman St.
Dagon Township
Yangon
(+95-1) 221-872
www.mm-marychapman.org

Myanmar Women's Development Association & Home for Girls

17 Wingaba St.
Bahan Township
Yangon
(+95-1) 542-925

Parahita Kyar Monastic School for Orphaned Boys

Kamayut Dudayon Street
Ward Number 6
Hlaing Township
Yangon
(+95-1) 524-852

Viola Woodward beautifies a Yangon pre-school and monastery

"Let's go on a field trip," I suggested to my third grade class.

Twelve beaming faces looked up at me and cheered.

I was in my second year of teaching at a private international school in Yangon, and I wanted to get my students out of the classroom in order to broaden their experiences. They were a joy to teach and eager to learn, but most of them were from well-off families and had been kept relatively sheltered. I asked the parents for ideas, and we decided to visit the United Nations Office near Kandawgyi Lake. That trip was a success, so we made a second field trip the following month to a garment factory on the outskirts of Yangon.

Following that, our next three trips were to the same place: the Growing Together School. I had discovered this community pre-school earlier while doing an online search, looking for volunteer opportunities in Yangon for Barry, my fiancé, who was planning to visit me. One of the requests on the school's website included a garden project, which sounded perfect for Barry, who grows beautiful roses and lilacs in his garden in Vermont.

After my desperate cry from halfway around the world—"I can't live here without you!"—Barry left his painting business and joined me for three months. The first time he and I biked to the Growing Together School, the front yard looked desolate: just weeds and sand, with some piles of wood in a corner. The school had budgeted funds for landscaping, so we went to a gardening place at People's Park and inquired about plants, flowers, and sand. After getting approval to spend the money, we played a waiting game as deliveries were scheduled and re-scheduled.

In a few short weeks, the school's yard was magically transformed. The garden in the front was planted with palm trees, along with grass and plants inside the fence. Following another suggestion by Barry, we added a brick path/entryway. Then the scavenger hunt began. We found a pump sprayer at a garden center, and made several trips downtown to "Paint Street" to buy high-quality paint, primer, brushes, TSP, scrapers, paint stirrers, rollers, and a roller pan. We couldn't find the pan, so we improvised with a cardboard box and plastic bags.

We tracked down maroon paint for the school's fence to match the porch railings, but another decision remained. What to do about the cement wall that the school shared with the Zawtika Monastery? We asked the monks for permission to paint the wall, and they happily agreed to the idea, opting for "monk red" as their color of choice.

Then it was finally time for the paint professional to begin his work. Barry cleaned the monastery wall with bleach, scrubbed it with TSP, primed it, and gave it three coats of paint. When all was finished the wall looked good. So good, in fact, that the monks decided that their gate needed painting too. Upon consultation, the monks requested peach as a contrasting color. We also fixed the lettering above the gate, the holes in the cement, and the windows in the wall.

At that point someone noticed that the inside wall looked shabby, so Barry cheerfully (I think!) agreed to continue painting the interior of the monastery. By now, it was getting expensive to buy so much paint, so a yellow starburst above the gate sufficed as the final touch.

When I showed photos of the school to my third graders, they expressed an interest in donating plants to complete the entranceway. I checked with my principal, and he supported the idea. Teachers also donated money for plants, and we bought an additional assortment of flowers to add more color and fragrance to the garden. We brought about ten potted plants to the school on our first field trip, along with books and crayons for the pre-schoolers. My students enjoyed their time with these little kids so much, playing games and singing songs together, that we made plans to return.

Two years before, I had left my tomatoes ripening on the vines in Vermont to travel thousands of kilometers to teach at a small school in a country about which I barely knew anything. Now I was returning home with so many wonderful memories and hoping that I had left some small impressions behind in a small corner of Yangon, along with a beautifully painted monastery gate and a lovely flower garden.

Growing Together School

At the time of publication, the school was heavily damaged by Cyclone Nargis. The once-charming garden and carefully painted fence are now in need of new volunteers to help bring this wonderful place back to life.

5 Theingi St.
Taketa Township
Yangon
www.growingtogethermyanmar.org
contact.gtf@gmail.com

Meeting needs

Myanmar is one of the poorest Asian countries, and there is always a need for help. Any traveler interested in volunteering in Myanmar will find lots of informal opportunities once in the country. Looking online is one place to start, which is how I found out about Growing Together. On the school's old website, a garden was specifically listed among the needs. That may not strike most people as a big need, but in Myanmar such beautification projects are quite important to people. I noticed that even small shacks in the surrounding neighborhood had gardens, even if they were just a few pots of tropical plants or vines creeping up rickety fences.

YANGON & SOUTHERN MYANMAR

YANGON & SOUTHERN MYANMAR

Painting a monastery

Many monasteries around Myanmar have walls and gates that are in need of a new coat of paint—as we soon discovered. After we started painting the school, one thing led to another... and then there were the monks with ideas of their own. They were as pleased as punch that these Americans dropped from the sky and painted their gate and walls so beautifully! They gave Barry a book of Buddhist stories in English as a thank-you present. If you visit a monastery that looks a bit shabby, ask if the monks would like a paint job. Most would be thrilled to have volunteers help with such a task. In downtown Yangon, paint supplies are available at many shops on 30th Street ("Paint Street").

Sandra Gerrits
feels under pressure
at a Yangon blind school

In Myanmar, as in most other countries, blind people have fewer job opportunities. That's why I was happy to find the St. Mary's Workshop for the Blind in Yangon. The school offers massages provided entirely by its blind staff, giving the students a means to support themselves and their families.

When I paid my first visit, I thought I might have come to the wrong place. Located behind what appeared to be an abandoned church, the unassuming brick structure didn't look like a school at all. The big barn-like building turned out to be the massage "salon" and was housed on the property with several smaller buildings where the blind students and their families have been living since the 1960s after the original school for the blind was nationalized and those buildings taken over by the government. These "new" buildings at the current location were donated by foreign benefactors.

The massage space is nothing fancy. The main room has a concrete floor with five simple wooden platforms; there are three additional platforms in a separate room. Each platform is covered with a bamboo mat and includes a pillow for comfort. Still, St. Mary's turned out to be one of the best massage places I've visited in Yangon—not just for the local style of massage but for all types.

The first time I visited they asked whether I preferred having a masseuse or a masseur. I thought that was a nice option, although for me it didn't matter. I just wanted a good massage. Most people know about Thai massage, but the style in Myanmar is quite different. While Thai massage involves a lot of stretching, a local massage is done mostly with the pressing of thumbs and fingers. The masseurs say that this "opens up the muscles." It sure feels that way to me.

This type of massage is a great way of detoxing and energizing your body.

It is especially therapeutic when your muscles are cramped and stiff after a long plane ride or an overnight bus journey. I also like getting one just before I am ready to board a flight back home. In general, I enjoy softer massages, and local massages can be a tad on the painful side. The masseurs at some places seem to think they aren't doing their job properly if they don't give me a massage as hard as most locals prefer it. Then again, I'm a wimp. Fortunately, the students at St. Mary's will ask how firm I want the pressure.

On more than one occasion I went to St. Mary's with very sore muscles, only to leave with a spring in my step. I felt as if I'd had a seriously good workout, but with a more relaxing end result. And by having it done by these talented blind students, I also always feel that I'm contributing to a good cause.

St. Mary's Workshop for the Blind

The massages at the school are not done on the clock, so it is not unusual to have one that far exceeds the hour. Prices are very reasonable: 2,500 kyat for a one-hour massage. The traditional local massage can be a bit hard for most Westerners, but you can ask for a lighter version. The massage staff can speak a bit of English, although just enough to explain the massage options. It also depends on who is working there. Some of the children and adolescents can speak English better than the adult staff.

96 Kyundaw Rd.
Sanchaung Township
Yangon
(+95-1) 537-326

AYEYARWADY DIVISION

Sudah Yehuda Kovesh Shaheb befriends Chaungtha beach vendors

I was sitting on the beach in Chaungtha when I heard someone behind me say, "This is your first day, you are enjoying yourself. Tomorrow, you will enjoy even more."

I turned around to see who was making this optimistic prediction. A teenage girl stood with a batch of homemade green coconut leaf hats balanced on her head.

"What about the day after tomorrow then?" I asked her.

"Day after tomorrow you will be sad, because you will be getting ready to leave."

She was of slender build and had *thanaka* paste on her impish face. She told me her name was Tin Tin Aye. She was not sure of her age or her date of birth. I was saddened to hear that she had quit primary school six years earlier because her parents couldn't afford for her to continue. For the past three years she had been selling hats on the beach every day. If she was lucky, she could sell up to ten hats a day at 100 kyat each, bringing in a bit of extra income for her family.

We were soon joined by more young beach vendors, Pa Pa Win and E To Win, friends of Tin Tin Aye. These girls had also dropped out of school. During the weekend, when the beach was full with visitors from Yangon, the children did a brisk business selling hats and other items. But I had arrived on a Friday afternoon, and the crowds had not materialized yet, so they had time to sit around and chat. They told me how they made rounds on the beach early every morning, and after selling a few hats, returned home for breakfast. For the rest of the morning they busied themselves making more hats and other items to sell before heading back to the beach around noon.

The next morning, as I was having breakfast at my hotel with friends from Yangon, I saw the girls waiting outside. I decided to donate 100 kyat to each of them, the price of one hat, to help them begin the day. Later that morning, Pa Pa Win saw me on the beach and gave me a seashell bracelet. The next morning, the girls were once again waiting for me, this time handing me a seashell necklace.

After I expressed an interest in seeing the girls' village, Tin Tin Aye invited me to her house. She held my hand and guided me through the narrow streets, saying hello to her acquaintances along the way. We came to a cluster of open-windowed huts,

sitting amidst a fair amount of filth and clutter. Tin Tin Aye apologized that construction was not finished.

Her home was nothing more than a small square area of wooden slats resting on four strong pieces of lumber that held the structure aloft. Three sides had rudimentary wooden panels covered with plastic wrapping. There was no running water, and I do not remember seeing any electrical connections. The cooking was done on a raised platform adjoining the house, with wood for fuel. There was no place to hang clothes inside; just a neatly folded stack of belongings in one corner. Tin Tin Aye's father, a jovial man with teeth reddened from chewing betel nut, greeted me warmly. Her mother also seemed genuinely happy that I was visiting her home.

The girls then took me on a tour of the rest of the village. At a small grocery shop nearby, I bought some noodles and eggs for their families. By the time I had finished paying the shopkeeper, a crowd had started to form around us, the usual curiosity about a foreigner visiting the village. Besides buying this food, I was thinking about what else I could do for my new friends. It was such a pity that I couldn't get them to resume their studies, but I had to respect the parents' decision to withdraw them from school.

Instead, the next day I asked the girls to come with me to the market. I wanted them to choose material with which they could make skirts and blouses. They were smiling from ear to ear at this treat. They chose pastel-colored fabric for themselves and ready-made clothes for their brothers.

Spending money to buy clothing, eggs, and a few kilos of rice is nothing. Helping three families cost me slightly more than a couple of cups of coffee at Starbucks. As for sacrifice, it's relative. I had been planning to fly to Sittwe later that week to see a friend, and then continue north to visit the ancient ruins at Mrauk U. But I thought about how much that trip would cost. The airfare to Sittwe alone would be enough for me to buy books, pencils, crayons, and clothes for every child in the village. I decided that instead of spending four days traveling to tourist places, simply in the name of adventure, I would use the money saved on such a trip and give it to these village girls and their families. The following day I took the children to a market where we bought shoes, clothing, and a variety of food.

During a return trip, three months later, I invited the families to come to Yangon. With the help of my friends there, I arranged accommodation at local homes, and a restaurant offered a discounted rate for food during their stay. I took them around to pagodas, amusement parks, and the zoo. This was their first trip to Yangon and they were thrilled.

I am always touched by the generosity of people who have little. We travelers give a bit of what we have, but the people of Myanmar offer so much compared to what they have. While the homemade gifts they presented to me when I left Chaungtha were nice, including items that were very important to them, like old photos, what was most precious to me was the gift of their friendship.

The gift of language

On later visits I was able to arrange for some of the children to take English classes at a nearby monastery, Sa Ka War Taung, whose head monk is U Pyin Nyar. I also gave notebooks, books, and food to the monks at the monastery, and donated a small amount of money for its building program, which includes the construction of a school. Tourists visiting Chaungtha are encouraged to visit any of the monasteries in town and make a donation toward the education of some children. To find a monastery, you can start at William Restaurant (the one on Bogyoke Street) in Chaungtha. The owner, William, also known as Win Htay, speaks good English and is very helpful. Ask him for the names of monasteries and schools in the area.

Lai Lai Chaungtha Beach Hotel

The rates are reasonable for a beachside resort. Foreigners pay $22 for a single room and $30 for a double. Locals pay less than half of that.

Chaungtha Beach
(+95-42) 22587
lailaibeach@lailaihotel.com.mm

MANDALAY DIVISION

Jan Polatschek teaches homonyms and idioms in Mandalay

I love Mandalay. I hate my hotel room. While looking for new lodging, I discover the Unity Hotel. At the reception desk is a lovely and gracious young woman named Nyi Nyi. With a smile, she says, "We will be happy to welcome you." I check in the next day.

After breakfast, before my climb up Mandalay Hill, I invite Nyi Nyi for coffee. She smiles. She declines.

The next day, before my tour of the nearby ancient capitals of Inwa, Amarapura, and Sagaing, I ask again. She smiles. She declines.

Finally, on the third day, after I return from my river trip to Mingun, where for good luck I pat the tail of a huge stone elephant, I try once more. Nyi Nyi smiles. "You have asked me three times. Now I will say yes."

Yes!

Public social relationships between men and women in Myanmar are conservative and discreet. A "date" means that the girl shows up with a chaperone—or two. Nyi Nyi introduces me to her cousin and a

friend. During our dinner, I comment on their excellent English skills. They tell me they attend an evening class at a local monastery school. I admit that many years ago, as a high school teacher in New York City, my specialty was teaching English to immigrant boys. "Juanita is tall. Conchita is taller than Juanita. Carmelita is the tallest." Nyi Nyi invites me to lead a class at her school.

The next evening we take trishaws to Nyi Nyi's language class, which is held at Thatmaga Yama Monastery on the east side of town. The head monk greets me warmly and escorts me to the classroom. Twenty-seven eager young adults await my lesson. They sit on long wooden benches, their notebooks and pens arranged on tables of wooden planks. The side walls are open to the air; the roof is woven bamboo. In the front of the room is a large modern whiteboard and markers.

For two hours, we progress from idioms (*pay through the nose, cat got your tongue*) to grammar (*ride, rode, ridden*), to spelling (*tough, thought, thorough*), to homonyms (*cite, sight, site*), to geography (*archipelago, volcano, caldera*), to religion (*priest, cardinal, rabbi*), and back again to idioms (*play it by ear*). English ain't easy. Everyone is curious. They ask personal questions. Married? Children? Age? And if I use a word they do not understand, someone opens a dictionary and reads aloud.

I'm on fire. I can feel my energy rising, as I am pressed and prodded by my conscientious students, who are active and enthusiastic and motivated. They remind me of the young boys I once taught in New York, determined to master a new language. "Mr. Jan, please explain, 'Pepsi beats the others cold.'"

In "remote" areas of the world that I've visited, English proficiency is a highly prized skill, yet the opportunity to study with native speakers is rare. Students appreciate even one class or a brief meeting with a caring and nurturing teacher. When I was in Indonesia, for example, I met a shy but motivated university student who was majoring in English literature. She confided that I was the first foreigner she had ever spoken to.

I suspect that is also the case with some of the students in this classroom. Nyi Nyi and her classmates share the same enthusiasm and gratitude that I found in other Asian countries. I use all my skills to encourage everyone to participate, but a few women are quiet and shy. Sitting in the front row, Nyi Nyi is also reticent. But she continues to smile. Like her classmates, she is happy. These optimistic students in Mandalay are thankful for any contact with the "outside" world. I am thankful for the opportunity to meet and teach such a wonderful group of charming young men and women.

After class I share a simple soup and rice supper with the head monk. He is also appreciative of my visit. "Please come again," he tells me. I *will* return to Mandalay. I love to teach. I hope I'm good. And dare I hope that Nyi Nyi will be there to share another dinner and another class?

Thatmaga Yama Monastery

This is also known as the Japan-Myanmar Monastery. Similar English-language classes are conducted at monasteries in towns throughout Myanmar. Regardless of the city, the staff at most hotels and guesthouses should be able to direct you to one where your teaching talents can be put to use.

62nd Street (28/29)
Mandalay

Win Thuya establishes a public library in Bagan

Apart from local government schools, when I was growing up in Bagan there were no places for students to enhance their educations, such as libraries, computer centers, or language institutes. The turning point in my life came at the age of twenty-two when I moved to Yangon and trained to become a tour guide. Here, in my country's biggest city, I found new challenges, new educational opportunities, and new experiences.

Those experiences included discovering libraries at the British Council and at the Alliance Française, where I took French classes. I like reading, and browsing the shelves and seeing so many books in one place was incredible for me. The

MANDALAY & CENTRAL MYANMAR

libraries seemed to have everything I could want. I observed a lot of youth who spent their time learning vigorously at the libraries in Yangon. I felt pity for my friends back in Bagan, who had no similar facilities where they could expand their knowledge.

This gave me the idea to start a library for the public—especially students—in Bagan. In Myanmar, millions of dollars are spent each year on various archaeological projects, but only a small percentage of money goes for public education. With the help of my employer, Gulliver Travels in Yangon, I found a building to rent in the community of New Bagan. After registering the library and getting a business license, we opened in August 2006.

The library's primary goals are to distribute books, journals, and newspapers, and to encourage a reading habit among local youth. The library opened with around eight hundred books and magazines, mostly in the Burmese language. This included secondhand books, out-of-print editions, new books, and also some English versions of Burmese novels. We started with just two bookshelves, two long tables, and a bench, all of which were donated. Since our opening we have added two more shelves and hundreds more books, thanks again to donations. We have a staff of two, and one of my friends takes care of the management.

You might think the opening of such a small library is not big news, but it is indeed for the people of New Bagan. This library is not for a minor-ity, but for all the people in the community. There is no charge to use it because we want it to be a place that the public can access easily. In the future we plan to hold symposiums and writers' conferences. We also want to organize summer classes such as English conversation, computer basics, and supplemental courses for those who are working in the tourist industry.

I am based in Yangon where I collect books, magazines, and journals. I usually take the donations with me when I return to visit my family; if I am unable to go myself, I arrange for friends to take them to the library.

Besides increasing the selection of books, my hope is that that the library will eventually expand to include multimedia and computer rooms. Though there is enough space for these facilities, there is not enough money to do everything I want to do. But with the help of donors and tourists who visit Bagan, we can make this a reality. It is my dream that Kuthodaw Library will play an important role in assisting Bagan's youth in their continuing quest for knowledge.

Kuthodaw Library

Near the morning market on the main road, the library is open daily but closed for an hour or two around lunchtime.

(+95-61) 60593
New Bagan
http://kuthodaw-library-bagan.blogspot.com/
www.gulliver-myanmar.com

nanopost@mail4u.com.mm
(Library)
wthuya@gmail.com (Win Thuya)

Magwe Division

Pascale Reinhardt savors a gentle breeze in Yenangyaung

The guesthouse where I stay in Yenangyaung overlooks rice fields and pagodas, which are nestled between sand dunes. Every evening I sit on the terrace and watch an incredible ever-changing sunset. My gaze crosses the wide Ayeyarwady River, traveling toward the Rakhaing Mountains. Seated on this terrace made of gray hand-carved stones, I write, rest, and reflect upon my encounters with the people I have met in this relatively isolated town. I am grateful that my traveler's luck has brought me here.

This guesthouse belongs to U Eric Trutwein. I met this remarkable man in Yangon upon the recommendation of mutual European friends who, like me, bring donations to Myanmar every year. Our encounter would lead me to discover Yenangyaung, an extraordinary community of open-hearted people. It's a place where I pledge to return as often as possible. Though it's not located near main tourist destinations, it is a worthwhile trip for anyone who wants to discover the simple and poignant side of rural life in Myanmar.

Eric chose his birthplace for the guesthouse, naming it Lei Thar Gone, meaning Gentle Breeze Inn. From uncultivated land, between waves of sand, he has created an incredibly peaceful haven. He constructed a bridge for a road, bored a deep well to find water, cleared the grounds, and built the stone house. Fossilized wood pieces surround flowerbeds, and stone statues decorate every path. Pottery hosts flourishing plants, tin-plated watering cans wait by the lily pond, mango bushes bear mature fruit, and the bougainvillea and rose bushes blaze with colors.

The garden is an incredible luxury in this dry zone, where the porous land gulps water, and traditional village cisterns dry out in a matter of months. Locals sometimes have to walk ten kilometers to fetch water. One can meet them on footpaths, carrying their precious loads on shoulder poles. Building cement cisterns is one of the many projects sustained by the NGO that Eric heads in Yangon. These cisterns are a vital asset for the poor people living in the area.

Lei Thar Gone is more comfortable than many hotels I stayed at in Myanmar. Two terraces shadowed from the sun host my tai chi sessions. The larger terrace, like a boat's prow, gives me the feeling of sailing a silent ship over the wide landscape. Inside, my quarters are cozy and decorated tastefully with local fabrics and bamboo furniture. A Shan mulberry paper guestbook contains the memories of the few former guests, and I find fresh fruit, bottled water, drinks, and snacks in the refrigerator. Although they speak little English, the staff members do everything they can to make my stay pleasant.

Lei Thar Gone serves as a resource for people interested in understanding, and supporting, life in this arid region of central Myanmar. As anywhere in the country, but perhaps more so in this area, people are struggling to get by. Some of the adults migrate to bigger cities in search of jobs and never return, leaving behind their children and elderly parents to fend for themselves. Eric and his family subsidize some of these poor families, offering education and work for many orphans, and providing food to more than fifty elderly women. Eric's two brothers take part in running the projects. Glen is the cook and also in charge of managing the cisterns' construction sites; Eugene is the bookkeeper.

Eric's next goal is to complete the building of an orphanage of sorts. This unique home will be for children and elderly women, who will mutually care for one another. This will give the orphans a clean, caring place to live and study, with meals provided. The women will be invited to live in another house on the compound. Often, they are the children's grandmothers, but were separated from the family because they were too poor to feed the children or provide for their education. Eric's plan will help reunite such families and let the women care for the children with the help of older orphans and specially trained staff.

During my stay, Eric invites me to go with him to visit the elderly women he has been helping. I am heartbroken to see the torn bamboo shacks where they are living in rags. One woman is combing her hair when we arrive. I make a mental note to bring not only toys for the kids, but also some pieces of fabric and perhaps combs for the ladies the next time I visit.

Another day, I am invited to a party organized at Lei Thar Gone. Glen has cooked up *monhinga* for seventy people. The orphans, freshly bathed and faces covered in *thanaka*, arrive in a pickup truck. They are shy and look at me from a distance. We spend a lot of time taking pictures. One of the older youngsters soon learns how to use my camera, and takes at least two hundred shots. The children pose, looking very serious; everyone stands upright and very still.

In an attempt to make the kids smile, I start making monkey, elephant, and hen noises. In the final series of pictures, everyone looks happy. So am I, here in the middle of these lush grounds with wonderful people. In Mandalay I purchased small plastic balls with rattles inside and carried the light but bulky load all the way to Yenangyaung. Now they are distributed to the children. They wave their goodbyes with the rattling toys gripped in their tiny hands.

As I watch the sun set over the motionless sea of green land and white sand, I wonder about the strange crossing of destinies that brought me so far, to experience so much. Myanmar and its people are dear to my heart and a strong desire to come back has grown inside me. I do not understand much of what happens in this country, but I know that whenever I am away from it, I have left a small part of myself behind.

Getting to Yenangyaung

Yenangyaung (literally "stream of fossil oil") is located about one hundred kilometers south of Bagan in Magwe Division, on the Nyaung U to Pyay highway. The journey from Bagan takes about three hours by car. Though it will take longer, ask your driver to take you to Salay. It's well worth a visit so see the lovely teakwood monastery and old colonial-era buildings. Plan to arrive in Yenangyaung in the afternoon, stay at least two full days, and depart on the third in time to catch a flight from Nyaung U (Bagan Airport) back to Yangon or onwards.

Lei Thar Gone—Gentle Breeze Inn

The inn has three large rooms and can house a maximum of six guests at a time. Each of the nicely decorated accommodations is fully furnished and very comfortable. The upper room has two large terraces (one to enjoy sunrise, the other sunset) overlooking the green, flowered grounds, Ayeyarwady River, and Rakhaing Mountains in the distance. If you would like to stay at Lei Thar Gone, plans need to be arranged with Eric Trutwein at least three working days ahead of your arrival. The guesthouse will need to send someone out to meet your car and guide you in, but the journey is worth it.

(+95-1) 681-881 (Yangon office)
egsimco@mptmail.net.mm

Social responsibility

Water is scarce in this dry zone. Eric had to have a well dug 120 meters deep. Although your hosts will never request it, please be careful while using water. Likewise, electricity is scarcely distributed in town, and the house's neighborhood only gets power one evening out of three. You may opt for a candlelight dinner, or choose to give up the sound of crickets at night in exchange for that of the gasoline-operated generator. But remember that petrol is expensive in Myanmar.

Exploring Yenangyaung

When possible, the Trutwein family will show you around town and the surrounding villages. They will take you to small houses built in the dust, where the people they subsidize live. You will be warmly welcomed everywhere and will have the opportunity to witness how the money you are willing to donate is being spent. A minimum donation of $45 per guest, per day, is requested.

SHAN STATE

Guillaume Rebiere gets an education in Pindaya

I am in Pindaya, visiting an old man who runs a bookshop. He is sitting in front of me while we play Scrabble by candlelight. Customers come and go, renting books, some flashing surprised looks when they see me, a foreigner.

I have spent most of the day here, after visiting the nearby caves of Pindaya earlier in the morning, talking with the man about books and his life. He fed me lunch, offered me tea, and gave me a tour of the town. One of the things we talk about is what can be done to help poor people in the area. I tell him the story of a village school that I visited recently.

I had been traveling with a group of Burmese friends, and we were driving down a sandy road in the middle of the flat plains surrounding Bagan, far from the itineraries usually followed by tourists. Herds of goats resting among clusters of palm trees disappeared behind the cloud of dust raised by our jeep.

People are definitively poor in this area of Myanmar. Only two things can grow in this dry and unfertile soil: palm trees and ground nuts. Farmers have to drive many kilometers in their ox carts and wait in line for hours at wells to fill their tanks with water. Here, a few dollars could really help people. But how? And for how long?

Earlier in that day our guide had taken us to his home village. My friends and I were struck by the poor state of the local school. Under a simple roof made of bamboo leaves, the studious children were reciting a lesson written on a board. In Myanmar, teachers are greatly respected, and getting a good education is still considered a more important goal in life than having lots of money. But this school did not have even enough to provide books, notebooks, and pencils for all the students.

Seeing the earnest children in this classroom, I could not help but remember some kids I saw earlier that week in Mingun; they had dropped out of school and spent their time following tourists and begging for money. Thinking that irresponsible tourists might turn Myanmar into a country of uneducated beggars made me sick.

So, rather than just giving the school some money, my friends and I decided to go to the nearest town and buy notebooks and pencils. When we returned, our jeep pulling into the village, the teacher who had accompanied us was the first one to jump out. He could not wait to show the children what he had brought back with him. Judging by the children's joyful shouts as the teacher was distributing the lot, this was the best gift we could have given them.

After I finish telling my story, the old man in the bookshop nods with a smile. Like me, he thinks it was the right choice in giving supplies, rather than money, to the school.

I lose at Scrabble. It is time to leave. I am wondering how to thank this kind man for giving me so much, when he has so little. I look around the small shop, which is also his home, and notice a small mattress rolled up in a corner of the room. He could surely use some money, but would such a gift be appropriate?

Instead, I offer him the books I am carrying with me and buy three more from his shop. He thanks me. We shake hands like old friends and I return to my hotel. Tomorrow I leave for another city, but memories of the bookshop owner and the village school will remain with me forever.

Getting to Pindaya
See the fact file on page 146.

Responsible giving
Although it has already been mentioned, it cannot be emphasized enough. When traveling in Myanmar, you might be struck by the poverty of some people, but easing your conscience by giving them money is not a solution. It is a part of the problem. In particular, never give any money to children; you will turn them into beggars and encourage them to drop out of school, which is not a gift to them.

If you want to help people who have offered you hospitality, remember to treat them with dignity, as equals and not as beggars. Always try to make your relationship with them an exchange. If they have a shop, buy something even if you don't need it. Consider offering a gift, as their warm welcome was meant as one for you. But don't give something you have already used as it would be insulting.

Ray Waddington challenges the orphans of Inle Lake

Inle Lake is one of the most popular tourist destinations in Myanmar. Who could resist more than two hundred square kilometers of calm, clear water surrounded by mountains, leg-rowing fishermen, floating markets, and indigenous villages? As an anthropologist, the latter was my main reason for traveling to the area, but my research online had uncovered another more personal reason, one that helped to make my short stay among the most memorable of any of my travels.

Mine Thauk is a small village on the eastern shore of the lake. It's not included on the itineraries of most tourists who use boatmen to ferry them from one end to the other. After all, compared to the other attractions that conveniently fit into a one-day organized tour—floating gardens, floating markets, groves of ancient *stupas*, and monasteries with acrobatic cats— a village like Mine Thauk appears unremarkable. But for those who want to get off the beaten path and help a good cause, this is an experience you won't find elsewhere in the area.

Mine Thauk is the location of a boys' orphanage and one of Myanmar's very few girls' orphanages. During my short visit I got to know some of the most resilient children I'm ever likely to meet. Some were not even orphans in the true sense of having no living mothers and fathers. Instead, they had parents who were simply too poor to care for them any longer.

One boy and his sister, barely school age, had been found abandoned in a rice field by local villagers looking for food. A slightly older girl had been sent away from her family after her parents' divorce because her father's new wife was unwilling to accept her. The heartbreaking stories went on, but despite their pasts, all the children I met told me they were looking forward to bright futures.

During my visit, my hosts took me to a well-lit classroom in the boys' orphanage to meet and talk to some of the children. As a way of both getting to know the boys and encouraging them in their studies, I decided to set a challenge for each one, basing it on his stated career choice or the subject he liked best in school.

I asked a nine-year-old boy from the Pa-O ethnic group, who said his favorite subjects were math and English, to write the word for his age in English.

As the room went quiet he quickly got up from his chair, walked over to the blackboard, picked up the chalk and wrote "nine." I led the applause and the others quickly joined in. Then, as though my challenge was not difficult enough for him, he wrote the formula for "nine times nine equals eighty-one."

Another nine-year-old Shan boy liked soccer and dreamed of being a professional player. There wasn't a soccer ball in the classroom, so I drew one on the blackboard and asked him to tell me in English what it was. He was shy in front of the others and spoke so softly that I couldn't tell for sure if he said "ball" or not. I asked him to write the word in English on the board. He did, and was so proud of his accomplishment that he asked to have a photo taken with his successful answer showing in the background.

Then I was taken to the girls' orphanage. As with the boys, setting a challenge for these girls was my way of breaking the ice and getting to know something about them. A thirteen-year-old Shan girl liked science and wanted to work for the Red Cross. Her challenge was to tell me just one fact about the organization. I discovered that this young girl, living in a country with limited access to information, already knew more about the Red Cross than most Western adults.

Next I met a six-year-old Pa-O girl who was one of the true orphans. Because of her young age, finding a challenge for her that was neither too easy nor too difficult turned out to be a challenge for me. Since she said she liked English, I eventually decided that she was to count aloud up to five.

I started her off by holding up my first finger, saying aloud "one," then holding up my middle finger and silently indicating for her to continue. She did it without any hesitation. Then she surprised me and the other girls by stretching out her other hand and, although she had to pause a few times to think, made it all the way to ten without help. Like many of the other children I met that day this little girl wanted to prove she was more than up to my challenge. I don't think I've ever seen a prouder gleam in a child's eye.

Mine Thauk Orphanage

Mine Thauk is located on the eastern shore of Inle Lake, about ten kilometers south of Nyaungshwe. There are two ways to reach it, by a short boat ride on the lake or by road. If coming by boat, try to find the *Inle Glory*. Ask around in Nyaungshwe for the driver, Ko Yan Naing. Proceeds from his boat fee go directly to the orphanages.

When you get off the boat at Mine Thauk village, ask the locals for the orphanage director, U Tet Tun, or for the *parahita*. Most boatmen know where the orphanages are located and can walk with you. From the boat landing area, you must walk about twenty minutes uphill. The girls' orphanage will be on your right, and just past that on the left is the boys' orphanage. If coming by road you will pass the dirt road leading to the orphanages on your left side (just before the "Drugs Free School" on the right) before you reach the village.

You can cycle the distance from Nyaungshwe to Mine Thauk in about one hour. The road is mostly paved and mercifully flat, and the scenery along the way is lovely. Bike rental at most places in Nyaungshwe is 1,000 kyat per day. If such a trip sounds daunting, you can also hire a motorcycle driver to take you there.

Mine Thauk Village
(+95-81) 29406

What to give

There are about fifty boys and fifty-five girls staying at the orphanages. You are welcome to donate during your visit. U Tet Tun will be happy to accept dollars or kyat, and can provide you with a written receipt. Some countries currently impose trade sanctions on Myanmar that extend to direct charitable donations by their citizens. If you wish to send a check or make a bank transfer after you have visited, you will find information at Stichting Care for Children.

www.careforchildren.nu

GENERAL MYANMAR

*Myriam Grest
suggests becoming a
godparent in Myanmar*

My friend Marjut called to tell me some big news. She was housing twin baby girls, just a month old, in the garage of her home in Kalaw. Their mother, Marjut's seamstress, had died a week after the babies were born due to complications from a Cesarean.

The girls' future did not look promising. Their father, a trishaw driver and maintenance man, could not return to work because there was nobody else to watch over the babies, but he had no clue about what they needed or how to take care of them. The twins had rashes, their room was dirty, and there was no money for infant formula. Other relatives (grandmother, aunties, uncles, half-sisters) were either not able to take care of the girls or couldn't be bothered.

A week after Marjut's phone call, she came to Yangon with the twins, Anna (May May Than) and Sofia (Min Min Than). My daughter begged me to take her to look at them, and once we saw those fragile little babies, our hearts just opened. With tears in her eyes,

Marjut said she didn't know how she was going to be able to support them.

Marjut first became involved with helping the orphans of Myanmar in 2000 with Finnfund, a Finnish industrial development fund. This partnership originally supported ten young orphans who could not go to school due to lack of money, or because the child needed to work to support himself or a remaining parent.

Seeing so many orphans in need, Marjut formed Myanmar's FinnConnect, a small, non-profit, non-political NGO and humanitarian association that supports orphans with education, counseling, and job training. Through the organization she launched the Early Childhood Development Program for infants through age five, and under the umbrella of the Godchild Program, FinnConnect helps children pay for periodic expenses such as annual school fees. It also helps to buy books and other school supplies, sports equipment, and clothing.

Through Marjut's affiliation with FinnConnect, she was able to pay for the hospital and funeral costs of the twins' mother, as well as purchase the necessary accessories and infant formula for the first six weeks of the babies' lives. But money was running out, and the father had already received offers to sell the twins. It was time to make a decision. Marjut said that she could continue taking care of the babies if my travel agency in Yangon would make an annual contribution to FinnConnect to help with expenses.

Most of the time the twins stay at Marjut's little wooden house in Kalaw, where the climate is cooler than in Yangon and the cost of living is cheaper. The twins go to a local nursery school on weekdays and also take swimming lessons several times each week. They also like to "help" Marjut with the cooking at home. But even my yearly support to FinnConnect is not enough to take care of all the twins' needs, so FinnConnect is hoping to find more sponsors—"godparents"—for them.

With Anna and Sofia, as well as the other orphans in the FinnConnect program, the main goals are to take care of the child's physical and emotional needs, as well as boosting confidence through participation in various activities. All of the children in the program come to Marjut's Kalaw house on holidays and are encouraged to bond with one another. If funds allow, the group also arranges summer holiday trips and pays for the children's hobbies.

Despite the economic difficulty, Marjut is determined to take care of the twins as best she can. "I would not uproot these beautiful and healthy little girls in order to place them elsewhere," she told me. "The girls are now very attached to me and this is their home as long as I personally can help."

FinnConnect

Marjut Sieppi
(+95-81) 50026 (Kalaw)
(+95-1) 644-533 (Yangon)
marjut.htay@mptmail.net.mm

How to help

The required commitment is a minimum of five years. The hope is that the support will continue until the child has finished ten years of basic education. The basic cost for a child is $2,000 per year. One nutritious meal costs about 1,200 kyat ($1). For babies without a mother, infant formula, diapers, medical costs, and nanny care add to the expenses.

Myanmar Travel

Pansodan Office Tower
3rd Floor, Room 3/A
189/195 Pansodan St.
Kyauktada Township
Yangon
(+95-1) 204-046, 391-015
www.myanmartravel.net

Kyaw Zay Latt introduces orphanages around Myanmar

For a long time I have been interested in helping orphans and homeless children in my country. These kids don't have parents to love and care for them, so they must struggle for even their basic needs. Most, for example, are not able to go to school because they lack money.

After I started my career as a tour guide in 2004, I finally had the means to do more to help. The first orphanage I ever visited was Aye Chan Tha in Taikkyi Township, north of Yangon. I went there with a group of German tourists who wanted to visit some independent orphanages in the area.

At Aye Chan Tha we found about sixty boys being cared for by a Buddhist monk and four assistants. There were nine dormitories with eight bunk beds crowded into each room. The classroom contained a blackboard and several rows of low tables, but no chairs. The children all sat on the floor. Their playground was a bare patch of muddy ground on which the boys played soccer, while others practiced volleyball using a net strung between two trees. Their meals consisted almost entirely of rice with small sides of chicken or beef curry. But despite the poor facilities, the children appeared to be happy and grateful that they were being cared for. They were most appreciative of the items that we brought them: books, chalk, pens, pencils, coloring books, and soft toys.

When I talked to the children, some of them told me they didn't know their own birthday or the names of their parents. When I asked a few what they would like to be when they grew up, they acted surprised at hearing such a question and did not know how to answer. But that wasn't very strange. For most poor children in Myanmar, their future careers are determined by what their parents do. In other words, children of farmers want to become farmers.

One boy told me that he wanted to become a bus conductor because he usually saw lots of money in the hands of the conductors. About one-third of the children said they wanted to become soldiers or policemen, which probably reflects their desires to turn their situations around and be in a position of authority.

Seeing the children's gratitude that day was a heartwarming experience for me, and inspired me to assist other orphanages. Most orphanages in Myanmar struggle to buy enough food for their children, and the situation has been even more critical since late 2007 when gas and food prices skyrocketed nationwide.

In the orphanages, I now see many more kids who are hungry, thin, and sick. In many cases there are insufficient beds—one orphanage had only three beds for twenty children—so many of the kids must sleep on the floor. The beds themselves are filthy, as are the toilets, showers, and cooking areas. Sometimes there is no running water. At one orphanage I noticed that there weren't any screens on the windows, allowing mosquitoes to enter the room.

There are many things that tourists can do to help orphanages in Myanmar. You can donate a few dollars from your travel budget to buy new clothes, sandals, or sports equipment like footballs, wicker balls to play *chinlon*, and badminton sets. Anything you can do to address the poor living conditions for the orphans is greatly appreciated.

I encourage tourists to visit an orphanage while they are in Myanmar. Charity travel is a relatively new concept in Myanmar, but it is possible to organize a tour for travelers who are keen to help needy children. There are orphanages in Yangon, Mandalay, and the Inle Lake area that you can conveniently visit during your stay.

The children are glad to receive you as guests, even when you are not able to make a donation or give presents. They are thrilled when tourists take the time to teach them some English or play games or sports with them. Even something as simple as talking about your life, or showing them photos of your travel experiences, will bring smiles to their faces.

What to give

The most welcome presents are pencils, pens, notebooks, English-language instruction books, hats, soccer balls, badminton sets, and toys. Apart from the language books, most of these items are available at local markets. If you would like to make a cash donation while traveling in the country, it's best to make it in kyat. If you are bringing presents for the children from your home country, it may help to have an official letter from the orphanage in order to qualify for an excess luggage allowance from the airline. In such cases, I can help to organize this, but be sure to email me at least one full week ahead of your arrival in Myanmar.

eugenelatt@gmail.com

How to volunteer

In theory, volunteer work by tourists is not allowed in Myanmar, but some have been able to temporarily volunteer as English teachers at orphanages. First, visit an orphanage and ask if they would like someone to teach English. You should stay at a nearby licensed guesthouse, even if the orphanage offers to provide free accommodation. Information on many of the orphanages below can be found at the following website.

www.themandalayprojects.com

Orphanages in need

Following is a list of orphanages on the tourist routes that are in desperate need of donations.

ACT Youth Development Center

Abbot: U Jotika Targwa
Tharettaw Village
Taikkyi Township
Yangon
www.actmm.blogspot.com

Aye Yeik Mon Girls' Orphanage Association

Abbesses and Founders: Daw Khang Mar Nandi and Daw Nanda Htay Ri

22nd Street (62/63)
Mandalay
(+95-2) 61214

Kin Ywa Orphanage and Monastic Education School

Chief Abbot: U Wilartha

Shwe Pyi Aye Quarter
Mawlamyine
(+95-9) 532-1018

GENERAL MYANMAR

Mahamuni Buddha Vihara Parahita
Local coordinator: Ko Soe Than
Sittwe
(+95-43) 21765

Myanmar Buddhist Orphanage Association for Boys (MBOA)
Abbot: U Sandimar
Director: Ko Ko Kyi
Corner of 30th Street and 62nd Street
Mandalay
(+95-2) 36774, 61187

Paya Phyu Parahita (White Pagoda Orphanage)
125 Kanbawza St.
Ye Aye Gwyn Quarter
Taunggyi
(+95-81) 22664

Parahita (Monastic Orphanage)
116 Sasana Myay
No. 5 Quarter
South Okkala Township
Yangon

Su Htoo Pan Thiri Mingalar Kandaw Parahita
Aye Mitta Street
Thanlyin
(+95-56) 21926

Janice Nieder offers a wish list for giving in Myanmar

Kidding around
When traveling to a poor country such as Myanmar, I always face a dilemma about giving gifts, especially to the local children. What might begin as a generous act can turn into a nightmare when hordes of children descend upon you. One can never bring enough gifts for a whole village. I also don't want to contribute to the problem of children expecting—and begging for—gifts every time they see a foreign tourist.

Instead of giving candy or toys to children in Myanmar, a better idea is to simply give them your time and attention. I found that a good way to break the ice with village kids was to pull out a Frisbee and show them how to throw it. Another fun activity was to take turns looking at a bug under a magnifying glass. I also brought an ink pad and a rubber Mickey Mouse stamp and let the kids decide if they wanted to be stamped on their hand, arm, or forehead.

For those special occasions when you do want to offer a gift, perhaps to the child of a family that has befriended you, I have had great success with flavored ChapStick, hair clips for girls, cartoon character toothbrushes, posters (soccer themed for boys), glow-in-the-dark plastic jewelry, and paper kites, as the children of Myanmar are avid kite flyers.

A healthy planet

While I was in the town of Kyaing Tong in eastern Shan State, I went to the market with my guide to buy gifts that we could distribute to some of the villages in the area. The guide knew these villagers and their needs, so I gave him money to buy whatever he felt the people could use the most— aspirin, salves, vitamins, Band-Aids, etc. Many villages are in desperate need of medicine, but you should never be the one dispensing anything, especially from your home country, even if it's just aspirin or vitamins. A tourist like me has no idea what, if any, other medicines these people might be taking, plus the villagers can't read labels in a foreign language and won't know when and how to take the medicine.

Worth a thousand words

I've found that no matter where I travel in Myanmar, people are as curious about my country as I am about theirs. The children I met loved to see pictures of my hometown, and of my family and pets. If you have any photos of other places you've visited in Myanmar, these make nice gifts, as many locals never get the chance to travel around their own country and would love a souvenir photo of someplace like Shwedagon Pagoda or Golden Rock. You might also hand out things from your hometown, such as pins, banners, stickers, or caps, and bring a laminated map to show where you live. Before leaving on a trip, I contact my local Chamber of Commerce and ask if they have any free souvenirs that I can give out.

Educational supplies

Schools in particular are always in need of pencils (colored ones are a fun treat), notebooks, and writing pads. Along with these more obvious donations, a map of the world and/or an inflatable globe will be greatly appreciated. These items are also useful for children living in orphanages and for novice monks at monasteries.

Monasteries

Visitors are welcome to donate money to monasteries, or give gifts of fruit, pens, notebooks, soap, or other items such as flashlights and batteries — very useful during the frequent evening power cuts.

How to give

If you do want to give anything to a group of children or village while you are in Myanmar, rather than attracting a crowd that expects gifts or "money present," one solution is to quietly give whatever you bring to a person of authority. This could be the village chief, a teacher at a school, a head monk at a monastery, the director of a local orphanage, or even parents.

RESOURCES FOR THE ROAD

Practical advice to help you prepare for your travels

Walk into your local bookstore and you will be hard-pressed to find much, if anything, about Myanmar. If you do, chances are the book will be political, or perhaps a biography of Aung San Suu Kyi. But if you mine the shelves of secondhand shops or surf online, you can dig up a fascinating array of literature that gives you a better understanding of the country's culture and history.

For insight into the current political landscape, and why the situation is as complex and convoluted as it is, it helps immeasurably to read about the history of the country. Along with the list that I have compiled, Ma Thanegi and James Spencer weigh in with their favorite volumes. Their choices are interesting both for their insider angles and for the glimpses they offer into the disparity of opinions about Myanmar.

Perhaps the most famous book written about the country is George Orwell's novel *Burmese Days*, based on his years there. But, as you will read, James calls it "the granddaddy of them all," while Ma Thanegi faults it for not showing the "true nature" or the "humor and kindness" of both the Burmese and the British. Pick up a copy and draw your own conclusions, and then discover how relevant the book is today with Emma Larkin's *Secret Histories: Finding George Orwell in a Burmese Teashop*. Larkin follows the trail of Orwell in the cities in which he lived and worked, but her book ends up being "more of a portrait of modern Myanmar and the relationship of the people to their rulers," according to James.

Finding guidebooks can also be an exasperating task. Once again politics rears its ugly head. Some companies deem it "unethical" to publish guides about Burma/Myanmar, so currently there are only two major English-language guidebooks: Lonely Planet and Insight. Both are packed with useful information, particularly LP, but as in any guide, some information can become dated quickly. Travelers in search of updates, as well as more in-depth info, will find it useful to check out online sources.

Monks studying at a monastery near Mandalay

The internet, of course, has become fertile and invaluable ground for current information on Myanmar, though due to its nature, one has to watch out for erroneous or outdated reports. Still, as a resource it can't be beat. There are dozens of websites and blogs that focus on Myanmar, including several travel websites with active readers' forums. These can be valuable for obtaining current information, as well as recommendations on restaurants and hotels. I can't tell you how many wonderful places I've discovered—everything from teak monasteries to fabulous teashops—all due to a recommendation that I read online or from advice in a forum that someone posted.

Along with books and blogs, there are other ways to "learn" a country, and we've included those, as well. Cooking is certainly one way to get to know Myanmar, as you will discover in Robert Carmack's essay on cookbooks, and naturally a shared language is a key to better understanding, which is why Don Gilliland has provided a varied list of ways you can teach yourself to communicate with the locals. For further enlightenment, keep turning the pages. Let's hope your journey of discovery never ends!

Book Recommendations

XXXXXXXXXXXXXXXXXXXXXXXXXXXXXX
ooooooooooooooooooooooooooooooo

FICTION

The Glass Palace
by Amitav Ghosh

This is an engaging novel that gives a good feel for a very turbulent period in Burma's history. Beginning with the fall of Mandalay in 1885, *The Glass Palace* takes you from Burma to India and then to Malaya with a colorful cast of characters spanning three generations. Ghosh's vivid descriptions of Mandalay's old palace, streets, and citizens offer an enlightening perspective for today's travelers.

The Lacquer Lady
by F. Tennyson Jesse

The Lacquer Lady makes a nice complement to *The Glass Palace,* as it's also set during the reign of Thibaw, Burma's last king. It is both a love story and a fascinating account of the chaotic and bloody period when Thibaw ruled. Burmese and Western (British, French, and Italian) characters populate this novel, giving it a cultural balance. Of note in the cast are Supayalat, the demanding woman who became Thibaw's queen, and her friend, Fanny, the Burmese-Italian woman who features prominently in the outcome of the story. The author visited Burma in the 1920s, doing extensive research and talking to locals who remembered Thibaw and the royal family.

The Lizard Cage
by Karen Connelly

Set inside a Burmese jail in the 1990s, this riveting novel focuses on Teza, a popular singer who has been arrested for anti-government activities, and a young orphan boy who works in the jail. There is a predictable political slant, including the horror at the treatment of prisoners, but the story is well written, even poetic in parts, and the characters are especially intriguing. A disturbing but absorbing read.

The Piano Tuner
by Daniel Mason

With an unconventional angle, this is yet another novel set in 1880s Burma—a time ripe for a writer's imagination. Elements of politics, religion, history, and music intertwine in this story of a piano tuner who is sent from London to Burma in order to tune the piano of an eccentric army officer stationed at a remote outpost in the northeast of the country.

Saving Fish from Drowning
by Amy Tan

This novel features an eclectic, and eccentric, cast of American tourists—including a recently deceased tour group leader who keeps track of her clients' travels "from above"—who find themselves taken hostage by a group of ethnic rebels during a boat tour of Inle Lake. You may think twice about taking such a cruise after reading this bizarre tale! Tan uses the plight of ethnic groups, struggling to survive amidst government "relocation" programs, to set the stage for a wild and fascinating story.

NON-FICTION

The Burman: His Life and Notions
by Shway Yoe

Shway Yoe was the nom de plume of Sir James George Scott, an influential administrator who was stationed in Burma during the nineteenth century. Scott's humor and vast knowledge of his adopted country bring the pages of this book alive. Although it was written in 1882, I haven't found a better primer for learning about Burmese culture and customs anywhere.

A Burmese Legacy
by Sue Arnold

An excellent memoir by a British woman with Burmese roots: her parents both had British fathers and Burmese mothers. Arnold visited the land of her ancestors back in the mid-1980s. Some of the book's passages involving her family history get a bit tedious, but most of the story is engrossing. Another twist is the author dealing with her failing eyesight. Now blind, she still writes for a newspaper in England. Although her homecoming took place many years ago, this chronicle of the country contains plenty of sharp insights into its society and, of course, politics.

Golden Boy and Other Stories from Burma
by Saw Wai Lwin Moe

This book is a collection of folktales, fables, and legends as told by Burmese parents to their children.

Besides providing good entertainment, these stories reveal the fantastic magic and ancient wisdom of the enchanting "Golden Land." A short read, but highly enlightening.

In Farthest Burma: The Record of an Arduous Journey of Exploration
by Frank Kingdon-Ward

This book details the 1914 expedition of the author, a famed plant collector and explorer, along the eastern branch of the Ayeyarwady River. It is considered by travelers and botanists to be a classic account of old Burma. Kingdon-Ward's descriptions of the people he met and the plants he found in this remote region are equally vivid.

On the Road to Mandalay: Tales of Ordinary People
by Mya Than Tint

When the author traveled around the country giving lectures in the 1980s, the many "ordinary people" he met inspired him to write this book. These thirty-four simple, truthful portraits of people as diverse as waitresses and fortune tellers give a good overview of everyday life in Myanmar.

Shans at Home
by Mrs. Leslie Milne

This is a colorful account of the Shan States, where the author lived from 1906-1907. In some ways, it's much like Shway Yoe's *The Burman*, offering an abundance of information and insight into local customs and practices. While residing in the town of Namkhan, Mrs. Milne was the only foreign resident, but she made the most of her time in the area, absorbing numerous aspects of Shan life. The book also includes dozens of black-and-white photos taken by the author.

The Soul of a People
by H. Fielding Hall

This is another wonderful introduction to the country ... written way back in 1898! Hall was a district magistrate stationed in Burma during the waning years of the nineteenth century. He clearly loved the people and culture, as is proved in this passionate account of his time in the country.

The Trouser People: A Story of Burma in the Shadow of the Empire
by Andrew Marshall

For something more recent (published in the past decade), this is a good read. Inspired by the tales of Sir James George Scott, Marshall finds adventures of his own during travels around the country, particularly in Shan State. This is more than a travel book, offering revealing looks at the country's historic past and the turbulent present. Marshall met members of various ethnic minorities, including the Wa, notorious headhunters who now reputedly run a thriving narcotics business. He shares Scott's sense of humor and adventure, giving the book page-turning appeal.

The White Umbrella
by Patricia Elliot

This is a biography of Sao Hearn Hkam, Mahadevi (Princess) of Yawnghwe in Shan State, though the book also gives

a lot of information about her family, the Shan State, and Burmese politics. Outspoken for a woman of her era, Sao was also the wife of the first president of Burma. After living with her husband in Rangoon, she later became a rebel leader in Shan State and eventually lived in exile in Canada. Sao's story follows momentous events from the twentieth century, including Burma's rocky road to independence, the struggles for Shan State independence, and the proliferation of the narcotics trade in the Golden Triangle region.

RECOMMENDED SOURCES

DCO
www.dcothai.com

From historic travelogues to volumes by *To Myanmar With Love's* own Ma Thanegi (see the following essay), this Thailand-based online store has many books about Myanmar in stock.

Google Books
http://books.google.com

If you can't find the book itself, this is the next best thing. Google Books offers the text of numerous volumes online, including many of the obscure books in this chapter.

Myanmar Book Centre
www.myanmarbook.com

This is a division of Nandawun Handicraft Centre in Yangon (see page 262). Its website is not the easiest to maneuver, but it does offer the opportunity to shop for a good selection of Myanmar titles online.

Orchid Books
www.orchidbooks.com

A "wide range of books devoted to Asia" includes a large selection of titles about Myanmar. I particularly like their "Bibliotheca Asiatica" series, which includes reprints of classics by the likes of W. Somerset Maugham, James George Scott, and Frank Kingdon-Ward.

Used book websites
www.abebooks.com
www.alibris.com

For tracking down used copies of many titles mentioned in this chapter, AbeBooks and Alibris are reliable starting points.

White Lotus Press
www.whitelotuspress.com

Offering original titles and reprints, this press covers a range of subjects, from historic journeys to puppetry and politics. Intriguing titles such as *An Ill-conditioned Cad* just beg to be read.

*Ma Thanegi
offers her essential
Myanmar reading list*

When the people of Myanmar must say something, but with great reluctance at committing an immodest act, we say that we need to shift our faces to the back of our heads: *shay myet hnar, nauk htar.* So here's my face way at the back of my head while recommending some of the books I have written.

Let me assure you that I do it only because there are almost no other books on the same subjects, and because many Western writers have made serious errors in depicting Myanmar— things that no one born here would do, writer or not. I thought I could do some damage control. Also, a lot of negative press surrounds my country. When writers trash my culture or the people, even if unintentionally, I feel personally insulted. I have a deep attachment to my heritage, and my chief aim is to share information that is not commonly known about Myanmar.

BOOKS BY MA THANEGI

Burmese Marionettes: The Illusion of Life

A guide to the world of puppetry in Myanmar, including tales of the role puppets played in royal affairs of the past.

Myanmar Architecture: Cities of Gold

A record of architectural traditions as well as related history and cultural norms up to the colonial era. Many of the old-style timber buildings featured in the book will soon be gone, since the large plots on which they sit have been passed down to descendants who will have to sell the land in order to claim their inheritance.

Myanmar Painting: From Worship to Self-imaging
with Dr. Khin Maung Nyunt and Sein Myo Myint

A complete history of the art of Myanmar from ancient times to the present.

The Native Tourist: A Holiday Pilgrimage in Myanmar
This travelogue follows an eighteen-day bus pilgrimage to sixty pagodas across Myanmar. A review by Michael Smithies in Bangkok's *The Nation* called it "a very readable account of an internal journey ... in a land one does not immediately associate with pilgrimages (or bus tours)." Try to find the uncensored, 2004 second edition from Silkworm Books.

ADDITIONAL TITLES

The book that is best known to many readers is *Burmese Days* by George Orwell, but it hardly shows the true nature of the Burmese—or even the British. In Orwell's novel every single character is either mean, malicious, or greedy, and without a shred of the humor and kindness of both races. The titles below, however, give insights into various aspects of life in Myanmar and truly reflect the personalities of ordinary—and yet extraordinary—people, while being great reads at the same time.

The Burmese Family
by Mi Mi Khaing

First published in 1962, this is a beautifully written and insightful book on family traditions in Myanmar by Mi Mi Khaing, the late scholar, writer, and educator.

She explains Burmese family traditions as they are bound by the local culture.

Canoe to Mandalay
by Major R. Raven-Hart

Written with delightful humor and published in 1939, this is an account of one man's odyssey to test the wild waters of the upper Ayeyarwady (then known as the Irrawaddy) River. The author had a keen eye and an open heart, enabling him to see the beauty of the land, and the pride and generosity of the people. It's obvious that he enjoyed himself immensely, and the reader shares this enjoyment with every word.

Elephant Bill
by James Howard Williams

A must-read book for anyone interested in animals or life in the jungles of old Burma. This is also a hilarious account of the wily timber elephants pitting their smarts against men—and often winning. However, this book is not only about elephants. Williams was in Burma during WWII as well, and scholars of the period will find his experiences most interesting.

Festivals and Flowers of the Twelve Burmese Seasons
by Khin Myo Chit

The people of Myanmar love festivals and celebrate at least one each month. Here Khin Myo Chit describes the annual celebrations and the seasonal flowers that mean so much to the people. Paw Oo Thett's lovely, translucent watercolors are a perfect fit for the text.

Golden Earth
by Norman Lewis

This tale of travel through the country in 1951 is enlightening, though Lewis had some strange takes on local practices; for example, the claim that fishermen believed they could save a fish from drowning by catching it, which has been passed along as if it were true and even served as the inspiration for the title of a novel by Amy Tan. In spite of these errors—which may well be jokes, as you can't really hear the chuckle in written words—this book gives insight into Burmese history and religion, as well as Lewis's feelings as he toured the country.

The Great Po Sein: A Chronicle of the Burmese Theatre
by Kenneth Sein and J.A. Withey

This book about a great dancer of the stage not only describes theatrical traditions but also gives a clear view of the lives of ordinary people. Performances in Myanmar are not at all like those of the West, but more like a large moving village led by a headman, touring the country and putting on plays.

The River of Lost Footsteps: Histories of Burma
by Thant Myint-U

Anyone who wants a levelheaded look at the country's political history should read this book. It stands out with its in-depth knowledge and objective tone. The author is the grandson of the late U Thant, who was the UN Secretary-General in the 1960s. Regarding the nuances behind the country's present political impasse, *The River of Lost Footsteps* serves as a voice of reason from someone who understands the value of the attitudes of both Myanmar and the outside world.

Trials in Burma
by Maurice Collis

This extremely interesting work is by a writer, judge, and administrator who lived in Myanmar during the early 1900s. Collis had integrity when it came to legal situations between the "natives" and the "White Raj," in spite of the prevailing attitude of most British at the time—that they were always in the right, or that they should not lose face even if they were wrong. Collis basically said pish to that, which makes his account of some of Burma's early twentieth-century trials all the more valuable.

Purchasing books in Myanmar

Both old and new copies of these titles, and many others not included in the list above, are available from bookshops in Yangon. Out-of-print editions are sometimes offered cheaply as photocopies. For a listing of bookshops, go to page 260.

James Spencer selects his five favorite Myanmar reads

What books should you read before setting out on a trip to Myanmar? Any list will be idiosyncratic and subjective, and my five personal favorites are no exception. Bar one, each of the books I have chosen is by a gifted writer, and all show a significant aspect of Burmese history or society. Two of my choices are from the British colonial period; this is no reflection of antiquarian interests on my part, but a recognition of the fact that Myanmar today remains very much a captive of its past.

Burmese Days
by George Orwell

Readily available in the secondhand bookstalls of downtown Yangon, this is the granddaddy of them all. Orwell was a member of the Indian Imperial Police in the town of Katha, north of Mandalay, in the 1920s, and this novel was his indictment of the effects of colonialism on both the colonizers and the colonized. Another Orwell classic is his essay "Shooting an Elephant," describing how the expectations of a Burmese crowd forced him to shoot an elephant that was in fact quite harmless. The essay can be found in full online at *The Literature Network*. www.online-literature.com

From the Land of Green Ghosts
by Pascal Khoo Thwe

Whereas most books about Myanmar are by foreigners and therefore inevitably describe the country from the point of view of an outsider, this is the work of an ethnic Padaung. Young Pascal grew up in the remote mountains of the Burmese-Thai border—where his grandmother still worshipped the spirits of rocks, trees, and streams—before eventually graduating from Cambridge University with a degree in English literature. In between, he had a life crammed with more adventure and experience than most of us can ever imagine.

The Gentleman in the Parlour
by W. Somerset Maugham

This is the master's record of a trip through Burma, Siam, and French Indochina (to use the colonial names) in the years between WWI and WWII. Whereas Orwell recorded Burma from somewhere near the bottom of the colonial pecking order, Maugham saw it from much nearer the top: rich and famous. What Willie wanted—entrance to the best clubs in Rangoon, a private chef in the depths of the jungle—Willie got. I particularly enjoyed his description of his temper-tantrum when the servants provided by a local prince failed to build his bamboo house promptly one evening—and his shame as he later reflected on his petulance and unreasonableness. A perceptive observer, he's still worth reading today.

Land of a Thousand Eyes: The Subtle Pleasures of Everyday Life in Myanmar
by Peter Olszewski

Land of a Thousand Eyes offers something that none of the other books here touches on: a factual record of day-to-day life in Yangon. Olszewski was in Myanmar to help train local journalists in the ways of a free press (one wonders what his students are doing today). True, his viewpoint is still that of a privileged foreigner, and his project was perhaps a little quixotic, but it gave him a rare opportunity to observe the lives of ordinary people. Olszewski is no stylist, and his lack of interest in politics drew the scorn of some reviewers, but until someone comes along with a better book, this will remain a unique introduction to the lives of ordinary urban people in Myanmar today.

Secret Histories: Finding George Orwell in a Burmese Teashop (AKA, Finding George Orwell in Burma)
by Emma Larkin

Larkin studied the Burmese language extensively before setting out on what was ostensibly a search for traces of Orwell's multi-year stay in Burma. But in following his trail around the country, her story actually becomes more of a portrait of modern Myanmar and the relationship of the people to their rulers, which many reviewers of this book have compared to Orwell's *Animal Farm* and *1984*.

Robert Carmack offers a tantalizing taste of Burmese cookbooks

I first discovered the world of Myanmar's cuisine as an armchair cook while reading Mi Mi Khaing's *Cook and Entertain the Burmese Way*. It was a small, hardcover, 1978 edition from a regional American publisher. On the cover, a sepia-toned photo of an intricately carved wooden façade was attributed to "Ananda Monastery in Bagan." I suspect now, after having visited the area, that it's actually Nat Htaunt Monastery. While Ananda is built of stone, Nat Htaunt is a teakwood structure on the outskirts of Old Bagan.

I have since located other editions of Mi Mi Khaing's cookbook, from a small pocketbook to a popular folio-sized version, yet this particular edition remains my favorite. I was immediately intrigued by a cuisine described as "the best of Chinese and Indian cooking, but with a distinctive flair all its own." After repeated trips to Myanmar, however, I would explain its food like this: Indian without the spice, Thai *sans* chili, and salads not too tangy.

Although many recipes can be very good, and it's especially easy to recreate the flavors yourself, the dishes as now cooked in this impoverished country lack the infinite variety of the world's three great cuisines along its border: India, China, and Thailand. Moreover, many dishes served in Myanmar are well and truly unctuous. The best explanation for this is that the generous coating of oil protects against air spoilage in a country where refrigeration is unreliable. Alas, in these health conscious "naughties" of the millennium's first decade, oily cooking falls distinctly out of Western favor.

Since locating Mi Mi Khaing's book, I've made it my quest to source other tomes about the dishes of Myanmar. Initially, I thought the hunt would be easy, as the footpaths along Pansodan Street in Yangon are literally lined with used booksellers. Unfortunately, English-language editions are scarce, and once found, recipes can seem indecipherable. How much is a *viss*, I pondered? Later, I learned it was 1.6 kilograms. And what are *seinza ngapi* and ladyfingers? Answer: high-quality shrimp paste and okra.

One of the best cookbooks I've discovered is Ma Thanegi's *An Introduction to Myanmar Cuisine*. It is certainly the most thorough, covering all facets of the country's cooking in 148 pages, which is encyclopedic compared to *Myanmar Cook Book* by Daw Ena Win, a minnow at only forty-five pages and with barely a couple dozen recipes. Like Ma Thanegi's book, it's a simple, straightforward introduction to the country's most popular recipes. Both locally published volumes contain color pictures of the "executed" dishes, ideal for novice cooks to see what they are actually cooking.

By contrast, cookbooks published by foreigners and/or published overseas look infinitely more professional, but this does not assure their authenticity. Typical of most such cookbooks, *The Best of Burmese Cooking* by Aung Aung Taik, *The Burmese Kitchen* by Copeland Marks and Aung Thien, and *The Flavors of Burma* by Susan Chan are heavily Westernized, catering to ingredients available in the country of publication.

Another good source for culinary knowledge is in regionally published books on the culture of Myanmar, such as *Colourful Myanmar* by Khin Myo Chit and *Myanmar's Attractions and Delights* by Ba Than. These books are fonts of information on food culture, featuring such tidbits as a treatise on why *bu thee gyaw* (gourd fritters) are so popular, the origins of *monhinga*, and short stories on glutinous rice and durian fudge. Sadly, most such locally published English-language editions are printed in miniscule batches—as little as five hundred to a few thousand copies—and can be difficult to track down.

As for the dearth of imperial-era cooking manuscripts, blame can be laid on colonial cringe and its prejudice against Burmese dishes. For example, the only ostensibly Burmese aspect of my 1932 copy of *The Burma Guides Cookery Book* is its title. Admittedly, it includes a grand total of ten local recipes—albeit all heavily Anglicized—plus an "easy vocabulary" that lists Burmese and Hindustan equivalents, presumably to make the Memsahib's shopping easier.

This is not to say that these books don't have their value. I located one copy of *Burmese National Dishes* by "Olivia," originally published in 1934. From this delightful tome of both "Hindustani" and Burmese dishes, I discovered that Mawlamyine (known as Moulmein at that time) was once renowned for its mammoth ginger root. Alas, that's no longer the case. When I last visited Mawlamyine, the markets were bereft of the rhizome, and locals looked perplexed when I even mentioned the town's former agricultural gem.

My search for cooking manuals continues, and truthfully I find it almost as exciting as exploring the country itself. I am doubly rewarded later, when I try my hand at cooking the recipes back home. Like Marcel Proust and his madeleines, my memories are triggered, taking me back to this tantalizing country.

Hunting for recipes

An Introduction to Myanmar Cuisine and *Myanmar Cook Book* are available in select hotel lobbies in Yangon, such as the Sedona Hotel and The Strand. Many of the city's bookshops as well as used booksellers along Pansodan Street, also have copies of these and other cookbooks. Another source of recipes is the in-flight magazines of various national airlines; both Air Bagan's *Lotus* and Yangon Airways' *SweSone* feature one regional recipe per edition.

Adventures in the kitchen

Hungry for something new? *Hsa Ba* is devoted to the cuisine of Myanmar and includes one hundred recipes. Some of these dishes look especially intriguing, such as avocado ice cream, yellow split pea fritters, and hand-mixed salad. The author of the site, Tin Cho Chaw, has written a cookbook that will be published around the same time as this guidebook.

www.hsaba.com

BOOKSHOPS IN YANGON

James Spencer browses the bookshops of Yangon

One notable aspect of Yangon's colorful streetscape is the large number of books for sale. Whenever I walk around the downtown area, I see outdoor book vendors all over the place. The heaviest concentration is found on the stretch of Pansodan Street near the corner of Merchant Street, about a block back from the Yangon River.

The bookstalls vary from a few hundred titles laid out on the footpath to a few thousand displayed on elaborate shelving. No matter how simple or sophisticated, these stalls are temporary, appearing early in the morning and disappearing again in the evening. The range of titles I have perused defies description: tattered airport thrillers, thick medical textbooks, the proceedings of learned societies, "teach yourself" language guides, glowing accounts of Soviet agricultural achievements, George Orwell's *1984*, and old *National Geographic* magazines.

A step up from the footpath stalls are the hole-in-the-wall bookshops. Probably they're related, as they seem to all carry the same stock. Customers browse from the footpath, pointing out to the titles they want from tottering piles packed inside. One of the best shops, Theingi Maw, is located near the corner of Bogyoke Aung San Road and Bo Son Pat Street. The owner has the good sense not to thrust books under your nose, and he carries a good range of titles that you might actually like to buy.

One place people keep recommending is the Inwa Book Shop on Sule Paya Road, and I can never understand why. It's really aimed at local students who are looking for English-language textbooks, dictionaries, and such. The single reason that I can see for visiting is that it carries fairly recent (usually a week old) and back issues of *Time*, *Newsweek*, and *The Economist*. If you feel that your week has a gaping current events hole that can only be filled by one of those magazines, this is the place for you. Alternatively, go to Zawgyi Café, one block from Bogyoke Market, and rent,

don't buy, the current *Bangkok Post* from the newspaper sellers who hang around outside.

Bagan Books, on the other hand, is a Yangon institution worth visiting. Its great attraction is that it carries reprints of classics that are otherwise unobtainable, or at least very difficult to find. On my last visit I was looking for books about white elephants, (there are four of these supernatural beasties revered in a compound out near the airport—well worth a visit), and found a copy of *Elephant Bill* (see page 255), James Howard Williams' 1950 memoir detailing his career as an elephant handler in the country. I also found Frank Kingdon-Ward's account of his travels through Upper Burma in search of orchids in the 1930s (see page 252), and in a *Journal of the Burma Research Society*, a memoir of a diplomatic mission from the king of Burma to the emperor of Vietnam in the 1820s, in which the king proposed that the two join together and partition Siam. When the ambassadors got back home they found Burma in the process of being partitioned by the British.

Two other bookshops are Myanmar Book Centre and Nandawun Handicrafts Centre which have the same owner and are in adjacent buildings. Nandawun also has a selection of valuable books, some so rare they are kept in a locked case, along with newspaper files dating from the 1960s. For the well-heeled book buyer there is the bookshop-cum-curio shop in Traders Hotel. It has a good range of glossy coffee table books, plus a few unexpected delights, such as a history of old Rangoon. It also carries a large selection of very beautiful photos from all over Myanmar, ready for framing. Be forewarned: books here are expensive.

Bookshops in Yangon

Bagan Bookshop

100 37th St. (Merchant/Mahabandoola)
Kyauktada Township
Yangon
(+95-1) 377-227

Inwa Bookshop

232 Sule Pagoda Rd.
Kyauktada Township`
Yangon
(+95-1) 243-216

Myanmar Book Centre & Nandawun Handicrafts Centre

55 Baho Rd. (near Ahlone Road)
Ahlone Township
Yangon
(+95-1) 221-271, 212-409
www.myanmarbook.com

Theingi Maw

This shop is located opposite Zawgyi Café.

Corner of Bogyoke Aung San Road and Bo Son Pat Street (30/31)
Pabedan Township
Yangon

Traders Hotel

223 Sule Paya Rd. (near the corner of Bogyoke Aung San Road)
Kyauktada Township
Yangon
(+95-1) 242-828
www.shangri-la.com

Zawgyi Café

The café is next to the FMI Centre.

372 Bogyoke Aung San Rd.
Pabedan Township
Yangon

WEBSITE RECOMMENDATIONS

Ancient Bagan

www.ancientbagan.com

As well as a detailed guide covering the history of Bagan and its many ancient pagodas, this site also includes information on area hotels, annual festivals, and other events. Nice photo gallery too.

Blogs

http://blogs.bootsnall/com/tags/Myanmar
http://myanmarblogdirectory.blogspot.com
http://www.travelpod.com/travel-blog-country/Myanmar/tpod.html
www.travelblog.org/Asia/Burma

Numerous travel websites feature country-specific sections for blogs, including *BootsnAll*, *TravelPod*, and *Travel Blog*. You will also find a good listing of blogs about Myanmar at the *Myanmar Blog Directory*.

Burma Research at the School of Oriental and African Studies
http://web.soas.ac.uk/burma

This site is aimed at academics and serious researchers of Burmese studies. You will find information on the current and forthcoming research activities of this group, along with notices of seminars and workshops.

BurmaNet News
www.burmanet.org

This website has links to current articles about the country, as well as updated news reports from a variety of sources. This is usually the first place I go for the latest news and information about all things Myanmar.

Enchanting Myanmar
http://67.212.226.228/enchantingmyanmar

This is the online edition of a quarterly magazine published in Yangon. The website is not always updated in a timely manner, but it's a real treasure trove of information, covering a wide range of travel and cultural topics that go beyond the predictable tourist fare. You'll find articles on various ethnic groups, remote destinations, archaeology, flora, crafts, and much more.

Inle Lake Tourist Information
http://myanmar.inlelake.info

This travel guide focuses on the Inle Lake area. It's far from comprehensive, but there is information on hotels and restaurants, as well as local orphanages.

The Irrawaddy
www.irrawaddy.org

Also a monthly magazine published in Thailand, *The Irrawaddy* is one of the most popular "Free Burma" sites. Not shy about expressing its anti-government views, it is nevertheless loaded with articles on a variety of subjects, not all of them political. It also has a good archive of interviews.

Kyaw Zay Latt
http://myanmarguide.blogspot.com
http://myanmar-society.blogspot.com
www.samsara-lane.blogspot.com

Kyaw Zay Latt, Yangon resident and tour guide, writes several information blogs, including *Insider's Travel Guide to Myanmar*, *Memoirs of a Tour Guide in Myanmar*, and *Peoples of Myanmar*.

The Myanmar Times
www.mmtimes.com

This is the online version of a weekly news and business magazine founded in 2000 by Ross Dunkley, an Australian journalist, and published in Yangon. You won't find anything political in these pages, but there is a nice variety of articles and information about events in Yangon.

WEBSITE RECOMMENDATIONS

Myanmar.com

www.myanmar.com

Billed as the ultimate guide to Myanmar, this website certainly offers a lot of useful information. Subjects run the gamut from news and travel to entertainment and traditional culture. The further you dig, the more goodies you unearth.

Online Burma/Myanmar Library

www.burmalibrary.org

If you are looking for information of any kind about the country, this is a comprehensive place to check. Articles are indexed alphabetically by subject and source. Altogether, there are classified and annotated links to more than eleven thousand full text documents about the country.

Travel Forums

www.passplanet.com/Myanmar
www.lonelyplanet.com
www.virtualtourist.com

Lonely Planet's Thorn Tree and *Virtual Tourist* have forums where travelers can post comments and suggestions. *Lonely Planet's* much visited readers' forum is an excellent source, and though the topics can sometimes be all over the place, it's fun wading through the dreck to find the good stuff. *Virtual Tourist* also has extensive information on Myanmar and an active readers' forum. Some of the contributors have posted details of their Myanmar trips on personal pages within the site. You can also find information by choosing a particular city and then surfing for more information. In additions to tips on restaurants, accommodation, and sightseeing, there are categories for "Tourist Traps" and "Warnings or Dangers." While it doesn't have forums, *Pass Planet* relies heavily on contributor/traveler information and updates. It has lots of useful, and often humorous, advice on various aspects of travel in Myanmar, and I found it helpful for trip planning.

Voices for Burma

www.voicesforburma.org

The founders of this site have taken a thoughtful pro-tourism approach to the country. They detail both the positive and negative influences of tourism. Here, travelers who want to help the people of Myanmar will find practical advice on how they can make their trip count.

Yangon Now

www.yangonow.com/eng

There are several online "city magazines" with information about Yangon, but this is the best one I've found. Not all the links work, but if you do enough clicking you'll find some fun tidbits. I like their updated listings of festivals around the country. Just don't mind the spelling errors.

LEARNING BURMESE

*Viola Woodward
builds a base of
useful Burmese words*

"Don't bother learning the language," a former ESL teacher at a job fair told me when she heard that I was going to work in Myanmar. "Most people there just want to learn English anyways."

Such strange advice, I thought. Shouldn't someone who teaches English as a second language also want to promote the learning of another language?

When I arrived in Myanmar five months later to teach at an international school in Yangon, that advice was still lingering in the back of my mind. But after a few weeks in my new country, I realized the counsel I had been given was nonsense. I felt that I really *needed* to learn this language. Gradually I picked up some useful words and phrases and enthusiastically practiced them with the Burmese teachers, guards, and cleaners at my school. Just saying *mingalaba* (hello) had people smiling and open to having conversations with me.

Inspired by such a positive response, I soon made a list, an eclectic yet practical assortment of words and phrases that I found myself using often. This selection, plus creative charades, made it easier for me to communicate and helped get me through many difficult situations over the next two years.

The expression for "I have" (*shi de*) was one of the most useful that I learned. It worked especially well when persistent kids were trying to sell me postcards for what seemed like the tenth time at Bogyoke Market. After I told them in Burmese that "I have" my share of postcards, they were more inclined to leave me alone. Other common words and phrases—such as "thank you," "sorry," "You're welcome," "How are you?" and "Have you eaten?"—were also handy and much appreciated by the locals.

Biking around the various townships of Yangon (my primary source of exercise and entertainment) forced me to learn the Burmese words for "come here," "go away" (useful for dogs and annoying boys), "bridge," "left," "right," "straight," "bus station," and "train station." These words were also convenient when I frequently found myself in a taxi with a driver who had no clue where I wanted to go.

Shopping necessitated a few more useful phrases, such as "How much?" and "Is there a discount?" I learned numbers so I could ask the market ladies the price of cucumbers. They would reply and waggle their fingers at me, so that I might have a chance of understanding them.

When speaking Burmese, I found that pronouncing the word with the correct tone is very important. The word for umbrella, for example, is *tee*. But if I spoke the same word with a downward inflection, locals would think I was asking for a hair trim! Sometimes I found that I could use words I already knew, ones that the Burmese have adopted from English and now use in everyday conversation: "photo," "discount," "okay," "sorry," "change money," "foreigner," "air-con," "snack," and "bye-bye."

So, should you bother to learn the language, even if you are taking a short trip to Myanmar? Of course! If you are out shopping, chatting, eating, drinking, taking taxis, and asking for directions—or needing a toilet—you will find it useful to know a few words or phrases. Not only will doing so make it easier to communicate, it will open up paths to establishing friendships.

I loved all of my daily interactions with the people in Myanmar, but the most memorable were the reactions to my attempts at speaking the language: occasional laughter, frequent amazement, and always lots of smiles.

Learning the language

For a variety of language-learning resources, continue on to the next essay.

Don Gilliland offers advice on learning Burmese

Burmese for Beginners
by Gene Mesher
www.paiboonpublishing.com

From Paiboon Publishing, *Burmese for Beginners* comes as a single book or as a set with the book and three CDs. Each lesson has vocabulary words, sentence examples, and conversations. There are also lessons on how to read and write Burmese script. The conversations include a few puzzling, if not useless, phrases—"There are no camels in Myanmar" and "My husband cuts his own hair"—but this is a good course overall.

Burmese Phrasebook

This pocket-sized Lonely Planet phrasebook includes Burmese script. That's always important to have. Whenever I botch the pronunciation, I can point to the script and ask a local to pronounce it for me. This book can sometimes be frustrating to use— many words and phrases I want are not listed—but it's a handy general source to help you during your travels.

Burmese: An Introduction to the Spoken Language
John Okell

www.cseas.niu.edu

The Center for Burma Studies at Northern Illinois University publishes this comprehensive course. The complete set comes with four books and thirty-four cassette tapes. Good sections on pronunciation help ensure you get those tones right. Different native speakers are used on the recordings, to give you an "ear" for these strange new sounds. Too bad there is no CD version on the market yet. Okell has additional Burmese language courses available through other publishers.

An Introductory Course in the Myanmar Language

The University of Foreign Languages in Yangon has compiled this course, consisting of a CD-ROM and 283-page book with lessons and vocabulary words. The listening drills are particularly helpful, ensuring that you get those tricky tones pronounced properly. It sells for $50 at Myanmar Book Centre & Nandawun Handicrafts Centre (see page 262).

Practical Myanmar
by Pranom Supavimolpun

Another pocket-sized volume, *Practical Myanmar* is not as practical as its title implies. Although it has extensive sections that cover food, shopping, hotels, health, and meeting people, there is no chapter about Buddhist etiquette. In addition, the exhaustive entries include many negative, unlikely-to-ever-use phrases such as "You are a damn liar!" and "Don't take off to gossip with the neighbors!" If you are serious about studying the language, this is handy to have as a resource, but it's not one I'd recommend for most travelers.

Travel Agencies

Following is a list of private travel agencies that I personally recom-mend, having used them for my travels or having received assistance from members of their staffs.

Enchanting Travels & Tours
www.enchanting-travel.com

This agency was started in 2005 by a brother and sister team, Myo Zin and Khin Swe Win Ko (she'll insist that you call her by her nickname, Jules). They provide a full range of ecotourism, sightseeing, and adventure tours, supported with knowledgeable and personable service. Enchanting's "Helping Hands for the Community" philosophy forms the backbone of its operations. Some of the more interesting tour options include balloon flights over the pagodas of Bagan, underwater dives, sea kayaking, jungle safaris, and steam locomotive trips.

3 Ma Kyee Kyee St.
Sanchaung Township
Yangon
(+ 95-1) 525-030
enchanting@myanmar.com.mm

Good News Travels
www.myanmargoodnewstravel.com

Good News Travels was the very first agency I used in Myanmar, and it's still my first choice when booking tickets. The company strives to make its tourism programs benefit every level of the local community by applying a systematic approach to minimize negative aspects of tourism. The owner, William Myatwunna, is extremely knowledgeable and helpful, and in 2008 was named one of the

"World's Top Travel Specialists" by *Condé Nast Traveler*. The head office is conveniently located in the heart of downtown Yangon, next to Bogyoke Market. There are also branch offices in Bagan, Mandalay, Inle Lake, and Sittwe/Mrauk U.

FMI Centre, 4th Floor, Unit 18
380 Bogyoke Aung San Rd.
Pabedan Township
Yangon
(+95-1) 375-050
(+95-9) 511-6256
goodnewstravels@gmail.com

Gulliver Travels and Tours
www.gulliver-myanmar.com
This friendly French- and local-owned company is operated like a family business, and you'll feel that personal touch as a client. One of Gulliver's stated aims is to "help you forge authentic connections with people who live here," based on the belief that it's the people of Myanmar who will ensure that visitors have an unforgettable travel experience. The agency also strives to help visitors better understand Myanmar's culture by giving back to the community. The company is happy to assist tourists who wish to make donations to local charities.

51A1 Inya Myaing Rd.
Bahan Township
Yangon
(+95-1) 720-151, 502-662, 526-100
infos@gulliver-myanmar.com
herve.flejo@gmail.com

Myanmar Travel Ltd.
www.myanmartravel.net
Founded by vivacious Swiss native Myriam Grest, who has lived twenty years in the country, Myanmar Travel Ltd. has a keen sense for capturing the spirit of Myanmar. Myriam and her dedicated staff offer personalized service and hand-crafted itineraries to meet each traveler's style. This agency's goal is to show visitors the treasures and unique culture of Myanmar.

Pansodan Office Tower
3rd Floor, Room 3A
189/195 Pansodan St.
Kyauktada Township
Yangon
(+95-1) 204-046, 243-125
info@myanmartravel.net

Swiftwinds Travels
www.swiftwindstravels.com
Established in 1992, Swiftwinds was one of the first travel agencies and tour operators licensed by the Myanmar Ministry of Hotels & Tourism. Apart from offering typical tourist packages, Swiftwinds specializes in nature-based tours, ethnic village tours, and river dolphin interactive fishing observation tours. Hpone Thant (you can call him Harry) and his colleagues can efficiently take care of any procedural, technical, logistical, or consultancy details you have during your visit. They can also obtain necessary permits and custom clearance. Needless to say, Swiftwinds can do it all!

care of any procedural, technical, logistical, or consultancy details you have during your visit. They can also obtain necessary permits and custom clearance. Needless to say, Swiftwinds can do it all!

02-03 United Condo Tower
39 Alanpya Pagoda Rd.
Dagon Township
Yangon
(+95-1) 384-816, 245-051
swiftwinds@myanmar.com.mm

Zarmani Creative Tours
www.zarmani.com

Zarmani is owned by a small group of experienced local guides, including the personable Nee Nee Myint. The love that they have for their country and its culture is evident in the services they provide. The entire Zarmani team loves to travel and share those magical experiences with tourists. They strive to provide accurate information and outstanding service, no matter what type of budget a tourist has. When choosing their suppliers, such as hotels or airlines, Zarmani always considers the service and ethics of the product. Their motto is "Your inner spirit will be lighter and brighter after having a trip with us to Myanmar."

34 D/9 Kaba Aye Pagoda Rd.
Bahan Township
Yangon
(+95-1) 701-049, 552-717
nnmyint@myanmar.com.mm
zarmani@mptmail.net.mm

Girl placing candles in front of a Buddha image at a Mingun pagoda

One writer discovers family among friends throughout Myanmar

DON GILLILAND DISCOVERS FAMILY
AMONG FRIENDS THROUGHOUT MYANMAR

I love to travel but wouldn't call myself a typical tourist. The fact that I've taken nine trips to Myanmar in the past three years is surely proof that my wanderlust strays from the ordinary. During my first few visits I admittedly indulged in the usual tourist activities. But after admiring all the glittering pagodas and rustic monasteries, and gazing upon tranquil lakes and craggy mountains, what leaves the most vivid impression on me is the people. That remains my motivation for returning so often: they move me, soothe me, and inspire me like no other.

I've made friends all over the country, but the ones I'm closest to live in New Bagan, a small town near the ancient pagodas of Old Bagan. On my first trip there I met a group of souvenir-selling kids hanging out in front of my hotel. Despite their frequent sales pitches, they were personable, polite, and a wee bit silly. We got along famously. Since that initial visit, each time I return I take a few of the youngsters on outings: a horse cart tour of the pagoda ruins, a boat trip on the river, or a longer trek to see a place like Mount Popa. These activities lead to invitations back to their homes for snacks or meals. Their families treat me like an honored guest, and I am continually humbled by their hospitality.

Despite my affection for the people in New Bagan, I consider skipping it during my upcoming trip. There are too many other places I haven't yet seen. If I bypass Bagan, I reason, I will have enough time to visit Monywa, Mawlamyine, and maybe even Pyay. But in April, as I'm making my plans, I get an email from my friend Nine Nine. Only sixteen, he dropped out of school last year so that he can earn money for his family by selling souvenirs full time. "This year very few tourists in Bagan, so our business is going to the ground," he writes. As a result, he plans to seek work at a teashop in nearby Nyaung U. The new school term will be starting soon and he wants to help his younger sister pay

---

Monks laughing at a monastery in Amarapura

her school fees. I immediately reconsider my itinerary, deciding that a visit to the Bagan area is necessary. I write back, informing Nine Nine that I will be arriving in late June. Hold off on the teashop idea, I suggest, I can help with school fees.

Then, in May, along comes Cyclone Nargis. Suddenly, a tourism industry that is already in the ground is under water.

As I continue to plan my trip, a friend in the US sends me an email, remarking how "brave" I am to be traveling to Myanmar at this time. Nonsense! The persistent notion that traveling around Myanmar is somehow dangerous has only been perpetuated by the recent disaster. Sure, the delta is devastated, but the rest of the country was spared the wrath of the storm and remains safe and easy to explore.

Of course, this doesn't mean that the cyclone isn't on my mind. Far from it. Struck numb by the tragedy, I check online for daily updates. I also collect money for relief efforts and plan to hand it over to aid workers in Yangon. In addition, I am bringing letters and/or money that people have given me to take to their friends. Like me, many other travelers have been touched by the people of Myanmar and are grieving over the situation. Knowing that I am going, a few of these kindred spirits have asked me to act as courier.

I spend the first three days in Yangon meeting with people and observing the damage that Nargis inflicted. I see raw stumps where tall, majestic trees used to sway; parking lots and fields stacked with logs; and buildings with patchwork roof repairs. Although visibly scarred by the storm, Yangon has quickly regained its everyday vibrancy. The sidewalks pulse with activity as vendors hawk their wares. Restaurants and teashops hum with the chatter of customers, and vehicles rumble through intersections.

When I arrive in New Bagan a few days later, though, the situation is different: it's hard to detect a pulse at all. Unlike those living in Yangon, residents of the Bagan area are almost totally dependent upon tourism for their livelihood, and many have been rendered jobless due to the sudden evaporation of foreign visitors. Many hotels in the area have laid off staff, or given them unpaid leaves. Some restaurants and gift shops are temporarily closed. At my hotel, at restaurants, and at the home of Gaw Soe, my horse cart driver, I hear the same refrain: "You are the first tourist we have seen in two months."

I am saddened by how the locals are weathering this new breed of storm. My friend Nine Nine pawned his guitar to buy medicine for his father. A restaurant manager I know sold his favorite watch to buy food for his family. I meet a tour guide who, facing the likelihood of few—if any—customers the rest of the year, is considering working overseas.

One day, I stop by Minyeingon Pagoda to see Ma Aung and Ko Ko, a couple I met through Peter, my friend in Bangkok. Normally, Minyeingon gets a trickle of tourists each day to watch the sunset from the pagoda's high terrace, and some buy Ko Ko's paintings. This month: not a soul. But it isn't just the income the couple is missing. Ma Aung asks me to drop by their house and take photos of their infant son to show Peter and his wife. "Please tell Peter that we miss him. He is like our family."

Obviously, the cyclone and the negative media coverage that ensued caused many travelers to cancel or postpone trips. My friends in Bagan understand, but that doesn't help to ease their worries. They need tourists now. To help out, I try to dine as much as I can at local restaurants, bringing along a few friends each time to pad the bill. When not restaurant hopping, I am invited to meals at family homes. I only have three days in town, so my schedule is quickly filled: dinner at Tun Tun's house, lunch at Nine Nine's place, a meal-like "snack" with Gaw Soe's family. Even Zin Maung Maung, a shy little ten-year-old, decides to join the action, voicing a simple invitation of "My house?"

The homes I visit are simple wooden ones with thatched roofs, some without running water or working electricity. The multi-course meals these generous people manage to prepare under such restraints are impressive—and delicious. Despite the economic hardships my friends are facing, I am showered with presents the night before I leave town: lacquerware coasters, sand paintings, *longyi*, T-shirts, and bags of tamarind flakes.

On the plane to Mandalay, there are only four foreigners, a sharp contrast to the tourist-laden flights I'm accustomed to. My first task upon arrival is obtaining wheels. I drop by Mr. Htoo's stand, where I usually rent a bike, but he isn't around, so I get one from another shop down the street. The next day, as I am cycling on 27th Street, Mr. Htoo flags me down. He has temporarily shut down his bike business due to the lack of tourists, and is now driving a trishaw to earn money.

I hire Mr. Htoo to take me to the MBOA orphanage, where I am scheduled to teach an afternoon English class. I figure this will save wear and tear on my legs, but more importantly give him some extra business. That evening we have dinner together at Aye Myit Tar, my favorite local restaurant. Mr. Htoo tells me that his first stint as trishaw driver was over a decade ago. Back then one of his customers, a Canadian tourist, donated six bicycles, enabling him to set up the rental business. "He changed my life," says Mr. Htoo.

I also visit the house of the famous Moustache Brothers comedy troupe. They recently held a benefit to raise money for cyclone victims, but other than that, they haven't had much to do all month: no foreigners, no shows. "We need tourists to come here in a jiffy," cracks Lu Maw, the brother well known for his constant use—and humorous abuse—of slang and idioms. Before leaving, I take photos of the trio as they strike their signature thumbs-up pose, all smiles, radiating the "never-say-die" spirit I have been encountering around the country.

I travel onto Nyaungshwe, the "Gateway to Inle Lake," where the situation is the same as in Bagan. A town fueled by tourism is coasting on fumes. Despite the hard times, what I find most moving is how everyone I meet refuses to be pessimistic. In what has become typical fashion, I am invited to meals with friends and acquaintances, including the monks at nearby Shwe Yan Pyay Monastery. Thein Linn, a jack of all trades who runs a travel agency, rents bikes, and sells books apologizes for *not* inviting me to his home; his wife is nursing an ill child and has no time to cook. Instead, he meets me at Unique Superb Food House for dinner. He is excited. He just met two tourists and is going to take them on a half-day trek tomorrow. Good news! But the situation remains pretty bleak when you are able to count the total number of foreigners in town on one hand.

After Nyaungshwe my plan is to return to Yangon and take a side trip to one of the towns on my original wish list. I change my mind several times before the obvious choice occurs to me: go back to Bagan. I know how much another visit will mean to my friends there, not only for the business I can throw their way, but also for the moral support. And I crave what they can give me: their steadfast friendship.

The bus to Bagan is an old one, the seats hard and narrow, the leg room negligible. There is no AC, but the open windows suit me just fine. Not surprisingly, I am the only Westerner on board. The journey takes more than ten butt-bruising hours, and at Nyaung U I hop into a horse cart for the final forty-minute leg. I am exhausted, but when I pull up to my hotel, my spirits soar at the sight of Gaw Soe and Nine Nine, along with an assortment of children and parents, all standing under the shade of a large tree, waiting for me. That mysterious tea leaf telegraph worked once again! Their radiant smiles wipe away my fatigue and I hop out of the cart to greet them. "My house for dinner?" asks Nine Nine.

The second day back, I hire Gaw Saw and his horse cart for a pagoda tour, though I could do this circuit on bike, as I have

many times before. I bring along Nine Nine and his friend, Tun Tun. As we bounce down dirt paths, Nine Nine opens up a bag of potato chips and offers me some. "No thanks," I decline. He pokes my arm. "We share," he demands with a grin. I return his smile and dip my hand in the bag. We share.

I get a kick out of the way these kids insist on sharing their snacks, but more precious to me are the shared experiences: climbing high up pagoda steps to find the perfect view; laughing at the antics of Mr. Bean in one of the restaurants where locals often gather to watch TV; or listening to Iron Cross sing a Dan Fogelberg song in Burmese and discussing what the lyrics mean in our respective languages.

Nine Nine is the brightest of all the kids I've met in Bagan. He wants to become a tour guide, but what about the immediate future? We discuss various business ideas before I agree to finance his plan to rent vendor space at one of the more popular sunset pagodas in Old Bagan. There, he can sell souvenirs, but not the usual lacquerware and postcard fare. I hope there will be a market for "Support your Local Horse Cart Driver!" T-shirts. But more than a good merchandise mix, his business dreams hinge on a post-Nargis tourism resurgence.

Back in Yangon, my last night before returning to Bangkok, it is raining. I navigate the patchwork of muddy puddles on the sidewalk and make my way to the appropriately named Monsoon Restaurant for dinner. As I wait for the food to arrive, I reflect on this trip. I've seen what relatively simple acts—paying school fees, donating bikes, buying a few cheap souvenirs—can do, and how much such acts are appreciated. The locals are also appreciative for the simple opportunity of welcoming visitors to their glorious golden land. Such gratitude inspires me to keep doing as much as I can to help Nine Nine and others I have met during my travels around the country. These people are more than my friends, they are family.

Food vendor's offerings on the streets in Yangon

Treats for sale on a Yangon sidewalk

CONTRIBUTOR BIOGRAPHIES, CREDITS, AND INDEX

Isabelle Abreu (Pg. 204)

Isabelle Abreu has spent most of her life working and traveling around the world. Southeast Asia is her favorite region. She is married and lives in Sydney, Australia.

David Allardice (Pg. 166)

New Zealander David Allardice is the driving force behind Ultimate Descents. He has spent the last twenty years in the Himalayas, exploring rivers and pioneering rafting trips in the region. Apart from his epic descents of many of Nepal's rivers, David has organized and been involved in exploratory first descents in the Pamir and Tien Shan Mountains, the Rhondu Gorges of the Indus River, and the rivers of Bhutan, Tibet, and Myanmar.

www.ultimatedescents.com

Aye Aye Maw (Pg. 206)

Aye Aye Maw was born and raised in Yangon. After high school she left Myanmar to attend schools in Bangkok, London, and the United States, where she received a finance degree from The George Washington University. Her favorite game used to be DDD: drinking, dancing, and dating. Not anymore. She now has a husband, Robert, and a son, Zey. They live in Colombo, Sri Lanka.

Serena Bowles (Pg. 62, 191)

Serena Bowles became hooked on travel during a round-the-world trip in 1998; she added Myanmar to her list of countries visited in 2005. She

is an avid photographer, and you can see her pictures, read more of her tales, and purchase her book, *O is for Overland*, on her websites.

www.serenityphotography.co.uk
www.underwater-girl.co.uk

Miranda Bruce-Mitford (Pg. 182, 212)

Miranda Bruce-Mitford is an academic and writer specializing in Southeast Asian Art. She studied social anthropology and Burmese language and literature at the School of Oriental and African Studies, where she took an MA in Oriental Religious Studies. She has been lecturer and tutor for the British Museum and SOAS Asian Arts Course and has escorted many tours to Southeast Asia. The author of *The Illustrated Book of Signs and Symbols,* she is currently writing a novel set in Southeast Asia.

John Buckley (Pg. 202)

John Buckley was born and raised in the ski resort town of Vail, Colorado. He lived with his family for one year on the remote island of Punlap in Micronesia when he was a child, and traces his current travel obsession to those loincloth-clad days. As an adult, his passion for travel took hold during a year abroad when he lived in New Zealand for six months, with further travels through Tahiti, the Cook Islands, Fiji, Australia, as well as South and Central America. He then set his sights on Asia. He is currently working in South Korea as an

Fisherman on Inle Lake

English teacher and writes the travel blog, *Mental Malaria*.

http://johnbuckley.travellerspoint.com/

Robert Carmack (Pg. 18, 23, 38, 52, 258)

Robert "The Globetrotting Gourmet" Carmack is the author of *Vietnamese Cooking, Thai Cooking,* and *Fondue.* Robert grew up in America's Pacific Northwest but has lived abroad for some thirty-five years. With equal aplomb, he can arrange a rare tour of the Japanese emperor's private soy sauce brewery, enjoy a multi-course meal of cobra in a tiny restaurant in rural Vietnam, or prepare a Shan-style curry with the hill tribes of Thailand. Robert also hosts gastronomic tours to Asia.

www.globetrottinggourmet.com
www.asianfoodtours.com

Tim Cox (Pg. 72)

Raised in the UK but now resident in New Zealand, Tim has spent over two years traveling in Asia. From lengthy overland trips through China and Southeast Asia to a couple of days in North Korea, he is always happy to return there, whether to eat curry, get lost in paddy fields, or contemplate life in a peaceful temple. His latest trip to Myanmar, this time with wife Kylie, was his third.

Julie Faulk (Pg. 120)

Born and raised in central Florida, Julie Faulk began her love affair with Asia in 1995 with a visit to Thailand. Since then, she has had trysts with

Cambodia, Laos, Indonesia, China, Myanmar, Japan, Singapore, India, Pakistan, and South Korea—where she taught for two years. Julie has traveled to many destinations in the Western world, but Asia will always hold her heart captive. She is currently working in Germany.

Sandra Gerrits (Pg. 23, 139, 142, 194, 228)

In 2004 Sandra Gerrits took a two-year sabbatical from her IT job in the Netherlands to travel around the world. Myanmar had not been on her list, but after a visit in 2006 she quickly fell in love with the country. She and her Burmese boyfriend now live in Yangon, where she teaches English to third graders. She still has the rest of her around-the-world trip to finish at some point in the future.

Jennifer Gill (Pg. 103, 161, 216)

Jennifer Gill left San Francisco in October 2001 for eight months of travel in Asia. In love with the freedom and adventure of living out of a rucksack, she moved to Taiwan where she taught English for three years, all the while stockpiling paychecks for the next big trip. She has chronicled her eighteen-month journey through Southeast Asia, China, Mongolia, Tibet, and India on her blog.

http://jengill.blogspot.com/

Don Gilliland (Pg. 21, 22, 25, 104, 115, 122, 209, 266, 271)

Don Gilliland was born and raised in Orlando, Florida, where he worked as a record store geek for eighteen years. Opting for something completely different, he moved to Thailand in 1996. He also ran the Lazy Mango Bookshop in Siem Reap, Cambodia, for two years before moving back to Bangkok and starting Dasa Book Café in 2004. Read his ramblings at his blog.

www.bangkokdazed.com

Jeff Gracia (Pg. 27, 29, 185)

A resident of northern California, Jeff Gracia took his first overseas trip as a teenager, backpacking through Europe in the 1970s. He's been bitten by the travel bug ever since and makes several trips abroad each year. His favorite destination is Asia: inexpensive, totally different, and with so many friendly, happy people. When he's not traveling, he operates a video production company.

Myriam Grest (Pg. 22, 80, 242)

Myriam Grest first came to Myanmar in 1985, where she promptly "got stranded" (at The Strand, of course!) and decided to stay. Seeing the need for a reliable tour operator in Myanmar, she formed Myanmar Travel Ltd. in 1994. Her love of adventure and her keen sense for capturing the spirit of the country have enabled her to become a successful businesswoman. She has one daughter, Yolanda, and splits her time between Yangon and Bangkok.

www.myanmartravel.net

Linda Hall (Pg. 132, 153)

Linda Hall must have been born with itchy feet. Her earliest memories involve wandering far from home. In her early twenties she traveled through parts of the Middle East, most of Europe, and Mexico. For the next decade she became "a responsible professional" and only went on annual holidays. In 1997, while sitting on the couch after work one evening, she realized, "This sucks, I'm not happy." Nine months later she boarded a plane for Bangkok and began a life in Southeast Asia which continues to this day. She currently lives in Vientiane, Laos.

Graydon Hazenberg (Pg. 60, 155, 189)

Graydon Hazenberg grew up in Thunder Bay, Canada. After studying mathematics and astrophysics, he hit the road to become a lifelong refugee from academia. His peregrinations have taken him to seventy countries so far (only 120-plus to go!), often by bicycle or on foot. Mountains, jungles, tropical reefs, and adventurous travel keep attracting him from his current base in Yangon.

Craig Hewer (Pg. 179)

With a Trinidadian wife and a son born in Japan, it's pretty clear that travel is part of life for Craig Hewer, an e-learning specialist based in Osaka, Japan. To escape the deadlines, timetables, and politics of corporate Japanese life, he often finds himself in Southeast Asia. His

CONTRIBUTOR BIOGRAPHIES

idea of a perfect afternoon involves a hammock, a good book, and a bottle of Singha.

Hpone Thant (Pg. 74, 158, 164)

A native of Yangon, Hpone Thant formed Swiftwinds Travels with a group of school friends. He is editor and publisher of the English-language quarterly magazine, *Enchanting Myanmar.* He also teaches tourism courses at the National Management College at Yangon University and the Tourism Training School of the Ministry of Hotels & Tourism. He was elected Secretary/CEO of the Union of Myanmar Travel Association (UMTA) in 2006.

Roger Lee Huang (Pg. 22, 145)

Raised in Taiwan and Thailand, Roger Lee Huang has studied in a small college town in Pennsylvania, debated politics at the London School of Economics, and tried a brief stint in Taipei as a research assistant on contemporary Western Art. After working in Yangon as an intern with the United Nations Office on Drugs and Crime, he now resides in Taipei.

Manjit Kaur (Pg. 40, 214)

A Malaysian-Portuguese, Manjit Kaur spent ten years with Singapore Airlines, where her wine passion began. In 1993, she arrived in Myanmar as pioneer startup crew for Myanmar Airways International. In 2002, after returning from Australia, she joined a Yangon supermarket chain as a wine consultant. A training facilitator by profession, Manjit

has set up a training facility that offers cabin crew orientation programs for locals. Look out for Manjit's first book, *Red, White or Spice,* about pairing wines with Asian food, coming soon.

Sudah Yehuda Kovesh Shaheb (Pg. 23, 88, 229)

Sudah Yehuda Kovesh Shaheb is an Australian educated in Australia, London, and Miami. He is one of the few physician-anthropologists who are lucky enough to practice both careers. His interest is in the welfare of the indigenous people of the Americas. He is a visiting Professor of Anthropology at the University of Havana in Cuba, and friend of various tribes in North America. When not traveling, which has been a lifelong passion, he spends his time in Paris, the United States, and Havana.

Kyaw Zay Latt (Pg. 22, 243)

Kyaw Zay Latt, nicknamed Eugene, is a Yangon-based tour guide. He offers excellent custom-built private tours and also leads tours for domestic travel agencies. A recommendation that appeared in *The New York Times* has helped to keep him busy in recent years. Armed with a degree in economics, he has a wide range of interests.

www.eugenelatt.blogspot.com

Ma Thanegi (Pg. 15, 21, 24, 36, 84, 117, 223, 254)

Ma Thanegi is a writer and artist who has participated in about thirty group shows and seven solo exhibitions since 1967. She is the author of numerous books and articles on the culture, arts, cuisine, and history of Myanmar. Painting is her first love and writing comes a close second. Eating falls somewhere in between.

Michael Meadows (Pg. 180)

Michael Meadows was born in Botswana, moved to Australia for high school, and only recently discovered the wonders of Asia. After working on an aid project in India for his engineering degree, he moved to Thailand to study philosophy. As well as attending the (very) occasional class, Michael travels extensively around Southeast Asia and loves every minute of it!

www.travelblog.org/bloggers/michaelpaddo

Ken Merk (Pg. 82, 106)

Ken Merk is an American who has spent most of his adult life in Asia. He hopes one day to retire to someplace with no internet, phones, or any other modern trappings. Preferably, this will be a place warm enough so that he never has to wear socks again. Ken is now actively scouting suitable locales for this endeavor.

Janice Nieder (Pg. 31, 246)

Janice Nieder could be the love child of Indiana Jones and Julia Child. She was a specialty food consultant for twelve years in New York, with a client list that included Tavern on the Green, Dean & Deluca, and Sign of the Dove. She is a world traveler, and her culinary adventures include

sharing a smoked monkey with the world's oldest living headhunter and judging truffles in Marche, Italy.

www.travelwriters.com/janicenieder

Caroline Nixon (Pg. 112, 143, 147)

Serving as a medical student elective in Chiang Mai, Thailand, in 1980 started Caroline Nixon's passion for traveling throughout Southeast Asia. Her favorite destinations are Myanmar and Cambodia. Her favorite pastimes include floating on rivers, cooking, and eating with friends.

Marydee Nyquist (Pg. 131)

Marydee Nyquist, a longtime resident of Myanmar, divides her time between the US and Southeast Asia. This former history teacher and world traveler now assists clients in planning Asian trips. Marydee also leads workshops in meditation and creativity, helping people learn to unblock their creative energies and shape the life of their dreams. She is co-author of *Career Spirit: Bringing Creativity and Compassion into the Workplace*, a work in progress.

www.cometomyanmar.com

Giles Orr (Pg. 17)

Giles Orr is a mechanical engineer, librarian, computer geek, and photographer from Toronto. He was born on the cusp between the Baby Boomers and Generation X, but his life has definitely felt more in tune with the latter, overeducated and frequently underemployed. Having spent a decade in Georgia, he delayed his return to Canada for a six-month trip around Southeast Asia. When he speaks, he sounds Canadian with a hint of the American Deep South.

Gill Pattison (Pg. 110)

Gill Pattison is a New Zealander and now a resident of Yangon. After long periods living in London and Hong Kong, she succumbed to her fatal attraction to the wacky and exotic, and moved to Myanmar, where she became involved in the local art scene. She opened River Gallery in 2005. She also organizes shows and exhibitions abroad during the low tourist season.

www.rivergallerymyanmar.com

Leif Pettersen (Pg. 49, 177)

In 2003, Leif Pettersen was "Kramered" by an unbalanced friend into leaving his idiot-proof career with the Federal Reserve Bank of Minneapolis and embarking on an odyssey of homeless travel writing. Currently based in Minneapolis, he travels often and writes a wildly popular blog about life as a travel writer and professional ex-pat.

www.killingbatteries.com

Jan Polatschek (Pg. 187, 193, 218, 232)

Jan Polatschek lives in Bangkok. His landlord loves him. When Jan returned from Kuala Lumpur, new wallpaper; when he returned from Phuket, a new wide-screen TV; when he returned from Mumbai, new bathroom fixtures. Now there's hot water in the sink! Jan writes travel letters and takes photos.

Next, a book? And who knows, maybe even a new bookcase.

www.travelwithjan.com

Morrison Polkinghorne (Pg. 23, 68)

Morrison Polkinghorne specializes in antique textiles and is an authority on both Asian and French weaving techniques. A frequent traveler to Southeast Asia, he considers Myanmar his favorite destination. He is also a guest lecturer at international conferences, and was labeled one of Australia's ten leading designers by prestigious *Belle* magazine. Morrison hosts annual gastronomic and cultural tours to Southeast Asia.

www.asianfoodtours.com
www.globetrottinggourmet.com
www.morrisonpolkinghorne.com

Anne Marie Power (Pg. 78)

Anne Marie Power is an artist from Melbourne, Australia. She has traveled extensively in Asia to exhibit, teach, research, and explore the art, architecture, and spirituality of those ancient cultures. Her interests while traveling also include fashion and food; she believes that a good café for coffee or a glass of wine with local cuisine are essential ingredients to the road well traveled. Examples of her artwork can be seen at her website.

www.annemariepower.com

Michael Pugh (Pg. 207)

On a solo, one-year, round-the-world adventure, Mike Pugh enjoyed betel nut, grilled kudu, Lao moonshine, fried scorpions, and more. He and his bride, Genevieve, dine on similar fare at their home in Chicago. He chronicled his travel experiences on his website.

www.vagabonding.com

Guillaume Rebiere (Pg. 21, 113, 119, 196, 238)

Guillaume Rebiere fell for Myanmar while falling in love with the woman that he eventually married there. He worked in Yangon for four years in advertising, public relations, and as a teacher. Experiences in the tourism industry and a passion for photography have taken him to some of the most remote sites in the world.

www.moonbeam-travels.com

Pascale Reinhardt (Pg. 235)

Pascale Reinhardt is a French psychologist and professional coach. She specializes in the areas of conflict and crisis management, and intercultural negotiation between Asia and Europe. Pascale lived in mainland China for several years and very often travels to Asia on business and teaching assignments. Her passion for Myanmar and its people has developed over the years and enhances her zeal for bridging cultures.

Mick Shippen (Pg. 63, 124, 162)

Mick Shippen is a freelance writer based in Chiang Mai, northern Thailand. His travel articles have been widely published. With a strong inter-est in local arts, he is fulfilling a commission for a book that will document the life and work of the traditional village potters of Southeast Asia.

James Spencer (Pg. 71, 101, 136, 257, 260)

James Spencer was born in Australia and has worked as a schoolteacher, diplomat, and for the UN in Iraq and Morocco. He is currently a freelance journalist based in Phnom Penh.

Stuart G. Towns (Pg. 90)

After riding the dot-com wave in Silicon Valley for as long as possible, Stuart G. Towns ended up settling in Bangkok, Thailand, in 2002. Ever since he arrived, he has been teaching IT courses at Bangkok University and traveling around Southeast Asia as much as his job and wallet will allow.

Ray Waddington (Pg. 239)

Ray Waddington is the president of The Peoples of the World Foundation, a secular, apolitical, non-profit organization based in the US. He established POTW to fund educational scholarships for indigenous people after witnessing the lack of educational opportunities available to them and the negative impact this has on their political representation. Dr. Waddington is preparing a travel/humor book based on his experiences. When he's not traveling to indigenous villages, he tours in the corporate world making a living as an independent software consultant.

www.peoplesoftheworld.org

Peter J. Walter (Pg. 55, 97, 169)

Born in the US, Peter J. Walter has been based in Bangkok since 2001 as a senior manager with L.E.K. Consulting. When not working, he enjoys spending time exploring Southeast Asia with his wife, Lyle, and their three children. Photos from his travels in Myanmar can be found at his Flickr site.

www.flickr.com/photos/60638581@N00

Laurie Weed (Pg. 28, 70, 138)

Laurie Weed is a freelance writer, editor, and vagabond who divides her time between San Francisco, California, and Southeast Asia. Her work appears in the Travelers' Tales *Best Women's Travel Writing 2007* and throughout the To Asia With Love guidebook series.

www.kismetworldwide.com/laurieweed

Wyn Tin Tut (Pg. 23, 33, 76)

A native of Yangon, Wyn Tin Tut is married with no children. She loves to travel, cook, and have fun—including her husband in the plans whenever she feels like it.

Win Thuya (Pg. 35, 233)

Win Thuya worked as a hotel receptionist in Bagan for four years after finishing his basic education. In 2000 he left his native village and moved to Yangon. He now works for Gulliver Travels in Yangon. In his free time he enjoys studying French and English, and traveling around Myanmar.

Viola Woodward (Pg. 19, 175, 226, 265)

Viola Woodward is a teacher from Vermont who loves to bike, travel, read mysteries, and avoid winter. She has taught in the Dominican Republic, Israel, and Myanmar, and can order coffee in several different languages. She is also good at balancing umbrellas on her head, dancing at birthday parties, and playing charades.

CREDITS

"David H. Allardice runs the Maykha River in Kachin State" reprinted in an edited form from "The Impossible River," originally published in *Enchanting Myanmar*. Reprinted by permission of the author. Copyright © 2003 by David H. Allardice.

"Hpone Thant tells tiger tales in Alaungdaw Kathapa National Park" reprinted in an edited form from "Is It a Hinmyo?" originally published in *Enchanting Myanmar*. Reprinted by permission of the author. Copyright © 2003 by Hpone Thant.

"Jan Polatschek clatters around Pyin U Lwin in a pony cart" reprinted in an edited form from "Riding Shotgun," originally published at *Travel with Jan* (www.travelwithjan.com). Reprinted by permission of the author. Copyright © 2006 by Jan Polatschek.

CREDITS

INDEX

Alaungdaw Kathapa National Park (Central Myanmar)
Accommodations
Log Cabin Camp, 166
Monasteries, 166
Sights/Attractions/Experiences
Alaungdaw Kathapa Shrine, 166
Exploring the park, 164-166

Amarapura (Central Myanmar)
Sights/Attractions/Experiences
U Bein Bridge, 62-63

Bagan, Old and New (Central Myanmar)
Accommodations
Bagan Thande Hotel, 99
Doing good works/Charities
Kuthodaw Library, 233-234
Food/Drinks/Dining
Mar Lar Thein Gi (Burmese curry), 39
Misan (Burmese), 28
Myo Myo Teashop, 36
Sarabha Restaurant (Burmese/European), 216
Silver House Restaurant (Burmese), 27-28
Tamarind flakes, 214-216

Yar Kyaw Teashop, 34, 36
Shopping
Lacquerware, 122-124
Royal Myanmar Handicrafts, 123-124
Sights/Attractions/Experiences
Alo Pyi pagoda festival, 72-74
Bicycle rental, 99, 187
Bicycling the area, 185-187
Boat from Mandalay, 182-185
Bus trip from Mandalay, 180-182
Minyeingon (pagoda), 97-99
Ninety-Nine (tour guide), 124
Shwesandaw Paya (pagoda), 212-214
Tamarind flakes factory tour, 216

Bago (Southern Myanmar)
Food/Drinks/Dining
Sayarma Gyi (Burmese curry), 40
Sights/Attractions/Experiences
Touring the town, 55-57

Bhamo (Eastern/Northeastern Myanmar)
Sights/Attractions/Experiences
Boat trip to Mandalay, 196-198

Border Towns
Sights/Attractions/Experiences
Myawady, 169
Payathonzu, 170
Tachileik, 32, 169

Chaungtha (Southern Myanmar)
Accommodations
Hotel Max Chaungtha Beach, 137
Lai Lai Chaungtha Beach Hotel, 231
Shwe Hin Tha Hotel, 137
Doing good works/Charities
Helping local children, 229-231
Teaching English, 231
Sights/Attractions/Experiences
Motorcycle excursion, 136-138

Gokteik Viaduct (Central Myanmar)
Sights/Attractions/Experiences
Train journey, 191-193

Hsipaw (Eastern/Northeastern Myanmar)
Food/Drinks/Dining
Black House Café, 101-103
Sights/Attractions/Experiences
Touring the town, 102

Kalaw (Eastern/Northeastern Myanmar)
Accommodations
Golden Kalaw Inn, 104
Food/Drinks/Dining
Hi-Bar, 216-217
Sights/Attractions/Experiences
Trekking, 103-104
Mr. Chain (tour guide), 104

Kinpun (Southern Myanmar)
Accommodations
Golden Rock Hotel, 59
Sea Sar Guest House, 154-155
Sights/Attractions/Experiences
Golden Rock/Kyaiktiyo, 57-60, 155
Hiking, 153-155

Kut Khaing (Eastern/Northeastern Myanmar)
Food/Drinks/Dining
Aung Chan Thar (Burmese/Shan), 33-34

Kyaing Tong (Eastern/Northeastern Myanmar)
Food/Drinks/Dining
General cuisine, 31-32
Golden Banyan (Shan), 31, 32
Market dining, 32
Sights/Attractions/Experiences
Ethnic villages, 80-82
Street parties, 82-83
Wan Seng village, 106-107

Kyauk Myaung (Central Myanmar)
Sights/Attractions/Experiences
Pottery makers, 63-65

Lahe (Northern Myanmar)
Naga New Year celebration, 84-85

Lashio (Central Myanmar)
Sights/Attractions/Experiences
Bicycling to Mandalay, 189-191

Lonton at Indawgyi Lake (Eastern/Northeastern Myanmar)
Accommodations
Lonton guesthouse, 149
Food/Drinks/Dining
Local cafés, 149
Sights/Attractions/Experiences
Touring the lake, 147-149

Mandalay (Central Myanmar)
Accommodations
Sedona Hotel Mandalay, 69
Doing good works/Charities
Aye Yeik Mon Girls' Orphanage Association, 245
Myanmar Buddhist Orphanage Association for Boys, 246
Teaching English, 72, 95, 232-233
Food/Drinks/Dining
Mandalay Night Market, 70

INDEX

Minthiha Teashop, 36, 211
Morning Star (teashop), 211
Nay Café (*chapatti* stand), 219
Nylon Ice Cream Parlor, 93-94
Pakokku Daw Lay May (Burmese
 curry), 40
Shwe Pyi Moe Café (teashop), 212
Soe Soe Mondhi Shop (*mondhi*
 noodles), 37
Teashops/general, 209-212, 219
Sights/Attractions/Experiences
Bicycle rental, 97, 179
Bicycling from Lashio, 189-191
Bicycling the city, 177-179
Boat trip from Bhamo, 196-198
Boat trip to Bagan, 182-185
Bus trip to Bagan, 180-182
Ma Soe Yein Nu Kyaung (monas-
 tery), 95-97
Mandalay Marionettes Theatre,
 71-72
Night on the town, 70
Shwe In Bin Kyaung (monas-
 tery), 95
Sunset views, 70
Thingyan (water festival), 68-69
Trishaws, 179-180
Vipassana Meditation Centre,
 139-141
Wild river dolphins, 158-160

Mawlamyine (Southern Myanmar)
Accommodations
Attran Hotel, 61
Doing good works/Charities
Kin Ywa Orphanage and Monas-
 tic Education School, 245
Sights/Attractions/Experiences
Touring the town, 60-61

**Maykha River (Eastern/Northeastern
Myanmar)**
Sights/Attractions/Experiences

Rafting/Kayaking, 166-168

**Mine Thauk at Inle Lake (Eastern/
Northeastern Myanmar)**
Doing good works/Charities
Mine Thauk Orphanage, 239-241

Mingun (Central Myanmar)
Doing good works/Charities
Mingun Home for the Aged, 161
Sights/Attractions/Experiences
Touring the town, 160-161

Mount Popa (Central Myanmar)
Sights/Attractions/Experiences
Zi O Thit Hla Forest, 74-75

Muse (Eastern/Northeastern Myanmar)
Food/Drinks/Dining
Tohu nwe (warm tofu), 34
Shopping
Border shopping, 33

Myanmar/General
Doing good works/Charities
FinnConnect, 242-243
How/what to give, 82, 224-225,
 238-239, 245, 246-247
Orphanages, 243-246
Painting a monastery, 228
Food/Drinks/Dining
Curry (Burmese), 38-39
Ethnic noodles, 36-37
Teashops (breakfast), 34-35
Wine, 40-42
Tamarind flakes, 214-216
Shopping
Shanachie Entertainment (on-
 line/music), 117
Shwe Myanmar (online/music), 117
Sights/Attractions/Experiences
Bicycling the country, 189-191
Boat travel, 160, 184-185, 197-198
Border crossing, 169-171
Buddhist etiquette, 212-214

Changing money, 49
Chewing betel nut, 207-209
Chinlon (game), 177
Longyi (traditional clothing), 202-204
Tipping, 52
Myeik Archipelago (Southern Myanmar)
Accommodations
Andaman Club Resort, 158
Myanmar Andaman Resort, 156-157, 158
Sights/Attractions/Experiences
Scuba diving, 156, 158
Touring the islands, 155-158
Namhsan (Eastern/Northeastern Myanmar)
Sights/Attractions/Experiences
Bus trip from Hsipaw/Kyaukme, 194-196
Tea plantations, 196
Ngapali Beach (Southern Myanmar)
Accommodations
Amata Resort & Spa, 139
Linn Thar Oo Lodge, 139
Food/Drinks/Dining
Brilliance Seafood Restaurant, 139
Sights/Attractions/Experiences
Touring the town, 138-139
Ngwe Saung (Southern Myanmar)
Accommodations
Myanmar Treasure Resort, 137
Sights/Attractions/Experiences
Motorcycle excursion, 136-138
Nyaung U (Central Myanmar)
Food/Drinks/Dining
Aroma 2 (Indian), 28-29
Nyaungshwe (Eastern/Northeastern Myanmar)
Food/Drinks/Dining
Golden Kite (pizza/pasta), 30,

41, 42
Unique Superb Food House (Burmese), 29-30
View Point Restaurant (Shan nouvelle), 23, 25, 41, 42
Sights/Attractions/Experiences
Bicycling the area, 193-194
Hot springs, 194
Shwe Yan Pyay Kyaung (monastery), 104-106
Traditional massage, 30
Paleik (Central Myanmar)
Sights/Attractions/Experiences
Snake Pagoda, 142, 143
Stupa/Pagoda Garden, 142
Pindaya (Eastern/Northeastern Myanmar)
Accommodations
Conqueror Resort Hotel, 145-147
Food/Drinks/Dining
Café across from resort, 147
Green Tea Restaurant, 147
Shopping
Shan paper workshops, 147
Pyin U Lwin (Central Myanmar)
Food/Drinks/Dining
Circular Road Teashop, 101
Golden Triangle Café and Bakery, 188
Sights/Attractions/Experiences
Anisakan Waterfall, 161-162
Chinese Temple, 101
Pony cart ride, 187-188
Shan Market, 101
Touring the town, 99-101
Pyinmana (Central Myanmar)
Accommodations
Aureum Palace Hotel & Resort, 126
Shopping
Morning market, 125
Sights/Attractions/Experiences
Touring the town, 124-125

INDEX

INDEX

Sagar at Inle Lake (Eastern/North-eastern Myanmar)
Accommodations
Shwe Inn Tha Floating Resort, 145
Sights/Attractions/Experiences
Pagoda complex, 144
Touring the town and lake, 143-145

Sittwe (Central Myanmar)
Doing good works/Charities
Mahamuni Buddha Vihara Parahita, 246

Swar Yarma Village (Central Myanmar)
Sights/Attractions/Experiences
Touring the town, 162-164

Taunggyi (Eastern/Northeastern Myanmar)
Accommodations
Paradise Hotel, 79
Doing good works/Charities
White Pagoda Orphanage, 246
Food/Drinks/Dining
Myanmar Vineyard (Aythaya village), 41, 42
Sights/Attractions/Experiences
Hot Air Balloon Festival, 78-80

Taungpyone (Central Myanmar)
Sights/Attractions/Experiences
Taungpyone Festival, 76-78

Travel agencies
Enchanting Travels & Tours, 267
Good News Travels, 267-268
Gulliver Travels and Tours, 268
Magado Travel, 79
Myanmar Bavarian Tours, 85
Myanmar Travel, 243, 268
Swiftwinds Travels, 268
Zarmani Creative Tours, 269

Yangon (Southern Myanmar)
Accommodations

Mother Land Inn 2, 122
Savoy Hotel, 132-134
The Strand, 52-54
Winner Inn, 134
Doing good works/Charities
ACT Youth Development Center, 245
Eden Centre for the Handicapped, 223, 225
Free Funeral Services Society, 224, 225
Growing Together School, 226-228
Kyimyindine & Insein School for the Blind, 225
Mary Chapman School for the Hearing Impaired, 224, 225
Parahita Kyar Monastic School, 224, 225
Parahita/Monastic Orphanage, 246
St. Mary's Workshop for the Blind (massage), 228-229
Su Htoo Pan Thiri Mingalar Kandaw Parahita, 246
Teaching English, 60
Wingaba Home for Girls, 223, 225
Food/Drinks/Dining
Aung Thuka (Burmese), 17-18
Aye Myit Tar (Burmese), 25-27
Bogyoke Aung San Market (*monhinga* noodles), 37
Café Aroma (coffee/dessert), 20
City Mart (coffee/groceries/wine), 20, 40, 41
Coffee shops, 19-21
Ethnic noodles, 15-16
Feel Myanmar 3 (Burmese/*monhinga* noodles), 21, 24, 37
Fook Mun Lau (Chinese), 24
Golden City Chetty (Indian), 23, 24, 49
Green Elephant (Burmese), 23, 24, 40, 42
Happy Café & Noodles (Kachin

noodles), 16
Le Planteur (French), 23, 24, 41, 42
Let Ywe Sin Tea and Store
(coffee), 21
L'Opera (Italian), 22, 24
Lucky Seven (teashop), 35
Monsoon (Asian), 22, 25
Moon Bakery (coffee/dessert), 20
Nilar Biryani (Indian), 49
Onyx (fusion), 22, 25
Padonmar (Burmese), 23, 25
Parisian Bakery and Café (cof-
fee/dessert), 20
Sagar Gyi Monhinga (*monhinga*
noodles), 38
Sandy's Myanmar Cuisine (Bur-
mese), 22, 25
Savoy Hotel (happy hour), 132-134
Sein Pan Pyar (*mondhi* noodles), 37
Shwe Kayar Gyi Teashop, 35
Shwe Mi (Burmese), 21, 25
The Strand Grill (lobster thermi-
dor), 18-19
Teashops/general, 206-207, 219
Thiripyitsaya Sky Lounge (coffee), 20
Thite Di Shin (Burmese curry),
24, 25, 40
Tin Tin Aye Monhinga (*monhinga*
noodles), 37
Yatha Teashop, 49
Zawgyi Café, 262
Zin Teashop, 207
Shopping
Augustine's Antiques, 114
Bagan Bookshop, 262
Bogyoke Aung San Market,
117-119
Bookshops/general, 260-262
Heritage Gallery (antiques), 118, 119
Hledan Market, 119-120
Innerspace (furniture), 113, 114
Inwa Bookshop, 262

Man Thiri Music Production, 117
Music (local CDs), 115-117
Myanmar Book Centre, 253, 262
Na Gar Glass Factory, 112-113
Nandawun Handicrafts Centre, 262
Pearl VCD Production and Distri-
bution, 117
River Gallery (art), 112
Theingi Maw (books), 262
Traders Hotel (books), 262
Trishaw (purchasing), 120-122
Violet Fashion (fabrics), 114, 115
Watch repair, 88-90
Yoyamay (ethnic handicrafts),
118, 119
Sights/Attractions/Experiences
Astrology reading, 204-206
Bicycle rental, 177
Bicycling the city, 175-177
Botataung Paya (pagoda), 91-92, 93
Fancy House (beauty salon),
131-132
Happy World Water Park, 134-135
Local artists, 110-112
Massage, 228-229
Moustache Brothers, 27
People's Park (pool), 135
Shwedagon Pagoda, 49-51
Sule Paya (pagoda), 90-91, 93
Theingyi Market, 54-55
U Hla Toe (tour guide), 52
U Tin Fish Sausage Factory, 54-55
Walking the city, 47-49
Yangon Swimming Club (pool), 135
Yele Paya (pagoda), 92, 93

Yenangyaung (Central Myanmar)
Accommodations
Lei Thar Gone, 235-237
Doing good works/Charities
Supporting the community,
235-237

Morgan Edwardson

Steve Goodman

Born in Miami, Florida, Morgan has worked in various cities around Southeast Asia. He currently lives in Bangkok and frequently travels to Myanmar. In his spare time he likes to eat "all things barbecued" and read mystery novels.

A former software company executive, Steve Goodman is a Phnom Penh-based photographer who has lived and traveled extensively in Southeast Asia since 2002. He holds a degree in philosophy from the University of Pittsburgh, and along with pursuing his career as a professional photographer, he enjoys traveling, reading, playing guitar, listening to music, meditating, and walking around to see what's going on in our world of inestimable beauty.

TO ASIA WITH LOVE SERIES

TO VIETNAM WITH LOVE
A Travel Guide for the Connoisseur
Edited & with contributions by Kim Fay
Photographs by Julie Fay Ashborn

TO THAILAND WITH LOVE
A Travel Guide for the Connoisseur
Edited & with contributions by Joe Cummings
Photographs by Marc Schultz

TO CAMBODIA WITH LOVE
A Travel Guide for the Connoisseur
Edited & with contributions by Andy Brouwer
Photographs by Tewfic El-Sawy

TO MYANMAR WITH LOVE
A Travel Guide for the Connoisseur
Edited & with contributions by Morgan Edwardson
Photographs by Steve Goodman

TO SHANGHAI WITH LOVE
A Travel Guide for the Connoisseur
Edited & with contributions by Crystyl Mo
Photographs by Coca Dai

TO NORTH INDIA WITH LOVE
A Travel Guide for the Connoisseur
Edited & with contributions by Nabanita Dutt
Photographs by Nana Chen

TO JAPAN WITH LOVE
A Travel Guide for the Connoisseur
Edited & with contributions by Celeste Heiter
Photographs by Robert George

TO NEPAL WITH LOVE
A Travel Guide for the Connoisseur
Edited & with contributions by Cristi Hegranes
Photographs by Kraig Lieb

For more information, visit www.toasiawithlove.com